THE SHADOW MEN

THE SHADOW MEN

THE LEADERS WHO SHAPED THE AUSTRALIAN ARMY FROM THE VELDT TO VIETNAM

EDITED BY
CRAIG STOCKINGS AND JOHN CONNOR

A NewSouth book

Published by
NewSouth Publishing
University of New South Wales Press Ltd
University of New South Wales
Sydney NSW 2052
AUSTRALIA
newsouthpublishing.com

© in this edition Craig Stockings and John Connor 2017
© in individual chapters is retained by the chapter authors
First published 2017

10 9 8 7 6 5 4 3 2 1

This book is copyright. Apart from any fair dealing for the purpose of private study, research, criticism or review, as permitted under the Copyright Act, no part of this book may be reproduced by any process without written permission. Inquiries should be addressed to the publisher.

National Library of Australia
Cataloguing-in-Publication entry

Title: The Shadow Men: The leaders who shaped the Australian Army from the Veldt to Vietnam / Craig Stockings and John Connor (editors).
ISBN: 9781742234748 (paperback)
 9781742242750 (ebook)
 9781742248233 (ePDF)
Notes: Includes index.
Subjects: Australia. Army – Officers – Biography.
 Australia. Army – Military Personnel – Biography.
 Leadership – Australia – History.
 Military art and science – Australia – History.
 Australia – History, Military.
 Australia – Armed Forces – History.
Other Creators/Contributors: Stockings, Craig, 1974– editor.
 Connor, John, 1966– editor.

Design Avril Makula
Cover design Blue Cork
Front cover images From left: Brigadier John William Alexander O'Brien, Major-General Gordon Legge, General Sir Cyril Brudenell Bingham White, Major-General Sir William Bridges, Colonel E.G. Keogh. See relevant chapters for image credits.

All reasonable efforts were taken to obtain permission to use copyright material reproduced in this book, but in some cases copyright could not be traced. The author welcomes information in this regard.

In Memoriam Jeffrey Grey

This collection includes three chapters written by Jeffrey Grey, who died suddenly on 26 July 2016. Jeffrey was a significant figure in the field of military history, both in Australia and internationally, and was the first non-American to be president of the Society of Military History. With Peter Dennis, he organised the Chief of Army's History Conference for many years. Jeffrey was the editor and a contributing author of the five-volume *Centenary History of Australia in the Great War*.

Those who knew Jeffrey will recall his sometimes gruff exterior, especially following the latest imposition from university administration, or the defeat of his beloved Brumbies rugby union team. The editors and chapter authors of this book will also remember Jeffrey as a trusted colleague or generous mentor. We dedicate this book to his memory.

CONTENTS

	Acknowledgments	ix
	Contributors	x
	Introduction *John Connor*	1
1	The First Commander: Lieutenant-General Sir Edward 'Curley' Hutton *Craig Stockings and Tom Richardson*	9
2	Duntroon to the Dardanelles: Major-General Sir William Bridges *Chris Clark*	37
3	The Enigma: General Sir Cyril Brudenell Bingham White *Peter Stanley*	59
4	Not Up to the Job? Major-General Gordon Legge *Chris Clark*	81
5	The Soldier as Technocrat: Brigadier John William Alexander O'Brien *Jeffrey Grey*	105

6	The Quiet Achiever: Lieutenant-General Sir John Northcott *Robert Stevenson*	119
7	Fall and Rise: Lieutenant-General Sir Sydney Rowell *Karl James*	153
8	A Military Intellectual: Colonel E.G. Keogh *Jeffrey Grey*	181
9	The Catalyst: Lieutenant-General Sir Thomas Daly *Jeffrey Grey*	195
10	Post-war Planner: Lieutenant-General Sir Mervyn Brogan *Tristan Moss*	211
	Notes	231
	Index	257

ACKNOWLEDGMENTS

This book could not have been produced without the contributions of many individuals. The editors thank the chapter authors for the quality of their scholarship, the skill of their writing, and their collegial spirit. Thank you for being part of this project.

We also express our gratitude once more to the talented team at NewSouth Publishing, whose vision, hard work and expertise brought this project to fruition.

Finally, we must express our appreciation to our colleagues at the Australian War Memorial and UNSW Canberra, and, most importantly, to our families and friends.

Craig Stockings and John Connor

CONTRIBUTORS

Chris Clark was head of the Office of Air Force History for nine years before his retirement in 2013. He was also a Visiting Fellow in the School of Humanities and Social Sciences at UNSW Canberrra (2003–16) until moving to Melbourne to live. A former army officer and Commonwealth public servant, he also previously worked at the Australian National University and Australian War Memorial in Canberra. In a writing career spanning 45 years he has written, co-authored and/or edited more than 20 books on Australian history – including biographies of Major-General Sir William Bridges (published in 1979) and Major-General Gordon Legge (1988) – along with chapters in half a dozen other books, and numerous conference papers and journal articles. His most recent book on the senior officer of the Australian Flying Corps in World War I (Lieutenant-Colonel Oswald Watt) was published in 2016.

John Connor is a senior lecturer in history in the School of Humanities and Social Sciences at UNSW Canberra. His books include *The Australian Frontier Wars 1788–1838* (2002), which was shortlisted for the Royal United Services Institute's Westminster Medal for Military Literature, *Anzac and Empire: George Foster Pearce and the Foundations of Australian Defence* (2011) and the 'Politics' chapters of *The War at Home*, co-authored with Peter Stanley and Peter Yule, as part of the five-volume *Centenary History of Australia and the Great War* (2014–16).

Jeffrey Grey was professor of history in the School of Humanities and Social Sciences at UNSW Canberra. He was the author or editor of 26 books in the fields of Australian and comparative and international military history, and published numerous articles, chapters and reviews in these fields. Most recently he was the series editor of *The Centenary History of Australia and the Great War* (2014–16). Professor Grey passed away on 26 July 2016.

Karl James is a senior historian in the Military History Section at the Australian War Memorial, Canberra, and completed his PhD at the University of Wollongong. He has worked on several exhibitions and was the curator for the Memorial's special anniversary exhibition, the 'Rats of Tobruk, 1941' on display during 2011. His books include *The Hard Slog: Australians in the Bougainville Campaign, 1944–45* (2012) and *Double Diamonds: Australian Commandos in the Pacific War, 1941–45* (2016). Karl is also a Departmental Visitor with the Strategic and Defence Studies Centre at the Australian National University, Canberra.

Tristan Moss is a researcher on the *Official History of Australian Operations in Iraq and Afghanistan, and Australian Peacekeeping Operations in East Timor* at the Australian War Memorial. He completed his PhD at the Strategic and Defence Studies Centre at the Australian National University, Canberra, in 2015. In 2016 Tristan was a teaching fellow at the Australian Command and Staff College, and worked on both the Serving Our Country project and the *Official History of Peacekeeping, Humanitarian and Post–Cold War Operations*. His first book, *Guarding the Periphery: the Australian Army in Papua New Guinea, 1951–75*, will be published by Cambridge University Press in 2017.

Tom Richardson is a researcher on the *Official History of Australian Operations in Iraq and Afghanistan, and Australian Peacekeeping Operations in East Timor* at the Australian War Memorial, and was previously associate lecturer in history at UNSW Canberra. He completed his PhD at UNSW Canberra in 2014. Tom's research interests include Australian military history, the Vietnam War and counter-insurgency.

Peter Stanley is a research professor at UNSW Canberra. He was formerly principal historian at the Australian War Memorial, where he worked from 1980 to 2007, and headed the Research Centre at the National Museum of Australia from 2007 to 2013. He has published 30 books on Australian military social history, British imperial and medical history and is a prominent commentator on Australian war history. His recent books include *Bad Characters: Sex, Crime, Mutiny, Murder and the Australian Imperial Force* (which jointly won the 2011 Prime Minister's Prize for Australian History), *Die in Battle, Do not Despair: The Indians on Gallipoli, 1915* (2015), and the 'Society' chapters of *The War at Home*, part of *The Centenary History of Australia and the Great War* (2014–16).

Robert Stevenson is a historian and a member of the team preparing the multi-volume *Official History of Australian Operations in Iraq and Afghanistan, and Australian Peacekeeping Operations in East Timor* at the Australian War Memorial. He holds a Master of Arts and a Doctorate of Philosophy (PhD) from the University of New South Wales and his PhD dissertation was awarded the Army History Unit's 2011 C.E.W. Bean Prize for the best postgraduate thesis on Australian Army history. A revised version of this thesis was published under the title *To Win the Battle: The 1st Australian Division in the Great War, 1914–1918* (2013), while his most recent major publication is *The War with Germany* (2015), a volume of *The Centenary History of Australia and the Great War* series.

Craig Stockings is currently working as the Official Historian of *Australian Operations in Iraq and Afghanistan, and Australian Peacekeeping Operations in East Timor*. Prior to this appointment, he was a professor of history at UNSW Canberra. His areas of academic interest concern general and Australian military history and operational analysis. Craig has published a wide range of scholarly articles, book chapters and books in the field. Most notably these include a history of the army cadet movement in Australia, *The Torch and the*

Sword (2007); a study of the First Libyan Campaign in North Africa 1940–41, *Bardia: Myth, Reality and the Heirs of Anzac* (2009); a reinterpretation of the German invasion of Greece in 1941, *Swastika over the Acropolis* (2013, with Associate Professor Eleanor Hancock); and most recently *Britannia's Shield: Lieutenant-General Sir Edward Hutton and Late Victorian Imperial Defence* (2015). He has also edited a number of books, including *Zombie Myths of Australian Military History* (2010), *Anzac's Dirty Dozen: 12 Myths of Australian Military History* (2012) and *Before the Anzac Dawn* (2013, with Dr John Connor).

INTRODUCTION

JOHN CONNOR

ANZAC DAY HAS BECOME perhaps the most important day for the Australian national identity. War, from the Australian frontier through two world wars to contemporary conflicts in Afghanistan and the Middle East, is central to Australian history. Despite this – with the exception of John Monash or John Simpson Kirkpatrick – most Australians could not name a significant figure of the Australian Army.

This is surprising, as the military forces of Australia could not have originated, developed and matured without the vision, devotion and sacrifice of the people who have served in it. Certain officers stand out for the significance of their contribution to the army. Despite this, they remain little known. Some of these individuals did their work behind the scenes. Others were once-important figures who have been forgotten with the passage of time. They have all become shadow men.

Margaret MacMillan, the best-selling Canadian historian, has described history as a house 'where the portraits of some of our forebears are displayed prominently on the walls while others are relegated to dusty boxrooms and attics'.[1] *The Shadow Men* aims to bring back to the light ten men who played key roles in shaping and moulding the Australian Army. These men may have been forgotten, but their achievements justify their return to public consciousness.

This book brings together a select group of veteran and early career historians to retrieve these people from the gloom. Biography – the story of a person – remains the most popular form of history, but as MacMillan pointed out in the 2015 Massey Lectures broadcast by the Canadian Broadcasting Corporation, historical biographies and the people who write them are often 'regarded with suspicion'. This form of writing has been criticised for placing too much emphasis 'on individuals in the mistaken assumption that "great men" or "great women" make history'. MacMillan recognises that broader social, political and economic forces 'must never be ignored', but she argues that it is 'the interplay between individuals and their worlds that makes history and brings it to life for those of us in the present'.[2]

Biography is an exacting form of historical writing. Gerry Walsh, who wrote more entries for the *Australian Dictionary of Biography* than any other person, described biography as 'one of the most difficult branches of a historian's craft'. The aim of historical biography should be, as British historians Jeremy Black and Donald MacRaild put it, to provide 'the contextualised life; the life as part of a wider sequence of events and occurrences'. The aim must be, as Stephen B. Oates, American historian and Lincoln biographer, states, to achieve the balance between 'life' and 'times'. If the individual disappears from the work for pages at a time, then there is too much of the 'times' and not enough of the 'life'.[3]

The authors in this collection have all succeeded in providing 'the contextualised life' of their subjects, from Federation and the establishment of an Australian army to the end of the Vietnam War. *The Shadow Men* begins with Craig Stockings' and Tom Richardson's exploration of the antipodean career of Edward Hutton, the British Army officer appointed in 1902 to be the first General Officer Commanding of the Commonwealth Military Forces. Virtually forgotten today, Hutton demonstrated great skill in combining the six colonial forces into the makings of a coherent national army consisting mostly of part-time citizen soldiers. He failed, however, in his attempt to convince the federal government that Australian soldiers should be automatically authorised to serve overseas in the event of the British Empire being involved in a major war. Ministers replied to Hutton that such a decision could only be made by the government of the day in response to actual events – as would occur in 1914, when the federal Cabinet, with overwhelming public support, responded to the outbreak of the First World War with the creation of expeditionary forces for overseas service. Stockings and Richardson find that Hutton's arrogant and intolerant personality led to his downfall. This ensured that Hutton would be the first – and only – Australian General Officer Commanding. The *Defence Act* of 1904 abolished his position and replaced it with a Military Board consisting of several officers.

If William Throsby Bridges is remembered today, it is for being the first commandant of the Royal Military College at Duntroon and for commanding the 1st Australian Division at Gallipoli from the landing on 25 April to his death on 18 May 1915. In Chapter 2, Chris Clark argues that Bridges' real contribution to the Australian Army lies in the eight years from 1902 to 1910 that he spent in the military headquarters at Victoria Barracks in Melbourne. As Assistant Quartermaster-General, Bridges had a wide range of responsibilities, from preparing annual budget estimates to devising defence schemes. He was sent on secret missions on behalf of the British to gather intelligence on the French colony of New Caledonia. Bridges also played a central role in creating the position of Director of Military Science at Sydney University, which offered a Diploma of Military Science and also provided much-needed courses in staff work for militia officers. It was Bridges' work in these, and many other roles, that leads Clark to identify Bridges as 'a most significant figure' in forming Australian defence policy in the first decade following Federation.

Cyril Brudenell Bingham White was mentioned by Charles Bean more times than any other person in the Australian First World War official history. However, because White was a staff officer who devised the military plans, rather than a commander who conducted the battle, it is difficult to identify the extent of his influence on operations at Gallipoli and on the Western Front. Furthermore, if White deserves credit for the Australian Imperial Force's (AIF) successes, then he also deserves blame for the AIF's defeats. Peter Stanley argues in Chapter 3 that White's most important contribution was to develop the administrative system that enabled the AIF to assert its national autonomy and also remain an effective component of the larger British

Empire force. The system that White established was subsequently used by the Australian Army in the Second World War and in Korea, Malaya and Borneo.

Gordon Legge created the 2nd Australian Division and led it into battle at Gallipoli and later on the Western Front, but Chris Clark points out in Chapter 4 that Legge's contribution to the Australian Army has gone unrecognised. Before the First World War, Legge proposed the establishment of defence factories to produce uniforms, small arms and other military needs. He played a major role in the establishment of the Australian compulsory military training scheme, and was sent to London in 1912 as the Australian representative on the Imperial General Staff. Clark concedes that Legge's performance as a military commander had its faults, but argues he has received more criticism than other Australian Great War generals because his independent 'Australianist' viewpoint put him at odds with the majority of his contemporaries who had a British 'imperialist' perspective.

During the Second World War, Australia was forced to expand the local manufacture of weapons and ammunition due to the shortage of imports. In Chapter 5, Jeffrey Grey charts the career of Brigadier John O'Brien, who could be described as the ultimate shadow man. A relatively low ranking officer, O'Brien held a succession of key wartime roles in which he developed Australian defence production. He initiated the modification of existing weapons, such as the 25-pounder gun, so they could be transported and deployed in the jungles of New Guinea. He authorised the production of new weapons such as the Owen submachine-gun, and halted production of low-priority projects such as the Australian Cruiser tank. O'Brien succeeded in this vital task of providing Australian soldiers with appropriate weapons and equipment because he had a unique combination of skills as an artillery officer, an administrator and an engineer, with strong connections to engineering and manufacturing companies.

John Northcott was one of four lieutenant-generals in the Australian Army in 1945, but Robert Stevenson points out that if he is remembered today, it is generally for being the first Australian-born

Governor of New South Wales, rather than his military career. Northcott became Deputy Chief of the General Staff soon after the outbreak of the Second World War, and then commanded the 1st Australian Armoured Division and II Australian Corps. In 1942 he was appointed Chief of the General Staff – where he had responsibility for training and equipping the army and advising the War Cabinet – and retained this position to the end of the war. He then commanded the British Commonwealth Occupation Force – consisting of Australian, British, Indian and New Zealand personnel – in Japan until June 1946. Northcott was effective in these roles because he was knowledgeable, dependable, calm and loyal.

While Northcott had a steady rise through the officer ranks, Sydney Rowell, in contrast, experienced a dramatic fall, followed by an equally spectacular ascension to become Chief of the General Staff. As Karl James describes in Chapter 7, General Sir Thomas Blamey sacked Rowell as commander of New Guinea Force in September 1942. It would have been expected that this meant the end of Rowell's military career. He was exiled to the Middle East to command the dwindling number of Australian personnel in that theatre. However, his fortunes changed when he was sent to London to lead the Tactical Investigation Directorate in the War Office. Here, almost uniquely for an Australian officer, he gained valuable experience overseeing the analysis of various aspects of military operations in Europe, including the German V2 rocket. Following Blamey's retirement in 1946, Rowell became Vice Chief and then Chief of the General Staff and played a major role in creating the post-war regular army.

The Australian Army has produced few intellectuals. In Chapter 8 Jeffrey Grey charts the career of Eustace Graham Keogh, the most important military thinker to emerge in Australia during the Second World War. The beginning of the war with Japan meant the Australian Army could no longer rely on British training documents and needed to create its own material, known as *Army Training Memorandums*, that were relevant to the Pacific campaigns. Keogh, who had served in the Middle East in the First World War and in the Middle East and the Pacific in the Second World War, joined the Directorate of Military Training in Melbourne in January 1945. Keogh was demobilised following the end of the war but returned to the Directorate as a civilian, where he encouraged military personnel to study military history as an integral part of their career development. In 1948 Keogh launched the first issue of the *Australian Army Journal,* and he wrote six books on military campaigns to assist officers with promotion exams. In retirement, he became a historical adviser for the long-running Second World War TV drama series *The Sullivans.*

Sir Thomas Daly was Chief of the General Staff during the Vietnam War from 1966 to 1971. Jeffrey Grey contends in Chapter 9 he is a shadow man because he maintained a low public profile despite his influence on the Australian Army. Daly was a regular officer who commanded a battalion in the Second World War and a brigade in the Korean War. His most important legacy was to commission a review into the army's organisation in 1969 in anticipation of a future withdrawal from Vietnam and the ending of conscription. This review replaced the obsolete state-based military districts that had been created at the time of Federation with a more effective system of functional commands (Field Force, Training and Logistics Commands). The reform also brought the army into line with the Royal Australian Navy and Royal Australian Air Force organisations.

Tristan Moss concludes this collection with his study of Sir Mervyn Brogan, the Chief of the General Staff from 1971 to 1973, who oversaw the army's withdrawal from Vietnam. After service in New Guinea in the Second World War, Brogan was identified as a promising officer. In the late 1950s he was attached to the British Far East Land Forces Headquarters and attended the Imperial Defence College in London. He succeeded Daly in Northern Command in 1962 and began preparing the Pacific Islands Regiment to become the defence force of an independent Papua New Guinea, as would eventually occur in 1975. As Chief of the General Staff, Brogan managed the army's withdrawal from Vietnam, the return to a volunteer army, and the restructure and reduction of personnel and units following a major conflict. Moss argues Brogan's greatest achievement was successfully guiding the army 'through an intense period of reorganisation, which represented the most significant period of upheaval' since Federation.

It has been said that there have been many books written on Australian military history, but often they are the same book published over and over again. This book breaks new ground and offers the reader new insights. By returning the shadow men to the light we will discover more about the Australian Army, and about the people who have served in it since 1901.

1
THE FIRST COMMANDER
Lieutenant-General Sir Edward 'Curley' Hutton

CRAIG STOCKINGS & TOM RICHARDSON

A LARGE SOMBRE-LOOKING PORTRAIT by Tom Roberts hangs on the wall of the 'morning tea' room in the Officers' Mess at the Royal Military College, Duntroon, in Canberra. Its subject is a middle-aged late-Victorian-era army officer who poses, rather pompously, for the artist (who is also his personal friend). It is not one of Roberts' finest. It is a rather dark and somewhat wooden piece – much like its subject. Within the Mess it blends into its military surrounds. Few people distinguish it from the other military-themed paintings on the walls. Fewer recognise it as a Roberts. Fewer still recognise the face upon the canvas. It is, however, this portrait's under-recognised significance that marks it as a striking representation of its subject, Lieutenant-General Sir Edward 'Curley' Hutton. In stark contrast to his current anonymity, Hutton was a giant of his time. His stamp on the post-Federation Australian Army was indelible and enduring. He is perhaps *the* most important single agent or figure that shaped the history of the army in the early 20th century, and his current obscurity is a reflection of the way in which the army's formative period has been overshadowed by the events of 1915 and beyond.

Lieutenant-General Sir Edward Thomas Henry 'Curley' Hutton, the first General Officer Commanding the Australian Military Forces.
Australian War Memorial, AWM P03875.002

Edward Hutton was born into a middle-class English family on 6 December 1848. He was educated at Eton and received his first commission into the 60th Rifles (King's Royal Rifles Corps). The commission continued the family's tradition of military service and was secured through the patronage and payment of around £450 by his step-father, General Sir Arthur Lawrence. Hutton's entrance into the Rifles marked the beginning of an outstanding military career cut short by personal failings that existed in equal measure with professional brilliance.

The apex of Hutton's career was his appointment as Australia's first General Officer Commanding (GOC), a position he held from January 1902 to November 1904. During his time as GOC Hutton laid the foundations for Australia's new national army, shaping the institution in ways that far outlasted his time in the post. The appointment also reflected Hutton's long career spent on the periphery of empire. He had commanded the New South Wales colonial forces (1893–96) and the Canadian militia (1898–1900), and fought in the Anglo–Zulu War, in Egypt, and in the First and Second Anglo–Boer Wars. In South Africa Hutton led troops drawn from the Australian colonies as part of the 1st Mounted Infantry Brigade, an experience that buttressed his existing conviction of the value of colonial troops and mounted infantry. As a member of the group of army reformers known as the 'Wolseley Ring' he had argued this belief with vigour, using his talent for public speaking to good effect. Hutton's career and reforming agenda were further helped by his marriage in 1889 to the aristocratic Eleanor Paulet and his appointment as aide-de-camp to Queen Victoria in 1892.

Hutton's service throughout the British Empire and his reformist bent combined to have a profound impact on the emerging Australian Army. Hutton arrived in Australia convinced of the need for a coordinated system of imperial defence, a view that had increasingly come to shape his career. Unusually for an officer in the late-Victorian army, Hutton had taken a scholarly approach to the strategic problems facing the empire – specifically, how best to craft a military organisation capable of both defending Britain's far-flung possessions and participating in a general European war.[1] Hutton's solution was that self-governing colonies maintain volunteer militia armies, capable of defending themselves and of being deployed overseas. It was a plan that promised to solve the empire's strategic problem while also not offending colonial sensibilities around citizen-soldiery and compulsory military service. Moreover, the plan conformed to Hutton's beliefs in the power of mounted infantry, the martial ability of the British race's colonial offspring, and the willingness of these colonial subjects to volunteer in times of crisis – beliefs seemingly confirmed in their validity by his experience in South Africa. Hutton and fellow reformers thought that these colonial volunteer armies would be capable of matching the mass conscript forces of continental Europe, equipping Britain to deal with a European war that many saw as not only inevitable but close.

Hutton's time in Australia was also defined by his forceful and polarising personality. One description of Hutton had him 'cast in the pro-consular mould, aggressive, imaginative, energetic, with a nearly limitless self-confidence', another as 'a propagandist, a missionary fired with apostolic zeal, and apostles do not think greatly of tact'.[2] Despite his education and marriage, Hutton never entirely left behind his middle-class roots, and as a consequence he rejected the cultivated anti-intellectualism of his aristocratic peers in favour of a rigid professionalism. 'To be a successful soldier you must work and work thoroughly and conscientiously', he told an audience at Eton in 1880, '[k]nowledge is power . . . Men will not believe in those whom they know to be ignorant.'[3] This sentiment drove Hutton and his reformist peers, who recognised that the army had to anticipate the problems it would face and the solutions for them in a time of great social and technological flux. Yet despite his contempt for the dilettantism of many of his fellow officers, Hutton still craved their approval.[4] Insecurity thus coloured his immense self-confidence, leading him to put even more emphasis on his professional achievements and to constantly seek recognition for them.

The combination of Hutton's dedication to his craft, ample intellect and enormous self-confidence produced an officer who was demonstrably brilliant, well aware of this fact, and consequently absolutely unwilling to consider alternative points of view. That others might not agree with him was a reflection of their lack of intelligence or hidden agendas at work, not fault on Hutton's part. The result was that he pressed his point on others and was resentful when it was rejected.[5] Hutton himself was well aware of his own flaws. In June 1902 he wrote to a friend who had served under him in South Africa:

> My very strong points constitute my weakness – for example my nature as you know is quick in perception and enthusiasm, amounting to strong impulse. These very qualities lead me to being impatient with others whose thoughts work slower than my own. I am strong in my views and the very strength which constitutes the value of most I try to do, betrays me sometimes into impressing my will too strongly upon those around me. I am my dear fellow very very conscious of my failings, and try as all the best of us try, to overcome them.[6]

Yet for all his recognition of his faults, Hutton was unable to master them. In particular, his belief that his military accomplishments and rank gave him an unassailable authority in defence matters boded poorly for his time in Australia. Yet this was ultimately two sides of the same coin. Hutton's self-confidence, intellect and drive gained him the position as GOC in Australia as the youngest substantive major-general in the British Army, and the negative manifestations of these same qualities ensured it would be his last posting of real significance.

Hutton arrived in Melbourne to take up his post on 29 January 1902. Despite the new Commonwealth's Department of Defence having been in existence for nearly a year, the lack of relevant legislation meant that almost nothing had been done to consolidate and organise the armed forces of the former colonies. Located at Victoria

Barracks in Melbourne, the department possessed only a skeleton staff consisting of the minister, John Forrest, his civil adviser, Captain Robert Henry Muirhead Collins, seven clerks, two messengers and a caretaker. The size of the staff reflected the department's lack of responsibilities in the absence of legislation. Forrest's priority, therefore, was the drafting and passage of a federal *Defence Act* that would give the department a legal footing and allow the reorganisation of the Commonwealth Military Forces to begin.[7]

That no *Defence Act* had been passed by the time Hutton arrived in Australia, despite over 12 months having passed since Federation, reflected the lack of consensus within Australian politics over the nature and role of the army within the Commonwealth. In March 1901 Forrest had asked the Federal Military Committee to draft a Defence Bill. Drawing on advice from the Colonial Defence Committee (CDC), the proposed Bill called for an 'active' force containing a mixture of paid militia and unpaid volunteer troops, buttressed by a small number of permanent soldiers. The Bill also made provision for the maintenance of a 'reserve' of men who had previously served in the active force, as well as rifle clubs and a cadet organisation. Taking a lead from Canadian legislation, the draft allowed for the Commonwealth military forces to be called out for active service anywhere inside or outside Australia at any time 'for its defence', and for compulsory military service in times of 'emergency'.[8] Forrest made sure that the final authority for the forces (and hence for these decisions) rested with the minister rather than the GOC or Governor-General, but otherwise accepted the committee's recommendations. As a matter of urgency, in June the draft was introduced to Parliament as the first Defence Bill.[9]

Forrest put forward a half-hearted defence of the Bill before departing for a funeral in Perth, leaving Prime Minister Edmund Barton to weather a storm of criticism in Parliament. The provisions for compulsory service and overseas deployment provoked deep anxiety within many parliamentarians, who saw the potential for a slippery slope into European-style mass conscription and a permanent standing army.

Such a force might be used during domestic crises, as the Queensland militia had during the shearers' strike in 1891. Other disagreements sprang up over the relative merits of volunteers and militia and the extent to which the two systems should and could co-exist. Some advocated more radical measures. Labor MP William Morris Hughes called for a national militia with compulsory annual training for all males, fashioned after the Swiss model. Others, inspired by the success of Boer commandos, called for the abandonment of a traditional military establishment in favour of a force anchored in rifle clubs.[10] Even with amendments, the Bill's second reading demonstrated that an acceptable conclusion had not been reached. Consequently, Barton motioned for the Bill to be discharged.[11]

For Hutton, the lack of a *Defence Act* represented an opportunity as much as a problem. The absence of legislation gave him the space necessary to push forward his own vision of how the Australian Army should be structured, in the process cutting through the confused and fragmented voices emanating from Parliament. Almost immediately, he began lobbying Forrest and Barton about the 'erroneous strategical assumption' that 'the defence of Australia was to be narrowed down to the defence of Australian shores'.[12] What was needed instead was a military force capable of 'a strong and vigorous offence' – a phrase that implicitly suggested deployment overseas.[13] To Hutton's delight, his words appeared to have an immediate impact. At a banquet held in honour of the new GOC on 15 February, Barton delivered a speech that seemingly echoed Hutton's arguments for a broader interpretation of Australian security. This was all the endorsement Hutton needed; he subsequently wrote to the British Secretary of State for War, William St John Brodrick, that he believed he could secure agreement for 20,000 mounted troops 'organised for service <u>wherever Australian interests are threatened</u>'.[14]

In reality, Hutton badly overestimated the significance of Barton's words, a mistake that foreshadowed the tone deafness to Australian politics that would help drive him from his post. The travails of the first Defence Bill were a clear indication of the difficulty Barton faced in building a consensus on the issue, and that Barton's views carried only limited weight. Moreover, one of the central concerns about imperial defence, the question of who would have authority over Australian forces deployed overseas, was thrown into sharp focus by the execution of Lieutenants Harry ('Breaker') Morant and Peter Handcock in Pretoria on 27 February. Barton had previously informed Parliament that while Australians were subject to the British Army legal system, Colonial Secretary Joseph Chamberlain had assured him that he would be consulted on any significant decisions. The news that Morant and Handcock had been executed without Barton being informed was therefore not only politically embarrassing but also direct evidence for imperial defence sceptics about the validity of their concerns. Barton never again gave his public support for this idea of compulsory overseas service in support of the empire.

As Hutton settled into his new role, he began to take stock of the forces under his command. From 1 January 1901 the armed forces of the six colonies had come under the control of the new Commonwealth government, forming the Commonwealth Military Forces. The force overall had a strength of 27,300 officers and men, from an authorised establishment of just over 30,000. New South Wales was the biggest contributor with 9338 men under arms, Tasmania the smallest with 2024.[15] Only around 1400 of the overall force were permanent soldiers, concentrated in technical arms such as artillery, engineering and staff corps. The remainder were divided between roughly 15,000 part-time paid militia and 11,000 unpaid volunteers, the preponderance of militia reflecting the abandonment of the volunteer model in South Australia and Western Australia. Of these part-timers, nearly 18,000 served in infantry units, while almost 5300 were in cavalry or mounted infantry units.[16]

These raw numbers were deceptive, however. The nomenclature, uniform, size and training of units differed dramatically not only between states but within them, a reflection in part of the way volunteer and militia units were raised by their communities rather than a central authority. Moreover, the force as a whole suffered from more basic problems such as a lack of ammunition, small arms, equipment and stores. These problems had been identified prior to Hutton's arrival by the Finn Report, produced by the Federal Military Committee the previous year.[17] Hutton thus needed to not only reorganise the forces under his command to fulfil the strategic function he saw as necessary, but also bring them up to a more acceptable standard. 'Thrown upon my own initiative', he later reflected, 'I had no recourse but either drift along with a slow tide and with a certainty of failure, or act upon the lines which I knew would achieve the result desired and desirable.'[18] Understandably he chose to act.

The place he began was the administrative and command structure of the new force. His first general order appointed eight officers to his staff, the 'Military Branch' of the Department of Defence, and outlined their duties. This was an extremely modest establishment that was lower than that recommended by the CDC and even smaller than the military headquarters of pre-Federation New South Wales. Even then, Hutton came under pressure to cut costs. Forrest complained to Hutton that he needed to show Parliament how the new headquarters structure saved money; its ability to discharge its duties was secondary. Further demonstrating the government's pursuit of savings, it was decided that the offices of Deputy Adjutant-General and Deputy Quartermaster-General would not be filled once their original occupants retired.[19]

As Hutton started the administrative work his post demanded, he also began to articulate his wider strategic vision. In late March 1902 he committed his thoughts to paper in a document entitled 'Minute Upon the Defence of Australia'. Filling the void left by the failed Defence Bill, the objective of the *Minute* was to outline 'a military system which shall be elastic, capable of expansion, and which shall form a carefully constructed framework into which the fighting material of this nation can be fitted when the emergency arises'.[20] Hutton was also careful to set the terms of the issue to suit his wider objectives. Thus the 'defence of Australia' encapsulated not only the 'defence of Australian soil' but also the 'defence of Australian interests wherever they may be threatened'.[21] While the primary objective of this new military system would be the defence of mainland Australia, Hutton intended that it would also be able to be smoothly integrated into a wider scheme of imperial defence if and when it emerged.

Hutton's system divided the CMF between two distinct roles: garrison troops, consisting largely of volunteer units, to protect 'certain pre-determined strategically [important] centres', and a 'Field Force' of militia for mobile and 'active' operations.[22] These two forces would have their training standards improved through the establishment of a series of schools for militia and volunteer officers, 'Staff Rides upon Field Service conditions', and the establishment of a military college modelled on the Royal Military College in Kingston, Canada, and 'the Great Public schools of England'.[23] Infantry, mounted infantry and cavalry would conduct 16 days of training annually, while engineers and artillerymen would undertake 20. Training would be conducted in a single annual camp for those in rural areas, and afternoon and evening training (with some short camps) for units in cities. In addition, Hutton recommended measures be taken to grow a body of men with at least some military skills outside the CMF. One such measure was government assistance for rifle clubs, on the understanding that shooting was conducted along military lines and members of the clubs were 'prepared to undertake in some definite form a direct share in the defence of the country'. The other measure was the establishment of a national system of cadets based on the existing Victorian model, with Hutton attaching 'great value to the military training thus taught and discipline thus impressed upon the rising generation'.[24]

Hutton had recommended a similar split between garrison and field forces in both Canada and New South Wales, but this reflected more shared strategic problems than dogma on his part. The likely threat to Australian soil was from ocean raids on the nation's widely spread cities; it therefore made sense to have garrisons in these locations and a more mobile force that could act as a reserve if needed. Yet the split also undoubtedly furthered Hutton's wider aims. The 'well trained, carefully organized, and well equipped' field force he envisioned would be able to be deployed overseas as well as serving at home – in part because he would ensure that it would be a 'thoroughly complete military organisation' possessing all the necessary departmental services, combat arms and trained staff.[25]

Hutton understood he faced risks in putting his case in writing, and shaped the *Minute* accordingly. He wisely left alone the question of compulsory service and made clear that the force would remain under the command of the Australian government and not a higher, imperial authority. Nonetheless, the furious reception the first Defence Bill had engendered made clear how sensitive the issue was. Consequently, Hutton was both relieved and encouraged by the reception the *Minute* received both in Parliament and in the press. Barton praised Hutton's plan as 'lucid and most able', and it was tabled in the House of Representatives on 23 April.[26] The *Sydney Morning Herald* declared that under the scheme Hutton would in short order have established 'a service equal to our requirements and worthy of our respect and confidence'.[27] The relief of the Adelaide *Register* at the absence of compulsory service justified Hutton's caution in shaping the *Minute*, while the paper's worry about cost pointed to a future hurdle. In Tasmania, the only note of concern was a provincial anxiety that the island state had not been explicitly mentioned. Encouraged by the broad reaction to the *Minute*, Hutton followed it in May with *The Defence & Defensive Power of Australia*. In addition to a spirited defence of the worth of Australian troops, the book contained a version of his imperial defence scheme, based on a paper he had given to the Royal Colonial Institute in London on 19 April 1898.

Within this broadly positive reception there were notes of doubt, however. Elements of the media and politicians remained leery of the deployable field force as the thin edge of the wedge on imperial defence. For the *West Australian*, the idea of the field force was in itself acceptable, but it also looked 'suspiciously like a feeler, thrown out, possibly under Imperial direction, to provoke an expression of Australian sentiment in regard to Imperial, as distinct from national, defence'.[28] Sir William Lyne, Minister for Home Affairs and acting Minister for Defence, expressed similar sentiments. Lyne, through Collins, made clear that the 'Minister does not agree with any proposal to give control, or implied control, over Australian troops to any but the Commonwealth authority'.[29] The objection once again was not to the idea of Australian soldiers serving overseas but rather to them doing so outside the control of the Australian government.

Despite the suspicion the *Minute* had created, Hutton's position differed little from that of Lyne: he had always assumed that in times of crisis, colonial governments would volunteer their support. Lyne's words thus made no real impact on the GOC. Another missive from the acting Minister for Defence did pose a threat to Hutton's scheme, however. Lyne directed (once again through Collins) that because of the Commonwealth's financial situation, Hutton was not to invest in any areas of the CMF based on 'any considerations of undertaking such external operations'.[30] This ran at right angles to Hutton's beliefs in how the field force needed to be structured. In a move that was entirely within character, Hutton simply chose to ignore Lyne's instruction. It was an early sign of the conflict with his political masters that would eventually drive him from Australia.

These storm clouds were still far on the horizon, though. By mid-April 1902, Hutton was in a positive frame of mind. The Prime Minister and wider community seemed happy with his vision, and Hutton had begun to take steps to turn that vision into reality. He had also supervised the raising of the first federal Australian contingents for the South African war, which had begun to depart in February. The government's parsimony regarding the size of his staff and his failure to secure a promotion to lieutenant-general were only minor irritants. Nor was Hutton overly worried about the lack of formal approval for his scheme, or the potential for opposition further down the track. In correspondence to Field Marshal Prince Arthur, the Duke of Connaught, Commander-in-Chief of Ireland, Hutton explained that it would 'require much patience and persistence to get all the recommendations carried through but I feel sanguine of success in the end'.[31] In a letter to Sir Arthur Bigge, private secretary to the Prince of Wales, Hutton confidently predicted that Barton and Forrest were likely to advocate the recommendations and principles put forward in the *Minute* when they arrived in London in June for the Colonial Conference.[32] The reply from the Prince of Wales sounded a note of caution. Hutton's proposals 'all seem excellent', wrote His Royal Highness, 'but I suppose you will be confronted with the old difficulty of money, or rather, the lack of it'.[33] It was a shrewd prediction, albeit one that only partially explained Hutton's eventual downfall.

It is testament to Hutton's energy and drive that, having laid the groundwork for his scheme in Melbourne, he embarked on a national tour in May. This tour served a number of objectives. It allowed Hutton to make himself known to the men under his command and to get a sense in person of their capabilities and shortcomings. It also served as a further way to build support for his scheme, with Hutton briefing senior officers on the planned reorganisation while also cultivating 'the sympathy and good-will of the press'.[34] At the same time, he began building the corps and services necessary for the 'thoroughly complete military organisation' he envisioned. The Royal Australian Artillery was raised in mid-1902 from various batteries scattered across the country, and in July 1903 a number of field, electric and submarine mining companies were combined into the Corps of Australian Engineers. Hutton's experience on operational service had also convinced him of the need for service branches, which, while unglamorous, were absolutely necessary for armies to survive in the field. Consequently, a medical service was raised, along with a military nursing service.[35] Hutton was also careful to ensure that, with some exceptions, by mid-1903 all states possessed elements from all of the arms and services – a sound course for both military and political reasons.[36]

Capping off a remarkable 18 months' work, in late July 1903 Hutton received formal approval from the government for his reorganisation plan. The last obstacle to the implementation of his scheme had been cleared. As always, Hutton made sure those in positions of influence knew of his success. The newly approved scheme was a 'sound and thorough organisation', he boasted to Sir Montagu Ommanney, Permanent Undersecretary of State for the Colonies, 'based on definite defence principles'.[37] Writing again to Bigge, Hutton reflected that 'the development of things military and of the present Scheme of Organisation has been unexpectedly rapid'.[38] In mid-December 1903 he wrote to Lord Northcote, who was soon to be appointed as Australia's third Governor-General. Hutton claimed that his achievements as GOC were 'very remarkable' and that few could have anticipated so little friction in effecting 'so many, and such vital changes'.[39]

In reality, however, by the time Hutton wrote to Northcote the tide was already turning against him. This was partly the result of actions he had taken and partly because of events outside his control. Regardless, Hutton lacked the ability to compromise or change. Instead, his almost total belief in his own infallibility meant that he saw resistance to his vision as something to be crushed through sheer hard work. In this respect, the boundless energy that had seen him achieve so much in his first 18 months as GOC began to count against him. His relentless pursuit of his vision regardless of concerns raised was interpreted as stubbornness, further alienating those around him. The result was that even as he boasted to Lord Northcote about a lack of friction, Hutton faced growing resistance and antagonism towards his plans and towards his person.

The first points of difficulty stemmed from events outside Hutton's control. Despite the war against the Boers ultimately ending in victory, there was a widespread belief within both Britain and the colonies that the war had been mismanaged. A series of reports and commissions conducted brutal self-examinations of the performance of the War Office throughout 1903–04. It was a process that ultimately led to important reforms but also contributed to a broader perception that the upper ranks of the British Army were incompetent, a perception that Hutton did not escape. For all of his faults this was deeply unfair to Hutton, who had consistently rejected the studied amateurism of many of his peers in favour of a hard-working professionalism. He had long railed against the anachronisms and inefficiencies of the British Army, and owed his rapid advancement in part to his association with the Wolseley Ring of army reformers. He had performed well when given command in South Africa, a campaign that showed his ability in the field and the validity of many of his wider ideas. Yet none of this seemed to matter in the face of the broader perception that British officers were incompetent.

There was also a certain bitter irony about Hutton's service in South Africa. The 1st Mounted Brigade had consisted of troops from across the British Empire, and their performance had convinced Hutton of the military potential of Britain's colonial subjects. The campaign had also made clear to him, however, the overriding need for professionalism in areas such as logistics and medical support – a lesson that heavily shaped his visions for the reorganisation of the CMF. The public view in Australia was almost diametrically opposed, however. South Africa had shown that untrained but enthusiastic amateurs from the colonies could hold their own with, or even outperform, British regulars. Regular soldiers, staff and military organisations were a drain on the public coffers.[40] Consequently, just as Hutton came to undertake the most difficult part of his reforms, the reorganisation of the garrison and field forces, public understanding was turning against the entire idea of a more professional force.

As this was going on, Hutton was also working to produce a revised Defence Bill. Forrest was determined to get it passed, despite a looming federal election and advice that he should wait until the next parliamentary session.[41] Debate was once again vigorous, but this time an amended version of the Bill passed and the *Defence Act* was formally proclaimed on 1 March 1904. Among other measures, the Act provided for the establishment of a Military Board of advice intended to discuss matters referred to it by the minister.[42] Based on ongoing reforms in Britain, and not initially formed despite the passage of the Bill, the Military Board was a seemingly minor command change that would in fact have serious ramifications for Hutton's time in Australia.

Despite having drafted it, Hutton disliked the Bill, describing it in a letter to Ommanney as containing 'much to be deplored'.[43] Although he had secured assurances that in an emergency the British government 'might rely with absolute certainty on the assistance of at least one portion of the Commonwealth troops', these troops would only be individuals who were willing to volunteer rather than whole units.[44] 'I did my utmost, directly and indirectly', he continued to Ommanney, to encourage 'a broader view of the necessities and the strategical and political situation in Australia as it appears to those of us who consider the question from a broad imperial standpoint', but was foiled by the 'ignorance and self-interest of politicians'.[45] The feeling was increasingly mutual. For many within Parliament, Hutton was becoming the avatar for all of the objections they had to imperial defence. Objection thus continued to build not only to Hutton's policies but also to his personality. This feeling in Parliament was not helped by Forrest's shift from Defence to Home Affairs on 7 August and Barton's departure from Parliament for the High Court on 23 September. Hutton lost two powerful figures sympathetic to the imperial perspective just as opposition to his reforms began to crystallise.

Opposition increasingly also came from the grassroots. When he had given provisional approval for Hutton's scheme in December 1902, Forrest had attached the caveat that the reorganisation must be 'effected with as little inconvenience or hardship to Corps as possible'.[46] It was a manifestly unworkable condition that Hutton, typically, chose to ignore. Yet it was also a directive that reflected the *social* role of military units throughout Australia. For many Australians, their local militia or volunteer unit was a source of pride: for those who served in them, a demonstration of patriotism, a civic duty, or an enjoyable social activity. Hutton's reorganisation threatened to upend this, removing units altogether from communities or changing them so significantly that many locals could no longer participate. Here was an issue that was deeply important to Australian communities in the early 20th century.

Hutton's reorganisations impacted on local units in a number of specific ways. His preference for militia over volunteers was reflected in the forced conversion of 1500 of the latter to the former.[47] It was, in one sense, an encapsulation of Hutton's reforms: a move that made a degree of military sense but ignored political realities. Hutton wanted more militia because it aligned with his long-standing convictions of the value of part-paid over non-paid soldiers, a view that had also been reflected in advice from the CDC to the federal government in March 1901. Yet this ignored the peculiar social nature and political power of the volunteer movement. Anchored in the middle and upper class, volunteer units were seen by those who participated in them as a vehicle for social advancement and prestige. Moreover, these men had the resources to mobilise popular and political opinion. The commanders of two prominent cavalry regiments, the Melbourne Cavalry and the New South Wales Lancers, fought protracted and very public battles against Hutton's attempt to transform their units into Light Horse. Such a transformation would have involved the loss of distinctive uniforms, weapons, volunteer status for the Melbourne Cavalry and, above all, social cachet. While Hutton ultimately prevailed, his wilfully blinkered view of the problem had ensured the aggravation of a key political constituency for only marginal gains.[48]

An issue that loomed even larger was the conversion of existing infantry units to smaller mounted ones. Many within urban areas could not afford the horses required, which led (as noted by the *Sydney Morning Herald*) to many cases 'of suitable men who are deterred from . . . taking up a commission by the expense they will have to incur'.[49] One outcome of these conversions was a growing friction between the mounted and non-mounted arms, and the issue became increasingly divisive within communities. This was evident in the Monaro district of New South Wales, for example, when the infantry company based at Cooma was replaced by a Light Horse squadron. Local member and future Minister for Defence, Austin Chapman, was inundated with complaints from residents about the change; meanwhile the press pursued a class angle, claiming that Hutton was attempting to exclude all but the wealthy by replacing 141 foot soldiers with a troop of 18 horsemen.[50] Such incidents were common throughout Australia.

Resistance to the physical reorganisation of the CMF was not the only problem Hutton faced. The failure to pass the *Defence Act* in 1901 had meant that the interim measures adopted for pay and conditions, which kept the existing colonial pay scales, continued until 1904. This meant that officers and men received different rates of pay depending on what state they were based in, creating a 'general feeling of dissatisfaction amongst both the officers and the men'.[51] Hutton had no ability to change the pay situation beyond protesting vigorously to Forrest that the system was 'manifestly unfair'.[52] Rather than improving the situation, however, his reforms only made it worse. Hutton's scheme had envisioned garrison troops being entirely unpaid volunteers, while the field force would be composed of partially paid militia. There was no orderly transition, however; instead, all designated garrison troops ceased to be paid. To make matters worse, units earmarked for the field force and thus entitled to pay did not receive it either. The result was uproar, particularly in Western Australia, South Australia and Tasmania, where all citizen soldiers had received some form of pay or allowances. Morale was seriously impacted, and both state commandants and members of Parliament protested vigorously to Hutton.[53] Reflecting the administrative immaturity that had helped cause the problem, Forrest's scrambled reaction was to restore temporary payment to two garrisons in Queensland and nowhere else.

The slump in morale created by the problems with pay and the backlash against Hutton's reorganisation began to be reflected in a decline in numbers. It soon became clear that the 26,000 personnel called for in Hutton's preferred force structure was simply unrealistic; by June 1903 the CMF was 3600 short of establishment strength, and numbers were continuing to fall. By June 1904 less than 20,000 troops were on the rolls. The decline in numbers proved ample ammunition for his growing body of critics. The Member for Wentworth, William Kelly, lambasted Hutton in Parliament: 'Everyone who has studied the question knows that, for some reason or other, there is the gravest lack of confidence through every rank . . . We have seen officers resigning and giving up the sword for the ploughshare.'[54] As with the pay problems, Hutton wore the blame for issues that were only partially his fault and which he had only a limited ability to change. In an effort to save money, Forrest had already frozen troop strengths in Tasmania and Western Australia, despite already approving Hutton's planned larger establishments in both states.

Hutton's reaction to this growing chorus of criticism was typically self-defeating. He was simply unwilling to consider that those opposing him had valid concerns, or to compromise on some issues in order to salvage others. As had been the case throughout his career, critics were dismissed as troublemakers, possessing vested interests, ignorant or simply persons who 'object to all changes'.[55] His belief that his rank and accomplishments spoke for themselves, and that those without military expertise should not question him as a result, also rankled. Hutton's reply to a request from the Minister for Defence for a response to parliamentary criticism was typical: 'I find it difficult to reply to the comprehensive criticism by ill-informed Members of Parliament who have neither the training nor possess the Military instincts to qualify them as critics.'[56] It was a spectacularly tone deaf effort that served only to further the growing rift between Hutton and his civilian superiors.

In some respects Hutton was correct, yet even in those instances his refusal to play the political game ultimately cost him. One of his most persistent and vocal critics was John Cash Neild, a conservative senator and the commanding officer of the volunteer St George's English Rifles. Neild had raised the English Rifles himself in 1896; just three years later a board of inquiry concluded that he lacked the judgment to command an efficient regiment, and in 1900 Major-General John French had recommended he be forcibly retired.[57] He was the definition of a vested interest, a man who commanded a military unit – a demonstrably ineffective one – because it gave him social status, notwithstanding the frequent ridicule his command prompted from the press and politicians on both sides of the floor. Tiring of Neild's sniping, Hutton sacked him on grounds of incompetence. This prompted uproar in Parliament, and the appointment of a Senate Select Committee to investigate Neild's charge that his dismissal was an effort to silence an elected representative. The committee ultimately found that Neild's incompetence justified his dismissal by Hutton, but the episode further eroded confidence in the GOC within Parliament.[58] As was so often the case during his career, being correct was not enough.

Obscured by these public spats, but just as dangerous to Hutton's plans, were ongoing funding problems. Hutton had assumed that the budget available to him would be equivalent to the combined expenditure of the six colonial militaries – a total of £937,000 in 1900. This was again a misreading of the political will, as there was a broad expectation in Parliament that Federation would result in savings in defence. Forrest was only able to get the initial defence estimates through the Committee of Supply by cutting £176,000 and promising a reduction of £84,524 in the 1901–02 estimates and a further £130,000 the year after that. Hutton therefore immediately found himself fighting budget cuts, even as he embarked on his reorganisation. By 1903–04 military estimates were a little over £581,000, a reduction of some £300,000 from 1901–02.[59] This was not enough money to maintain the existing establishment, let alone fund Hutton's scheme. He consequently asked for £486,000 over a four-year period from 1903 to 1907 to build the field force and garrison troops. The request was denied, and the defence budget in 1903 slumped to just 0.38 per cent of the year's Gross Domestic Product.[60]

Reflecting the atmosphere of austerity, in May 1903 Hutton was again ordered to reduce the size of his staff. His response was to threaten to resign, telling Forrest, 'I am not prepared to continue efforts which must be necessarily doomed to failure . . . and to continue responsibilities which I am unable to vindicate.'[61] Hutton complained to the Governor-General, Lord Hallam Tennyson, that he 'must fail unless I have assistance . . . I am justly entitled to a minimum number of officers to help me'.[62] Hutton did not mince words in his annual report, stating that he viewed the cuts with the 'gravest apprehension'.[63] Forrest refused to publish the report while urging

Hutton to amend it, in an effort to save the government's blushes. Hutton partially complied, but his relationship with the minister and the civilians within the Defence Department continued to deteriorate. Hutton continued to complain in his May 1904 report, writing that another proposed reduction of his headquarters staff from seven to six members would 'if carried out, render it impracticable for the General Officer Commanding to accept the responsibilities'.[64] Should the reductions go ahead it would be 'only a question of time' Hutton warned, 'for chaos and disintegration to replace the military order and system which is now being introduced'.[65] Hutton's complaints about the size of his staff continued until his departure in October 1904.

Hutton's headquarters staff was not the only area to suffer from budgetary pressures. Treasury released just £75,000 in 1903 for the purchase of warlike stores, despite the fact that more than £480,000 had already been approved over four years. This figure was itself £45,000 less than Hutton's conservative estimation of what he needed, which had included the continuing use of obsolete equipment.[66] Despite the lack of equipment, guns, arms and ammunition having been identified in 1901 as a significant problem for the CMF, just £370,000 was spent up to 1909 in an effort to rectify the shortfalls. Some states possessed no artillery carriages at all, a problem partially ameliorated by a reduction in the size of the permanent artillery force by 39 per cent. Hutton warned that this reduction could 'seriously compromise the security of the Commonwealth'.[67] In the event, funding for defence did not exceed the colonial total of £937,000 until 1906–07. Irrespective of popular and political opposition, these shortfalls ensured that Hutton's scheme was never properly implemented. Hutton himself cannot bear responsibility for this failure, however; the government, well aware of the prevailing political climate, had still approved his plan.

Despite the pressures he was under, Hutton continued to achieve some successes. A significant component of the 1902 *Minute* was Hutton's identification of inadequate training standards and his plans to rectify them. The social function of many volunteer and militia units meant that training, when it did occur, was largely confined to basic parade ground drill. Little effort was made to train in the field, and many artillery batteries had done little if any tactical or battle firing. The state of officers in the part-time force was a particular concern. The lack of realistic training in part reflected the inability of citizen officers to conduct it, and too often responsibility devolved directly onto the overstretched permanent instructional staff. It was this state of affairs that prompted Hutton's bitter complaints about the 1903 reductions in the numbers of permanents and his continued advocacy for a military college.[68] It also explained his lobbying for a pension scheme for permanent officers in order to avoid, as had sometimes been the case in colonial New South Wales, the retaining of officers on 'charitable grounds'.[69]

Hutton's solution to the problem of training standards reflected his professionalism and energy. He implemented a number of programs designed to give the permanent officer corps the experience necessary to command in wartime, including the creation of exchange systems with the British and Indian armies and the securing of places for certain officers at the British Staff College. Hutton also drew on his experience in Canada and established a Staff Ride system and the 'schools of instruction' called for in the *Minute*. He laid down a systematic training program, with annual field training generally conducted over the Easter period to minimise the number of days part-time soldiers had to miss work. Following the dictum of Hutton's early mentor Colonel R.B. Hawley that 'those who lead should be those who instructed', Hutton ensured that training at annual camps was undertaken by the officers of the units participating rather than the instructional staff.[70] Above all, the philosophy underpinning training shifted to one that emphasised a need for realism. The new musketry regulations, introduced in 1904, focused on practices with moving targets and rapid aiming in an effort to replicate battlefield conditions. These systems were far from perfect. Troops could not be compelled to attend their annual camps, and the reduction in permanent instructors reduced the effectiveness of the 'schools of instruction'. Nonetheless, Hutton's reforms improved the training standards of the CMF not only while he was GOC but until well after his departure from Australia too.[71]

Throughout his time as GOC Hutton continued to ignore the political forces building against him, even as they became more and more threatening. As noted earlier, Forrest had shifted from Defence to Home Affairs in August 1903. His relationship with Hutton had soured by that time, driven largely by frictions over the budget. Forrest was replaced by Senator James Drake, who lasted just 45 days before his replacement on 24 September 1903 by Austin Chapman.

It did not take long for the relationship between Chapman and Hutton to deteriorate, a reflection of both the ongoing budgetary issues and Hutton's continued blindness to the concerns of his political masters. As already noted, Chapman had heard first hand from his constituents about the deleterious effects of Hutton's reorganisation. He also now came to recognise Hutton's tendency to push the boundaries of what was acceptable in civil–military relations. Unlike Forrest, however, Chapman was much less tolerant of Hutton's forays. Once again displaying his sensitivity to any hint of credit being denied him, in March 1904 Hutton registered his distress about press reports concerning his new regulations, which suggested they had come solely from Collins.[72] Chapman leapt at the opportunity, rebuking Hutton that his complaint was 'written under a misapprehension of the responsibilities and position of the General Officer commanding'.[73] This relatively minor spat was followed by a more serious crisis when Chapman requested a copy of a ciphered message Hutton had sent to the Secretary for War in London. Hutton refused to divulge its contents as the original on the basis that if matched with a transcript, it would decrypt the code in which it had been written. Chapman was astonished at this response, and requested it again. Only the collapse of the Deakin government in April, and Chapman's exit from the ministry, prevented a further escalation.

The election of Australia's first Labor government posed further problems for Hutton. The new government's Minister for Defence,

Queensland Senator Andrew Dawson, was 'a hard-drinking, poorly educated orphan', who had worked as a miner, bullock driver and journalist.[74] He had also initially opposed the commitment of Queensland to the war in South Africa. It was hard to envision a man more ill-suited to managing the upper-class, conservative, imperialist Hutton. Moreover, Dawson was spoiling for a fight. Like many within the Labor Party he disdained military professionalism and believed Hutton had left the forces in disarray. The problem, then, was the GOC and not the financial restrictions he worked under. Hutton, for his part, dismissed the Queenslander as 'totally illiterate' and someone who could 'barely sign his own name'.[75]

Unsurprisingly given their existing views, the short time Dawson and Hutton spent working together was marked by intense and open acrimony. Dawson seized on the cipher issue as a way to assert his authority over Hutton and demanded to see a transcript of the message. Hutton was still formulating a response when the press got hold of the story.[76] Suddenly under public pressure, Hutton relented and provided a copy of the transcript. The message itself was innocuous; the issue had always been that of Hutton's willingness to obey civil authority. Prime Minister Watson was satisfied, but the relationship between Hutton and his political masters plumbed new depths. It was an untenable professional relationship, only broken by the fall of the Labor government and its replacement by the Reid–McLean ministry in August 1904. While Dawson later wrote of his 'happy relations [with] Collins and his civilian departmental staff', he acknowledged (with some understatement) that he and Hutton 'were, unfortunately not in touch or sympathy'.[77]

Any relief Hutton felt, however, was relatively short lived. Despite having been in office for less than four months, Dawson initiated a key reform that would ultimately be Hutton's undoing. Labor had come to power favouring the idea of raising a board to control the military forces rather than relying on a GOC. Dawson had consequently set up a committee, chaired by himself, to examine the command and administration arrangements for the military and naval forces. Perhaps unsurprisingly, the committee members rejected the idea of a GOC as 'the sole responsible adviser of the Minister on all Military questions'.⁷⁸ Instead they proposed to raise a Council of Defence to 'collate information and afford the Government advice on all questions of policy'.⁷⁹ A Military Board and a Naval Board would also be raised to administer their respective forces, while an independent Inspector-General would be appointed to 'ascertain and report upon the condition of the Military Forces'.⁸⁰ The idea of a military board had been provided for in the *Defence Act* of 1903, but had not been followed up. Dawson's advocacy of the reforms was motivated by a genuine desire to promote decentralisation, unite the civil and military branches of the department, and provide the government with a greater range of advice on defence matters. His difficult relationship with Hutton reinforced his views, rather than being the source of them.

The Dawson Committee's report was released just as the Labor government fell. Dawson's replacement as Minister for Defence was James Whiteside McCay, a lawyer and militia officer who would go on to command the 5th Division AIF. The new minister's background suggested he may have favoured Hutton's cause. Yet McCay's sympathies lay elsewhere, as shown by his request two weeks into his appointment for Hutton's opinion on Dawson's report and the GOC's suggestions for which officers might serve on the proposed council and board. The proposed reforms would bring Australia into line with the arrangements in place in Britain and Canada and help calm anxieties over the control of Australian forces by removing the imperial GOC. The removal of Hutton was a secondary objective but a welcome one nonetheless. It was a testament to how unpopular the GOC had become within the Australian Parliament that Hutton's arguments against the reforms fell on deaf ears. The *Defence Act* of 1904, an amendment to the Act of the previous year, was presented and passed in July, and assented on 9 December 1904.⁸¹ In a stroke, the position of GOC was abolished.

Following the passing of the amendment, Hutton wrote to Collins on 20 August 1904 asking that McCay inform the War Office 'of the termination of my command of the Military Forces of the Commonwealth on December 26th next'.[82] He planned to depart Australia on 15 November.[83] In passing on this news to the Prime Minister, George Reid, McCay could muster only a reference to his 'appreciation of services rendered'.[84] Reid passed the request on to Government House the same day, omitting McCay's polite words altogether. On the eve of his departure, Hutton chose to publicly vent his frustrations at the King's Birthday Banquet at the Melbourne Town Hall. The speech was yet another example of Hutton's tone deafness and lack of self-reflection. 'The difficulties with which I had to contend no man knows except myself,' Hutton began.[85] 'There are more tests of courage than the test of a battle-field,' he continued, 'I could not say anything for a soldier's hands are tied ... [but] If I have been silent it has not been for want of courage or love of fighting ... I fearlessly look Australia in the face, to the Press, Parliament and Public, and say that I have done my utmost.'[86] On 2 November 1904 McCay announced the formation of the Military Board, and the abolition of the position of GOC. Hutton departed Australia 13 days later 'with heavy heart', though, he also admitted, a 'feeling of relief which not unnaturally accompanies the termination of a period of great difficulty and strain'.[87]

Hutton ultimately failed to achieve his goal of building a military force capable of defending Australia and contributing to a wider system of cooperative imperial defence. When the general European war he had so long anticipated did arrive, Australia's contribution was not the militia field force Hutton had envisioned but an army raised specifically for the purpose of overseas service from individual volunteers. Hutton's failure sprang from many sources, but the dominant ones were the financial circumstances of the new Commonwealth and his own personality. The persistent budget pressures placed on Defence meant reform on a scale Hutton envisioned was never realistic. He had reason to be aggrieved given the government agreed to his scheme and then refused to properly fund it. Yet it was testament to the flaws in Hutton's character that he continued to relentlessly pursue his plans despite the enormous shortfalls in funding and the growing pressure from within the community. A more reflective, considered officer may have recognised the impossibility of achieving the entirety of his program and instead have elected to compromise in the hope of achieving at least some of his goals. Instead, Hutton continued to charge forward with his blinkers on. The result was that by mid-1904 he had aggravated his political masters to such a degree that they saw fit not merely to get rid of him but the entire position he occupied.

Hutton's absolute self-assurance meant that it was impossible for him to countenance professional failure for anything but a short period of despondency. He thus almost immediately began an intensive campaign to convince those around him, and himself, that he actually had been successful in Australia. 'I had achieved all that I had laid myself out to do in the three short years that had passed', he later mused.[88] Hutton argued that in less than three years he crafted a unified military system 'out of the motley defence forces previously existing in the six States of Australia, in spite of drastic retrenchment, and in spite of the halting administration of three successive Governments so widely divergent in their views'.[89] Although obviously self-serving, Hutton's argument had merits. There can be no question that when Hutton left Australia in 1904 the federal military force was more organised, better administered and more highly trained than the colonial forces he had inherited. His commitment to professionalism had also nurtured many officers – Cyril Brudenell Bingham White, Harry Chauvel, John Antill, William Bridges – who would subsequently make critical contributions to the Australian Army in peace and war. Prime Minister George Reid had predicted on the eve of Hutton's departure in 1904 that 'the people of this nation will see more and more clearly the results of the invaluable service that have been rendered to us, in the infancy of this nation, by General Hutton'.[90] In 1921 Charles Bean described him, not unreasonably, as 'a soldier of a brilliance only too rare' and that his 'mark will always be deeply pressed on the Australian Army'.[91]

Further reading

E. Andrews, *The Department of Defence*, vol. 5, *Australian Centenary History of Defence*, Oxford University Press, Melbourne, 2001

S.J. Clarke, 'Marching to their Own Drum: British Army Officers as Military Commandants in the Australian Colonies and New Zealand 1870–1901', PhD thesis, University of New South Wales, 1999

E.T.H. Hutton, *Military Forces of the Commonwealth: Minute upon the Defence of Australia*, Robt. S. Brain, Government Printer for the State of Victoria, Melbourne, 1902

———, *The Defence and Defensive Power of Australia*, Angus & Robertson, Melbourne, 1902

D. Leece, 'Who Was Edward Thomas Henry Hutton?', *Journal of the Royal United Institute of New South Wales*, vol. 63, no. 2, June 2012, p. 30

R.J.R. Lehane, 'Lieutenant-General Edward Hutton and "Greater Britain"': Late-Victorian Imperialism, Imperial Defence and the Self-governing Colonies', PhD thesis, University of Sydney, 2005

W. Perry, 'Lieutenant-General Sir Edward Hutton: The Creator of the Post-Federation Army', *Australian Army Journal*, no. 291, August 1973, pp. 19–27

———, 'Military Reforms of General Sir Edward Hutton in the Commonwealth of Australia, 1902–04', *The Victorian Historical Magazine*, vol. 29, no. 1, February 1959, pp. 34–57

C. Stockings, *Britannia's Shield: Lieutenant-General Sir Edward Hutton and Late Victorian Imperial Defence*, Cambridge University Press, Melbourne, 2015

———, *The Making & Breaking of the Post-Federation Australian Army, 1901–09*, Land Warfare Studies, Study Paper no. 311, Canberra, 2007.

C. Wilcox, *For Hearths and Homes: Citizen Soldiering in Australia, 1854–1945*, Allen & Unwin, St Leonards, 1998

J. Wood, *Chiefs of the Australian Army*, Australian Military History Publications, Loftus, 2006

2
DUNTROON TO THE DARDANELLES
Major-General Sir William Bridges

CHRIS CLARK

FOR MUCH OF THE 20th century, William Throsby Bridges (1861–1915) was remembered primarily for two things. According to his first biographer, war correspondent and official historian Charles Bean, the great achievements of Bridges' army career involved laying the 'main foundations of his country's fighting services in World War I' through the creation of the Royal Military College (RMC) at Duntroon and his command of the 1st Australian Division. By asserting this claim in a book devoted to the founders of the Australian Imperial Force (AIF), Bean no doubt meant to imply that it was not just Bridges' leadership of the division for which he was entitled to great credit but his initial role in raising and organising the AIF as a whole. As for Duntroon, Bean professed to be in no doubt about the importance of Bridges' work at the college, declaring it to have been 'one of the greatest personal achievements for which Australia is indebted to any one'.[1]

Since the time that Bean wrote his account in the 1950s, historians have begun disputing the nature and extent of Bridges' legacy to the Australian Army. Whereas Bean appeared convinced that, if Bridges had survived the first months after the AIF went into battle

Major-General Sir William Throsby Bridges, first Australian Chief of the General Staff.
Courtesy of the author

(instead of falling victim to a Turkish sniper's bullet three weeks after the Gallipoli landing in April 1915), 'it is probable that he would have emerged the greatest of Australia's soldiers',[2] others have taken the view that his performance at the head of 1st Division exposed serious deficiencies – to the extent that one rated him 'nearer the duds' on the generalship scale,[3] and another that Bridges occupies a mainly 'totemic position in Australian martial mythology' which was merely 'reinforced by the manner of his death'.[4] Central to the anti-Bridges case is his unattractive personality, which by most accounts was the opposite of magnetic. Those who knew or worked closest to Bridges left descriptions of him as aloof, diffident, remote, austere, severe and unsympathetic. The 1st Division's chief gunner at Gallipoli is claimed to have later described him as 'an uncouth, ignorant boor',[5] and even the wife of another officer on the division's staff angrily labelled Bridges 'a cur' for the way he treated her husband (who by 1918 was himself a divisional commander).[6]

Bridges' reputation for raising the AIF has fared somewhat better over the years, since it was undeniably a very considerable achievement to have brought into being a contingent of 20,000 volunteers from across Australia in the space of three months – even if there were significant deficiencies in the force's training, equipment and much else besides. Here too, however, the praise Bean heaped on Bridges' memory, for having taken wise and decisive steps to preserve the separate national identity of the AIF, has come in for later revision. While Bridges did choose a name that cemented the force's national identity, and stood firm to preserve its divisional structure against indications that the British War Office intended to parcel out Australian brigades among British formations, in neither case was his position exactly what it seemed.

There have since been arguments that the AIF's title was merely a recycled version of the planned 'Imperial Australian Force' (intended as a field force to help Britain fight a future war in Europe) that Australia's first Prime Minister was asked to sign onto at the 1902 Colonial Conference in London. The idea was rejected then, but by reviving it 12 years later – in slightly altered form – Bridges was almost certainly seeking to emphasise the imperial as much as the nationalist dimension of Australia's undertaking.[7] And in urging the War Office to accept a divisional-sized force that was offered by Australia he was merely complying with the expressed wishes of the Cook government then in office. 'It was not quite my idea of what we should send', he confided to Colonel H.G. Chauvel, then in London as Australia's representative on the Imperial General Staff.[8] Presumably he personally preferred the brigades option.

There is also clear evidence that Bridges' expectation all along was that command of the AIF would go to a British regular general – his first choice being his former mentor, Sir Edward Hutton. The reason for this was his personal belief that no Australian had the necessary experience of field command, including himself. It was only the determination of the Australian government that its military contingent to the war must be led by a local officer that propelled Bridges into this position, based on the fact that he, as Inspector-General of the Commonwealth Military Forces on the outbreak of war, was the nation's senior soldier.[9]

Far from championing the AIF's cause, Bridges was noticeably uninterested and cavalier in protecting its interests. In his rush to get the force to England, he was quite willing to disregard the threat it potentially faced on the high seas until the German Pacific Squadron had been properly accounted for.[10] And once the AIF had been diverted to Egypt to finish its training, he was conspicuously disinclined to resist persistent efforts to bring AIF medical and base elements at Cairo under local British control. He also attempted to divest himself of the role of AIF commander by shifting administrative authority for the force onto one of his British superiors, either Sir John Maxwell or Sir William Birdwood.[11]

Even Bridges' reputation as founding commandant of the RMC at Duntroon has not remained entirely intact. While the college still exists, on its original site and with its name unchanged, it is not the same institution that he created to provide a sustained educational and training experience over four years – one designed to foster a martial spirit in young men who were products of a community that lacked a significant military heritage or tradition before the First World War. Following the opening of the Australian Defence Force Academy (ADFA) in 1986, Duntroon began conducting a range of shorter officer training courses, allowing it to hold two graduations a year.[12] Even before the advent of ADFA, however, the college had long outgrown the stamp that Bridges imprinted upon the place as founder, though it took a committee of inquiry in 1970 to finally jolt the army into recognising the fact and modernise the regimen imposed on cadets.[13]

Despite the demolition (or at least partial dismantling) of the main planks of Bridges' claims to legendary status within 'Australian martial mythology', his 30-year military career cannot, and should not, be simply dismissed by those seeking to comprehend the early years of the army's history in Australia. Analysis and study of the decade before Bridges was appointed to establish the RMC in 1910 reveals a personal contribution to military affairs which – by itself – is deserving of respectful acknowledgment. Moreover, understanding Bridges' background and early years helps to highlight and explain the strengths and weaknesses that he brought to his previously recognised roles at Duntroon and during the initial nine months of the First World War.

The first and not least important aspect of Bridges' background concerns the fact that he was not a native-born Australian. Like a great many other 'Australians' of the late 19th century, he was actually an immigrant of British origins, having been born in Greenock, Scotland, a shipyard town on the southern shore of the Firth of Clyde, about 40 kilometres west of Glasgow. While some writers have alluded to Bridges' birthplace as though this was itself an explanation for his later 'dour' and humourless demeanour, in reality he possessed no Scottish ancestry whatsoever.

Bridges' heritage was actually English, but with the sort of widely travelled connections that heightened appreciation of the far-flung extent of the British Empire's boundaries. His father was a Jamaican-born Royal Navy officer, with more than a dozen years of sea service across the globe before he acquired an Australian wife, a member of the Throsby clan from Moss Vale, New South Wales, while stationed at Sydney in 1858. The family's presence at Greenock when William was born was therefore only a transitory interlude in a peripatetic naval existence that removed them from Scotland two years later, and took them to the Isle of Wight and London before his father was injured in a carriage accident and forced to retire in 1872.

The family moved to Canada and went onto the land near the present-day city of Barrie, about 80 kilometres north of Toronto. Young William completed a couple of years schooling at Port Hope, a town on the northern shore of Lake Ontario about 80 kilometres east of Toronto, before entering the military college established in June 1876 by the Canadian government at Kingston, Ontario. William Bridges was not in the first intake to the new college, but the second, which entered early in 1877, when he was aged 16. His stated intention was to train for a commission in the British Army.

Cadet Bridges had been at Kingston less than two years when his parents decided to leave Canada and move to Mrs Bridges' home town. Young Bridges' performance at his studies became erratic, and in June 1879 he left the college to take up a surveying position, arranged for him by his parents, in New South Wales. Although Bridges was therefore a drop-out and not a graduate of Kingston (as some writers mistakenly claim), he left Canada with a Certificate of Military Qualifications, which in due course would mark him out in the colonial forces of Australia in which few officers could boast formal professional training of any sort. He also arrived in Sydney as an 18-year-old already possessed of a world outlook that was imperial in its dimension.

For the next six years Bridges was employed in the roads and bridges department of the colony's civil service, working – first as superintendent, then as inspector – in northern rural districts far from Sydney. It was reportedly the unprecedented decision of the

New South Wales government in February 1885 to offer Britain a military contingent to assist with overcoming Mahdist 'rebels' in the Sudan region of North Africa adjoining the Red Sea that precipitated Bridges towards seeking an appointment in the colony's military forces. The usual story is that he hurried from his job at Narrabri in an attempt to enlist in the Sudan contingent, but failed to secure a berth in the force, which was fully subscribed before he reached Sydney. It was only the fact that the colony set about expanding its remaining defence forces after the contingent sailed on 3 March that Bridges was afforded a doorway through which to enter the military establishment.

The appointment Bridges received on 19 May 1885 as a lieutenant in the New South Wales Artillery was originally to have lasted only until the Sudan contingent returned, but when a vacancy opened in the permanent artillery forces in August that year he unexpectedly found his commission confirmed. There was considerable irony in the fact that Bridges owed his foothold on the initial rung of a regular military career to the first example of imperial military adventurism indulged in by an Australian colonial government; it can only be wondered whether this episode exercised a further formative influence over the military mindset of the nation's future top soldier.

For another five years Bridges' days were taken up with the dreary tedium of constant training in a peacetime military establishment. He did not allow himself to become jaded by this experience, however, but instead worked hard to become professionally competent in the gunner's art, with the result that he was quickly taken onto the staff of the school of artillery at Middle Head, Sydney. After he formally qualified as a gunnery instructor in 1889, he was promoted to captain and chosen to attend further advanced courses in England. Taking his wife and three children with him, Bridges disappeared from the colony for a period of two years. By the time he returned in February 1893, with a specialist Firemaster's Certificate in hand, the colony's defence arrangements were about to be transformed by another fresh arrival from England – in the person of Colonel

E.T.H. Hutton (see Chapter 1), a British regular who in May took up the command of the New South Wales forces with the local rank of major-general. Although Hutton was not yet imbued with his 'grand project' of binding the colonies to Britain in a cooperative imperial military partnership, he arrived in the colony with a vision of reorganising the local forces and raising their level of efficiency through better training.

It was Hutton who, recognising that Bridges' new qualifications made him the most technically proficient gunnery officer in the colony, had him promoted to major in August and appointed commandant of a new School of Gunnery. Hutton also probably came to consider that Bridges' background made him the closest thing to an imperial officer in his new command, and marked him out as useful for other purposes. When, in November 1893, Hutton was appointed to chair a joint naval and military committee that was required to consider general questions of local defence, he selected Bridges as secretary for the panel. Bridges also acted in the same capacity for two similar bodies, constituted in October 1894 and January 1896, to consider military matters ahead of Federation. Hutton later made clear that Bridges was receiving preferment in being assigned these roles, declaring that: 'Major Bridges had been specially selected by me for this duty, as I knew him to be an officer of great ability and promise ...'.[14] Although Hutton's period in command ended in 1896, by the time he left for England early in March[15] he could justifiably claim to have galvanised the colony's defence forces – and set Bridges' career on a path that ensured his rise to prominence.

While Hutton was unquestionably the major formative influence on Bridges' professional life in the period before 1901, there were other factors. On a personal level was a family tragedy that occurred a week before Christmas 1894, when one of Bridges' twin daughters – supposedly his favourite – drowned following a boating collision on Sydney Harbour.[16] According to Mrs Bridges, in the early years of her marriage her husband had been a fairly relaxed individual, given to sailing and reading novels in his spare time, but this changed dramatically. Immediately after the accident that claimed his daughter's life, and almost that of his elder son too, Bridges locked himself in his study for four days. Upon the door being eventually forced, he was found, insensible, at his desk. When Bean first heard of this story – almost certainly from Bridges' widow, after he contacted her in 1919–20 in connection with the official history – he felt that it was 'too intimate' to include in a biography, but 'it made clear to me that the old General was capable of feeling, which his treatment of subordinates didn't lead one to suspect in him'. It is possibly from this point that Bridges appeared especially driven in dedication to his military career, and that his persona underwent a change to the grim and humourless figure that he became known.[17]

The special regard in which Hutton held him also stood Bridges in good stead with Hutton's successor. This was Colonel G.A. French, a British regular officer who had previously served as commandant of the Queensland Defence Force for eight years before 1891. Arriving in Sydney from an artillery post in India on 27 April 1896,[18] George French led the New South Wales Military Forces as a local major-general until a year after Federation. Although he most probably knew about Bridges only from handover notes left by Hutton, French evidently also appreciated Bridges' special utility when matters arose involving imperial rather than purely colonial interests. It was probably this factor that led to Bridges being employed on a puzzling and murky assignment to the Pacific island group of Samoa for four weeks in May–June 1898. Although Bridges was officially on leave, later references he made to this episode hint that he was actually intelligence-gathering on behalf of the British War Office – something that almost certainly would have occurred only with the connivance of General French. During what was superficially a tropical holiday, Bridges managed to pay a visit to Tupua Tamasese Lealofi, who he described as 'the rebel king' – just six months before the situation in the island kingdom erupted into conflict over contested succession to the throne.[19]

Within two months of the start of the Second South African War (more commonly known as the Boer War) in October 1899, Bridges succeeded in getting away to the battlefront – but not in a capacity that provided any useful combat, command or staff experience. He was sent as a 'special service officer' attached to the British Army during early operations to lift the siege on the mining town of Kimberley and capture the first of the Boer capitals at Bloemfontein in the Orange Free State. This amounted to duty as an observer only, and lasted less than six months in any event after he fell ill with typhoid (enteric fever, as it was then called), an affliction that prevented him from taking up a staff post with the mounted infantry brigade led by Edward Hutton. Evacuated to England to convalesce, he gave evidence before a royal commission on the care of the sick and wounded in the South African campaign. Not wishing to be seen as strongly criticising the British medical system, he largely confined his comments to mentioning soldiers' dislike of being transported in horse-drawn ambulances on the rough and trackless veldt; his only complaint about his time in hospital at Bloemfontein was 'the amount of champagne they made me take'.[20] The latter comment was not as frivolous as it seemed, as drinking bottled wine was seen by medical authorities as preferable to the polluted water available during the epidemic that swept the British forces at the time.

Returning to Sydney in September 1900, Bridges was employed immediately following proclamation of the Commonwealth of Australia in a variety of additional staff jobs and bodies involved with handling the transition of the military forces to new federal arrangements – including a committee chaired by General French to draft a new *Defence Act*. He was still engaged on these duties when it was announced in December 1901 that Hutton would become the first General Officer Commanding (GOC) of the Commonwealth Military Forces. When Hutton duly arrived and in March 1902 named the small group of protégés who were to form his federal headquarters staff, Major Bridges was appointed Assistant Quartermaster-General – a post with responsibility for preparation of annual estimates, military intelligence and organisation, mobilisation, topography, and schemes of defence for Australia. This key position had been previously identified as requiring a staff-qualified British officer to fill. This sphere of activity would become the prime preoccupation of Bridges for the next eight years, much of this period spent at the Commonwealth military headquarters at Victoria Barracks, Melbourne.

Within four months of taking up his new post, Bridges became involved in a second secret mission to collect information on the defences of Noumea, the capital of the French colony of New Caledonia, on behalf of the War Office. The episode is highly instructive about Bridges' relationship with Hutton, since it seems almost certain that the mission was conducted without the authorisation or even knowledge of any minister of the Australian government and as such represented an entirely improper use of Australian military resources for British/imperial purposes. Although Hutton did his best to convince local politicians that the seizure of colonial possessions of Britain's rivals was a legitimate use of the field force he wanted to establish in Australia – even posing arguments such as fulfilling Australia's 'manifest destiny' in the Pacific, and pursuing an Australian version of the 'Monroe doctrine' – he was to remain frustrated to find no takers for the proposition among politicians of all parties, who remained deeply suspicious of imperial motives. That Bridges knowingly and willingly took part in the venture spoke volumes about his loyalty to Hutton as his mentor.[21]

Twelve days after arriving back from Noumea on 6 July 1902, Bridges was promoted to lieutenant-colonel – which seems a clear enough demonstration of Hutton's satisfaction with his performance as intelligence-gatherer. Eighteen months later, in March 1904, Hutton was upset when his Chief Staff Officer and Deputy Adjutant-General, Colonel John Hoad, used political contacts to secure government agreement to send Hoad to Manchuria with a group of British Army observers attached to Japanese forces at war with Russia. The GOC was not only outraged that Hoad had angled for the appointment in secret, but (as he told contacts at the War Office in London) he feared also that the prestige acquired from being with the Japanese Army would enable Hoad, a man with nationalist sympathies, to threaten Hutton's imperial plans for the Australian forces.[22] What was left unsaid in the tirade of abuse that Hutton now heaped on Hoad was almost certainly Hutton's belief that, if anyone was to go on such duty from Australia, the officer sent should have been Bridges. As it was, Bridges had to pick up Hoad's duties in addition to his own for the nine months Hoad was away.[23]

With Hutton's term as GOC due to expire at the end of 1904, government thoughts turned to what arrangements should apply to replace him. There was considerable dissatisfaction with having administration of the military forces under control of a British general inclined to act as an agent of the imperial authorities, so that deliberations began into alternative systems of local command. In August the Minister for Defence convened a committee to study the question, and ironically Bridges found himself appointed to it. The course recommended by the committee involved abolishing the GOC appointment and replacing it with an Inspector-General whose role was little more than audit, not command. Actual administration would be under a committee known as the Military Board, which would direct and control the military commandants in the states, while higher matters of policy were to be decided by a Council of Defence. Understandably, Hutton opposed the change, but – accepting its inevitability – he suggested that Bridges should be appointed to the senior post on the new board with the title of 'Chief of the General Staff' (CGS), a post newly instituted in the British Army.[24]

When the new administrative arrangements were formally adopted on 12 January 1905, soon after Hutton's departure, Bridges was duly appointed to the Military Board as one of three military members; the minister and the Defence Department's civilian chief accountant completed the membership. Personnel matters remained under Hoad as Deputy Adjutant-General, logistics came under a new post of Chief of Ordnance, and operational matters remained with Bridges under a new title – not of CGS, as Hutton wanted, but of 'Chief of Intelligence'. That Bridges had the key military role on the board was confirmed when the new Council of Defence was formally instituted soon after. The members of the five-man council were the Minister for Defence, the federal Treasurer, the Inspector-General of the Commonwealth Military Forces, Bridges, and the Director of the Commonwealth Naval Forces (which had also just come under a naval board of administration). It was in this forum, which met for the first time in March, that Bridges found himself leading opposition to proposals for the formation of an Australian navy, chiefly because it was clear that an enlarged naval force could only be funded by disbanding the army's field force that Hutton had been working hard to establish, plus at least a quarter of the nation's garrison troops as well.[25]

The Council of Defence also became the body in which Bridges began voicing a major concern that Australia had been purchasing considerable quantities of war *matériel* 'but very little knowledge' – a situation which, he said, presented the risk that before long there would be 'no officers fit to train and administer the Forces in peace and to lead them in war'. It was on these grounds that Bridges supported an offer made in April 1905 by the University of Sydney to provide instructional courses aimed at qualifying candidates for commissions in both the British Army and the Commonwealth Military Forces. Such a scheme would be invaluable, he told the minister, but warned that the university's proposed military education department would never form a substitute for a proper military college. After representing the minister on a sub-committee formed to explore the idea, he became heavily committed to getting the scheme up and running during the rest of 1905 – initially in the capacity of 'adviser' but from January 1906 as a formal member of the university's Committee of Military Education to oversee the new department.[26] His involvement with the university from this time and until 1909 probably contributed to the reputation for erudition that Bridges later acquired within the forces, as though academic learning was something that one might acquire through osmosis.

The installation of a new government in July 1905 led by Alfred Deakin also brought an important change of focus in thinking about defending Australia. The nationalist Deakin, now leading his second federal ministry, was inspired by the model provided by Switzerland as an example of the compulsory military service obligations that a democratic country imposed on its entire male population. Deakin and his defence minister, Senator Thomas Playford, were attracted to the idea of forming Australia's militia, as the Commonwealth Military Forces were also known, into a national guard based on a system of universal military training, fed by cadet training in schools, and backed by an expansion in the nation's capacity to produce ammunition, equipment and *matériel* in a range of new local defence factories. The new government was also attracted to the vision presented to it by its home-grown advisers that favoured the development of an Australian navy capable of defending local shores and sea-lanes – with or without an imperial naval presence.

These ambitions alarmed Hutton's protégé in Australia, because they disregarded advice provided directly by the Colonial Defence Committee (CDC) in London aimed at keeping defence arrangements in the dominions subservient to imperial ends. Even before the Deakin administration took office, in June 1905 Bridges had attempted to dampen political enthusiasm for the Swiss militia system by pointing out that no one in Australia had any first-hand knowledge about it, and suggesting that an officer should be sent to observe the 1906 Swiss army manoeuvres. After Deakin resumed office the following month the government took up this suggestion and chose Bridges for the duty. The government was not blind to Bridges' biases, however, and while also agreeing to extend his travel plans to London, to allow him to assist the CDC in its further deliberations on Australia's defence requirements, it instructed him to keep his personal opinions to himself – he was only to provide whatever factual information the committee may require. Deakin took the additional precaution of writing to the secretary of the London body, now styled the Committee of Imperial Defence, warning that any views he presented were 'neither those of the Prime Minister nor his colleagues'.[27]

Bridges returned to Australia in January 1907 wearing the rank of colonel, having been promoted while still overseas the previous October. He now found the Defence Department under a new minister, after Playford lost his seat at a federal election in December 1906 even though the Deakin government had been confirmed in office. The new minister, Thomas Ewing, was keen to see progress with the nation's defence preparations and began pressing Bridges on questions relating to matters that came within Bridges' responsibility. He was particularly interested in a scheme that had arisen while Bridges was away, proposing the creation of a corps of guides. The idea, the brainchild of two veterans of the Boer War, was seen as a valuable adjunct to enabling military commanders engaged on operations in the field to successfully manoeuvre their troops over ground unknown to them, using the local geographical knowledge of men who were trained surveyors.[28]

After Bridges was directed to meet with the scheme's proponents and work out the details of implementing the new body (which the Military Board had already placed funds on the department's budget estimates to raise), he greatly angered and disappointed the minister by suggesting the corps of guides was not ideally suited to meeting the actual information needs of Australia's military forces. After nearly a year of haggling with Ewing, Bridges finally had approval to raise a body based on a different concept. This was an intelligence staff corps of more than 70 militia officers formed into sections in each state, tasked with training for tactical intelligence work required for field operations in wartime, but during peacetime with collecting and distributing maps and other information on Australia and neighbouring countries needed for planning the conduct of operations in war. When formally established on 6 December 1907, the Australian Intelligence Corps (AIC) became a major step towards overcoming a deficiency that had hampered meaningful defence planning since Federation.

Although the AIC had its own officer commanding in Colonel J.W. McCay (who had formerly sat in federal Parliament and was Minister for Defence in 1904–05, when the Military Board was first set up), the new corps answered directly to Bridges and essentially provided the manpower for the work of the Chief of Intelligence which had previously been almost entirely lacking. While it took almost

12 months to man the state sections, eventually the corps would involve an array of outstandingly talented individuals, many of whom would become some of the nation's best known and respected professionals across a diverse range of fields. When the corps conducted its first week-long instructional course in Melbourne in January 1909, both Bridges and McCay did most of the lecturing.[29] Bridges also gave the keynote address, during which he emphasised the vital importance of the work they could be called upon to perform in war, amounting to the full range of general staff duties.[30] There was more than a kernel of truth in the later characterisation of the AIC as a 'citizen General Staff'.[31]

Even so, it was clear that there were limitations to what might reasonably be expected from a body composed almost entirely of part-time officers. There were also significant technical issues that needed resolution, especially in the matter of mapping. The technique adopted by the AIC involved adding cultural detail, contours and other data to state lands department maps and plans, but the maps turned out by this means had no reference system and could not be joined to provide continuous coverage. In November 1908 Bridges had acted to get advice on how to deal with these questions by consulting the head of the Geographical Section of the General Staff at the War Office. The response received from this source not only decided the scale and sheet size adopted for Australia's military maps, but convinced Bridges to obtain from Britain a small number of trained topographers from the Royal Engineers. When these non-commissioned personnel arrived in April 1910 they formed the core of a new permanent and full-time Survey Section within the Royal Australian Engineers, which eventually – on 1 July 1915 – became a separate Survey Corps within the Australian military forces. In the original Survey Section that Bridges caused to be formed lay the basis for the long-term project that was undertaken to provide complete map coverage of the Australian continent and Commonwealth territories.[32]

In many respects the AIC became the precursor of a fully-fledged general staff in Australia – or, as some said, was meant to provide what was wanted in a general staff at a time when the government seemed disinclined to approve such a body. As it happened, the question of raising such a staff had been rejuvenated by recommendations which came out of the Colonial Conference held in London during 1907, after the British Secretary of State for War proposed the creation of an Imperial General Staff comprising dominion sections linked to a central section at the War Office. This scheme was proposed as a useful means of achieving coordination and cooperation within the empire in time of war, and as such Deakin was not opposed to it even though he was not unmindful of the risk it could become a tool for infiltrating British influence over the administration of Australia's military forces. He agreed to send a senior officer to London to make necessary arrangements and study the proposal ahead of Australia formally committing itself to creating a local section. The officer chosen was Major-General John Hoad, who had stepped into the Inspector-General role in January 1907 after temporarily filling it (as brigadier-general) from September 1906.

During Hoad's 12-month absence from Australia, proposals were put before the minister for creating a separate Australian general staff regardless of whether it became ultimately linked to an Imperial General Staff. During June 1908 a scheme was submitted to Ewing that suggested the most appropriate title for the officer heading the new body should be Chief of the General Staff – the same as applied elsewhere across the empire. When the minister demurred, the Military Board the next month unanimously endorsed a response, drafted by Bridges, which argued that calling the post by some distinctly Australian name could only lead to confusion; the title of 'Chief of Intelligence' had always been a misnomer, the board members agreed, and was about to become even more inappropriate. In August duties at headquarters in Melbourne were reallocated, which in practical terms meant that Australia already had a general staff from that date, but it was not until a Labor government led by Andrew Fisher replaced Deakin's administration in November 1908 that Bridges was permitted to assume the CGS title, with effect from 1 January 1909.[33]

Deakin had probably intended to give Hoad the honour of becoming Australia's first CGS upon his return from Britain, and only the change of ministries had altered this. Even so, Bridges was not to enjoy the prestige of the office for long. As soon as Hoad arrived back in Australia in May, his recommendations for linking the local section to the Imperial General Staff in London were accepted by the new minister, Senator George Pearce, and Bridges was forced to trade places with Hoad by departing for the War Office to become Australian representative on the Imperial General Staff. Although the new Labor government collapsed late in May, it was too late to undo the new arrangements, which had been announced a week before – even if the returning Deakin (at the head of his third ministry) had been inclined to do so. Pearce, however, promised Bridges that it was intended to reappoint him as CGS on his return, and even complied with a request by Bridges that this pledge be put in writing. It was, moreover, the Fisher government that had put forward his name for an imperial honour, resulting in Bridges being appointed CMG (Companion of the Order of St Michael and St George) in July.[34]

If Bridges felt that he had been displaced at headquarters in Melbourne at a peculiarly dangerous juncture in defence affairs, his frustration over this situation can only have been compounded by questions that arose over his precise status and functions in London. Rejecting notions he was either an observer or an exchange officer, he argued that his role as official representative meant he should be seen as more than a mere 'lackey at Whitehall'.[35] He had yet to win his point when his presence in Britain was cut short in January 1910 by instructions he received to return home to establish an Australian military college. At first he attempted to decline the appointment, pointing out both the great personal expense incurred by moving his family, again, at short notice and his belief that the task required an imperial officer possessing special experience, but on the insistence of the Minister of Defence, Joseph Cook, he accepted. Although another change of government in April saw the return to office of Labor under Fisher, and a belated offer by Senator Pearce (again serving as defence minister) to reconsider Bridges' recall, by May he was back in Australia. From his perspective, the only good aspect to the unwanted appointment was a promotion to brigadier-general that he received upon return.[36] Although briefly considered for reappointment as CGS late in 1911, this opportunity coincided with a period of long service leave that he sought to spend with his family in England and obliged Pearce to discount him as a candidate.[37]

The four-year period that Bridges spent as commandant of the Royal Military College at Duntroon was never a cherished highlight in his army career. The site chosen for the new national capital was a remote rural locality at the time that he acceded to Pearce's wish to find a location there for the college. Any sense that he had been sidelined from the cut and thrust of vital decision-making at the nerve centre of military affairs in Melbourne was likely to have been acute. When H.G. Chauvel visited Duntroon in December 1912, it was to find 'old Bridges . . . quite affable', but Chauvel was horrified by the bucolic atmosphere of the place and told his wife that 'the monotony of it would kill me'. Two years later Bridges proposed that Chauvel succeed him at Duntroon, but Chauvel wanted none of it; he much preferred to go to London in Bridges' old post with the Imperial General Staff and asked that his name not be put forward for the college.[38] The costs associated with siting the college 'in the bush' had also put Bridges' relations with Senator Edward Millen, the Minister for Defence who succeeded Pearce in mid-1913, under bitter strain.[39] The sense that Bridges was unimpressed with his circumstances as founding commandant was apparent to public commentators, with one newspaper observing – even before the college opened – that he seemed 'as happily placed as an elephant on a tight-rope'.[40]

Added to the professional difficulties associated with the work Bridges had been tasked to carry out at Canberra were a number of personal factors of which most people would have been entirely unaware. Because there was no suitable accommodation immediately available for his family at the site of the nascent national capital, Bridges had been obliged in 1910 to leave his family in England. It was not until mid-1912 that he was able to bring out his wife and children, installing them in the cottage that formerly housed the Duntroon manager's family (from the days when the place was the homestead of a sheep station) until construction of the commandant's residence was finally completed in December. This long period of separation was made even more painful by the death in January 1911 of his second son in London, following two stomach operations to deal with complications from peritonitis suffered some years earlier. Again, Bridges was deeply distressed by this loss. He was too shocked to reply to the cable from his wife giving him the dreadful news, causing her to ask the High Commission to send a second cable five days later.[41]

By the time that Bridges' term as commandant was due to expire (in May 1914) speculation that he would become the next Inspector-General had been circulating since the previous September, it being noted in the press that this was 'the most important post in the gift of the Federal Ministry, and ... will virtually constitute him head of the Commonwealth army'.[42] Bridges was certainly in contention for the post, and in early March Senator Millen had asked General Ian Hamilton, the Inspector-General of Oversea Forces in the British Army who was then visiting Australia, what he thought about Bridges' suitability.[43] Writing to a colleague the following day, Hamilton recounted that he replied that Bridges did not have the magnetism and charm, nor the strength of character, 'which would carry the sympathy, concurrence, or have great weight with ... troops'; in his view, Bridges 'might make an excellent C. of S. [Chief of Staff]' but was not Inspector-General material.[44]

Despite this advice, Millen pressed on as planned – presumably because the government did not like the alternative of appointing another British Army officer to succeed Major-General George Kirkpatrick. Unaware of any of this, when formally offered the post in April Bridges played hard-ball by telling Millen that he was not happy at being offered neither promotion nor pay equal to that received by Hoad when he was Inspector-General. Only after Millen 'sweetened the pot' with a modest increase in salary, and agreed that Bridges could raise the two issues again in the future, did Bridges accept.[45]

Bridges had been Inspector-General barely two months when Australia found itself – with the rest of the British Empire – caught up in the unfolding catastrophe later known as the First World War. Although his career was essentially that of an able staff officer who had received practically no opportunity to command troops, this fact was probably not obvious to the Australian government when it gave him command of the AIF and of the 1st Division. It was to these aspects of his background that several commentators later alluded, with speculation on 'how the best soldier in Peace ... [would] acquit himself in War',[46] and the observation that Bridges was probably fortunate, in view of his personal unpopularity, that his first command was that of a division because a brigade 'is really the last command in which an officer comes into intimate contact with his men'.[47]

But for all that, Bridges had unquestionably been a most significant figure influencing the formulation and implementation of an Australian defence policy in the decade after Federation. The fact that he was identified as a 'Hutton man' in seeking to constantly strengthen the imperial connection with Australia's defence forces was not always viewed as the negative factor that it has often been seen subsequently. Bridges can still rightfully be regarded as the first notable home-grown general of the Commonwealth's army.

Further reading

C.E.W. Bean, *The Story of Anzac: The First Phase*, vol. 1 of *The Official History of Australia in the War of 1914–1918*, 11th edition, Angus & Robertson, Sydney, 1941

———, *Two Men I Knew: William Bridges and Brudenell White, Founders of the A.I.F.*, Angus & Robertson, Sydney, 1957

C.D. Clark, 'The "Invasion" of New Caledonia', *Australian Army Journal*, no. 279, August 1972, pp. 9–19

———, 'General Bridges: The Reluctant Commandant', *RMC Historical Journal*, vol. 2, 1973, pp. 31–6

C.D. (Coulthard-)Clark, *The Citizen General Staff: The Australian Intelligence Corps 1907–1914*, Military Historical Society of Australia, Canberra, 1976

———, *A Heritage of Spirit: A Biography of Major-General Sir William Throsby Bridges, KCB, CMG*, Melbourne University Press, Melbourne, 1979

———, 'Major-General Sir William Bridges: Australia's First Field Commander', D.M. Horner (ed.), *The Commanders: Australian Military Leadership in the Twentieth Century*, Allen & Unwin, Sydney, 1984, pp. 13–25

———, *Duntroon: The Royal Military College of Australia, 1911–1986*, Allen & Unwin, North Sydney, 1986

———, 'Australia's Monroe Doctrine: An Attempt to Keep the Islands English', *Pacific Islands Monthly*, vol. 57, no. 12, December 1986, pp. 40–2

———, 'Australia's First Spy', J. Laffin and P. Badman, *Special and Secret*, Time-Life Books Australia, North Sydney, 1990, pp. 12–13

———, *Australia's Military Map-Makers: The Royal Australian Survey Corps 1915–96*, Oxford University Press, South Melbourne, 2000

J. Connor, *Anzac and Empire: George Foster Pearce and the Foundations of Australian Defence*, Cambridge University Press, Melbourne, 2011

J. Mordike, *An Army for a Nation: A History of Australian Military Developments 1880–1914*, Allen & Unwin, North Sydney, 1992

P. Pedersen, 'Burning Bridges', *Wartime: Official Magazine of the Australian War Memorial*, issue 50, 2010, pp. 20–5

3
THE ENIGMA
General Sir Cyril Brudenell Bingham White

PETER STANLEY

IN SEPTEMBER 2015 AT a ceremony beside the obelisk over Brudenell White's grave in Buangor, near Ararat, Victoria, more than 200 people – White's descendants and family, officials of ex-service organisations, local people and representatives of the Australian Defence Force – gathered to witness the dedication of a panel recording White's contributions to the Australian Army. They had travelled to the tiny town, 70 kilometres north-west of Ballarat, to pay tribute to a man whom media reports described as 'one of Australia's lesser known war heroes'; indeed, described by a representative of Ararat Legacy as 'forgotten. Completely forgotten.'[1] *Completely* forgotten? Hardly: Cyril Brudenell Bingham White gained more references in Charles Bean's official history than any other Australian, and has been accorded more biographies than any other Australian Great War general besides Monash. His role in forming and directing the Australian Imperial Force (AIF) was such that he figures in practically every study of the force's organisation, administration, command and conduct in battle.

General Sir Cyril Brudenell Bingham White, one of the founders of the AIF, who rose to become Chief of the General Staff.
Australian War Memorial, AWM 001110

Even so, White remains arguably a 'shadow man' of the Australian Army, obscured, as it were, by the glare of his celebrity and by the very adulation he has attracted. Of the several books written about him, one was written by Charles Bean, whose veneration for White coloured, if not clouded, his judgment, and two were written by relatives – hardly dispassionate authors.² He has been accorded a PhD thesis ('Champion of Anzac' by John Bentley) that can best be described as flawed by an undue emphasis on sociological theory at the expense of historical evidence.³ Apart from an assured essay by Guy Verney, in David Horner's *The Commanders*, and an authoritative entry in the *Australian Dictionary of Biography* by Jeffrey Grey, White has largely not been subjected to scrutiny that draws on the full range of the official and private records available.⁴ This discussion reflects on White's life, character, achievements and relationships and suggests that he deserves a more sustained critical study, one that might draw him in all shades.

White's family background appears to have been that of the pastoral gentry of colonial Australia. His gentility is undoubted: as a junior officer White seems to have mixed easily with the colonial and British officers with whom he served, able to ride, talk about horses and use the right cutlery. If he lacked polish he certainly learned quickly – his time at the Staff College at Camberley in 1906 seems to have been as much devoted to becoming accustomed to mingling as an equal with rising, senior and even aristocratic British officers, forming connections which stood him in good stead soon after. But White's social origins are rather murkier than they might seem from the family portraits. His father, John, had been briefly an officer in the Rifle Brigade, one of the more exclusive British regiments. But John White sold out his commission in the Rifle Brigade, seeking to make his fortune in Victoria. This he manifestly failed to do. Taking up sheep runs in western Victoria, John lost money, which he blamed on bad seasons, the boom and bust of drought and plenty, but which could just as well have been caused by inexperience or poor judgment. He shifted around the colony (including St Arnaud, where Cyril, who used the name Brudenell, was born in 1876, the seventh of eight children) but never quite prospering. In a familiar expedient in colonial Australia, John and his wife, Maria, moved, to Queensland, repeating the pattern – Gympie, Charters Towers and Gladstone – only making a go of it when John abandoned the pastoral life and took up the less productive but more remunerative business of share dealing.

The vicissitudes of his father's fortunes explains Brudenell's patchy education – he left school at 16 (after some terms at 'Eton', a preparatory school with nominal but little other connection to its famous namesake). Brudenell, a younger son of a gentleman who enjoyed relative prosperity only later in life, must have been conscious that he could easily have lost that standing. Maria White secured him a position as a bank clerk through personal connections and her powerful character.

Despite the seeming abundance of White's biographies and papers, little is known of White's upbringing. Bean's portrayal is impossibly twee – Brudenell and his younger brother, Eustace, 'never quarrelled', it seems. 'Gentle, affectionate manners were natural to them, and both were always ready to help their mother.'[5] Bean recounts with a straight face the story that White, echoing the views of his mentor, Major-General Sir Edward Hutton, claimed that attending church on Sunday enabled him to play cricket all the better during the week. It is apparent that White's mother inculcated in Brudenell a strong moral sense. Among his 'Mottos for 1895' were 'never tell a lie'; 'have your own opinion'; 'be straightforward and not afraid of anyone'; 'do all work well'.[6] It is clear from an analysis of his career that he did not necessarily adhere to injunctions recorded as an earnest 19-year-old. As a military officer, and especially as a senior staff officer, he was inevitably implicated in decisions for which he was responsible for implementing regardless of his own views or values. Bean naively imagined that White held to these values throughout his life; the documents suggest that White's ethical positions and decisions were more complex or ambiguous.

As a bank clerk in Gympie, White studied before and after work –

a harbinger of the dedication he would bring to office work in uniform. At about 20 White joined the Wide Bay Regiment, gaining a commission in the Queensland Defence Force a year later after a prodigious effort studying for the examination, passing third overall in the colony with 77 per cent. After an unpromising start, posted to the outpost of Thursday Island as a gunner for most of the Boer War, he saw limited service in the final months of the conflict. He survived the indictment of his role in the troopship *Drayton Grange*, which returned in 1902 with 16 dead from the unsanitary conditions that its military officers – including White – had allowed to prevail, though White had placated the understandably restive troops. Within a few years, however, thanks to the influence of Edward Hutton (see Chapter 1) as a patron, and his own efforts and intellect, White began to prosper. In 1906 Hutton ensured that he became the first Australian officer to enter the Staff College at Camberley, and he worked at the War Office during the implementation of Viscount Haldane's reforms. As a protégé of Hutton ('one of the finest and greatest soldiers I have ever known', White wrote), he must surely have learned not just practical staff work but also the political realities and methods of the relationships between officers and between military officers and political superiors.[7] Hutton's support gave White entrée to a circle of rising and influential British officers, many of whom rose to senior commands in the Great War.

Back in Australia he worked under another patron, Colonel William Bridges (see Chapter 2), in military intelligence. Here his industry, intelligence and congeniality impressed his superiors, as did White's willingness to support them in the great game of the Commonwealth army, played out over the balance of allegiance between empire and nation, between 'Australianists' (such as John Hoad and Gordon Legge) and 'imperialists' (such as Hutton, Bridges and, indeed, White).

As a young reporter mixing with staff officers in the 'fly-infested dining rooms of country hotels' during annual camps, Charles Bean realised that headquarters was 'the arena of struggle between ambitious leaders jostling one another in their manoevres [sic] to reach positions of influence'.[8] The biographies and studies of the careers of the officers who rose to command in the AIF strongly suggest what a snake-pit the Gradation List was. Bean believed that White remained aloof from the grubby competition for preferment, posting and promotion, but there is no evidence that he did not harbour ambition. Indeed, his success in gaining most of the prizes going (aide-de-camp (ADC) to Hutton; postings to Camberley and the War Office) suggests that, if anything, White played the game better than his counterparts.

White identified with the imperial cause; but ambivalently. In 1908 he wrote to Hutton to assure him that he was 'glad if I am a humble agent' of an Imperial General Staff.[9] There is an irony at the heart of White's service before 1914. His training at the Staff College had imbued in him a profound understanding of and attachment to the needs of the empire rather than the part of it in which he happened to be born. His professional experience revealed the duality inherent in the decades when to be Australian was also to be British. White both dutifully planned both the defence of Australia against a Japanese threat independent of uncertain imperial support but also devised contingency plans for an Australian contribution to an imperial war. Simplistically portrayed as 'imperialist', he can be seen to have embodied the ambivalence inherent in a thoughtful Australian subject of the empire of the time.

As admirers such as Bean and the many correspondents in his papers testify, White was a most attractive and engaging man. Welcoming, self-effacing, with a sense of humour, White seems far from the arrogant, remote staff officer of legend. But there were other sides to the 'charming' White. As a 'Hutton man' and in favour with his protégés, White became something of a minor power-broker himself. In 1912 Lieutenant-Colonel John Monash, looking for a command after the abolition of the short-lived Intelligence Corps, sought an interview with Major Brudenell White. Trying to flush something out of White, he observed as an opening gambit that the Military Board seemed not to be able to find a post for him. 'No', White coolly replied, 'I do not suppose we will.'[10] So much for the 'charming' White.[11]

By this time, as a major and Director of Military Operations, White drew up the plans that allowed the rapid formation of what became the AIF in August 1914. He did not invent the idea of an Australian expeditionary force. George Pearce, Minister for Defence in Andrew Fisher's second Labor government, essentially accepted in 1911 that Australia would prepare for a future conflict by planning for such a force.[12] But during the First Balkan War in 1912 Brigadier Joseph Gordon and Major-General Alexander Godley (representing Australia and New Zealand respectively) asked White to devise a plan. It was White's proposal that the Australasian dominions would between them form a composite infantry division.

The happenstance of the absence of his seniors saw the 38-year-old White minding the office in Melbourne as acting Chief of the General Staff (CGS) in August 1914 when the European crisis tilted the empire towards war. Once Cabinet could be assembled and encouraged to make a decision it was essentially White's contingency plan that William Bridges, summoned to Melbourne from the Royal Military College (RMC) Duntroon, was asked to implement. With Bridges a familiar if demanding superior, White worked long hours with a small staff to raise and equip what became the AIF. While White seems to have assumed that it would serve alongside but not as part of British formations (at least retaining cohesion at brigade level) he also pragmatically insisted on largely using British war establishment tables. The two also shaped the complexion of the force's senior command, choosing mainly Australian citizen soldiers. Not surprisingly, they almost exclusively selected professional or landed middle-class and middle-aged Anglicans: men such as White himself, though there were no other contenders on offer.

White's role in raising, training and transporting the first contingent seems to have been routine, and he worked harmoniously with Bridges – not a man described as warm, but who appreciated brains and ability. In the planning for the Gallipoli invasion, however, White disclosed in his very first operational task a capacity for independent thinking that sits ill with his reputation for urbane acquiescence. In the conception of the commander of the Mediterranean Expeditionary Force, General Sir Ian Hamilton, the original plan for what had recently become the Australian and New Zealand Army Corps (ANZACs) in the landings had seen it earmarked for a beach at the foot of the peninsula, where the fleet's guns could in principle support it on both flanks. White disagreed, believing that the landing needed to be made on less constricted ground, foreseeing perhaps what actually occurred when the British and French landings were stopped a few kilometres inland. White argued that the force ought to land at the 'neck' of the peninsula, around Gaba Tepe. His insistence angered Bridges, who told him that he could stay in Egypt if he was not prepared to accept the decision. In the event, Hamilton changed the plan and General Sir William Birdwood's corps – though unfortunately not the entire force – was directed to land north of Gaba Tepe. Bridges, though crotchety, recognised White's motives and wrote of his gratitude for White's capacity and diplomacy in preparing for the invasion.[13]

On 25 April Birdwood's ANZACs failed to meet the objectives set for it. White wrote candidly that it was plain that 'as the day went on that we had failed'.[14] As chief of staff to the 1st Australian Division, the first formation ashore, he might have worn some of the blame, not least for failing to ensure that its brigadiers carried out their orders. It seems that neither he nor they faced any censure over the failure of 25 April or any other action on Gallipoli, at the time or since. Working for Bridges until his death in May and later for Major-General Harold 'Hooky' Walker, White also had a hand in planning the abortive break-out from the ANZAC lodgment which became known as the August offensive, and especially the debacle of the 1st Division's abortive and costly feint at Lone Pine. His complicity in an unrealistically ambitious and indeed unfeasible plan seems to have escaped scrutiny. This is, perhaps, because an individual staff officer's contribution cannot be distinguished in the surviving documents, but it also suggests that Bean's eulogies have become the basis of White's place in historians' regard.

And yet White was, it seems, vital to the division's operations. Agreeable and efficient, he was mainly liked and respected by his fellow officers in Bridges' headquarters. William Foster, at that time a captain and Bridges' senior ADC, reportedly regarded him as 'the one man we cannot afford to lose', a sentiment echoed by John Treloar, one of White's clerks: 'his loss would be felt by the Div[ision] very much'.[15] As Bridges lay dying in the hospital ship *Gascon*, Birdwood wrote to the Governor-General, Sir Ronald Munro Ferguson, that at least he had 'in Colonel White . . . a man who is . . . one of the best and most capable soldiers I have met for a long time'.[16] No one should doubt White's efficiency, dedication or influence, at least within the little world of the AIF's fractious command structure.

But dissident views exist. In August 1915 Major John Gellibrand criticised White's habit of keeping Administration (A), Quartermaster (Q) and General (G) staffs in watertight compartments, which produced duplication, ignorance and confusion. He claimed that White's policy left A and Q officers working under rather than with G officers, though Gellibrand, as a Staff College–trained former British regular, possessed the necessary experience and skills to do better. Peter Sadler wondered whether White 'deliberately use[d] his influence on Bridges . . . to block Gellibrand's advancement . . . as a rival to his own ambitions?' Sadler's answer was to quote Gellibrand's description of White in a letter to his wife as 'the cloven hoof'.[17]

By October 1915, now chief of staff to General Sir William Birdwood, commander of the ANZACs, White became involved in one of the episodes responsible for his celebrity. His role in planning the unexpectedly successful evacuation of the Anzac–Suvla area in December 1915 has been hailed as his first contribution to the AIF's operations in the Great War. Mark Derham, White's grandson, claims that 'the whole movement was his devising', arguing that because White ('a man not prone to boastfulness') said so in a letter to his wife, the matter is settled.[18] But White's contribution has been magnified in Australian accounts. It is one of the few episodes of White's career that has aroused anything resembling controversy. White has been portrayed as the genius behind both the evacuation and the deception plan that underpinned it: his daughter entitled her sustained encomium to her father, *The Silence Ruse*, after one of the most effective features of the deception plan. When I began writing *Quinn's Post, Anzac, Gallipoli*, I had been imbued with the conviction that White had been responsible for the evacuation plan. (In 1984 I had written the caption to his propelling pencil, displayed in what was then the new Gallipoli gallery of the Australian War Memorial, observing that it was with that very pencil that White had drafted the orders for the evacuation.) The relevant records suggest that the truth was more complex.

In the Australian records the impersonal passive voice habitually adopted in military writing conceals individual agency: 'orders for the withdrawal were issued', White wrote, not disclosing who issued them.[19] White's own papers offer little support for the extreme position taken by his partisans. In the British records, the file raised in the headquarters of the Dardanelles Army gives no prominence to White in the records of conferences, orders and signals preceding the evacuation.[20] The file shows that the responsibility for framing the evacuation was given to Cyril Aspinall, chief of staff to the Dardanelles Army. As was the practice, Aspinall's plans cascaded to White, chief of staff at Anzac (but not responsible for IX Corps at Suvla). The proof is that in fact Suvla was evacuated perfectly successfully, as was Cape Helles, the following month, without White's involvement. This is not to say that White did not execute his orders both efficiently and imaginatively – it is likely that he originated the idea of the 'silent stunt', accustoming the Ottoman defenders to the silence that would follow evacuation by instituting periods of silence. But there is no evidence that White actually devised the orders for the entire operation: that came from a conference on the headquarters ship *Aragon*. Alec Hill's judgment in this, as in so many matters, remains apposite: the evacuation succeeded, he wrote, 'thanks to planning of the first order by Brudenell White'.[21] He remains central to the success of the evacuation of Anzac, but we can no longer attribute to him sole responsibility for its planning and implementation.

What of White as the prime-mover in the 'doubling' of the AIF, regarded by his admirers as his second great achievement? As Birdwood's Deputy Adjutant and Quartermaster-General White reorganised and expanded the AIF in Egypt in the aftermath of the Gallipoli campaign. He is held to have virtually created the AIF that fought for the rest of the war. This is usually presented as a kind of national triumph, one heavily influenced by awareness of the sacrifice that followed.

On the evidence of the 51 'circular memoranda' that White wrote that formed the expanded force, his intention was to create formations that could work with the British armies of which they would form a part. In their establishments the new divisions, brigades, battalions and many ancillary units were based on War Office tables of organisation. White apparently made only three exceptions: he gave the Australian divisional artillery 36 guns (because no more were available), added a dental unit to each brigade's field ambulance, and for temporary and pragmatic reasons organised the field ambulances in two rather than three sections. (The changes were hardly major: British ordnance parks soon rectified the deficiency of artillery once in France, the dental units were a sensible addition, and the difference in ambulance sections became 'a source of confusion' for a time in France.[22]) Far from creating a miniature Australian army, White succeeded in forming a force British in its organisation and equipment, able to operate effectively as part of expeditionary forces in the Middle East and Europe.

The AIF certainly established a distinctive ethos, reputation and identity in both theatres: but it was not through White's ideas or actions. Even Bean, White's most ardent admirer, conceded that the idea of splitting the veteran Gallipoli battalions was Birdwood's. White's original idea, of posting selected officers and men to the new units, would surely have fostered division and discord rather than the unanimity and accord that the 'doubling' produced. Though White's work as a staff officer was without doubt efficient and orderly, the doubling was without question 'an outstanding administrative achievement': but no more.[23]

White's admirers are on safer ground in commending White's part in establishing a basis for what later generations would describe as the AIF's governance. This was necessary because the force was a part of larger British imperial armies but also belonged to a self-governing dominion. The negotiation of that relationship, one complicated by assumptions and imperatives on both sides, and which changed as the war continued, demanded a sound administrative basis if it was to work. This White provided, finding a way through a thicket of administrative, military, political and personal agendas to establish early in 1916 the mechanism of AIF Administrative Headquarters and subordinate staffs in France and Egypt, with a network of training, medical and convalescent establishments and the right personnel to make them work together. 'All the principles on which we now act', White wrote to his wife, Ethel, 'are the work of my hand.'[24] The episode is rightly seen as one of the shifts in the tension between nation and empire, in which war has been such a stimulus, and White's role was crucial.

Bean praised White for having established a 'system of control' of Australian forces within imperial formations that 'lasted through that war and was the model . . . in World War II also'.[25] This achievement provided a guiding principle not just on the Western Front, but also in Palestine in 1916–18, and even more in the delicate dealings between Sir Thomas Blamey and his divisional commanders and their British counterparts and superiors in the war in the Mediterranean in 1940–42. If the 9th Australian Division remained intact and able to deliver the decisive blow against the *Panzerarmee Afrika* at Alamein it is partly because Brudenell White saw the need for a relationship between the imperial and Australian partners that would work despite the disparities in force size, resources, authority and power. That ultimately might be White's greatest legacy, one that long outlasts the dubious contribution made by drip guns to the evacuation of Anzac in December 1915.[26]

Bean presented White's role as supremely rational. But what political decision – and the governance of the AIF was without doubt a political question – is decided without some tincture of influence, ambition and power? If White was as effective an influence in the AIF as he is represented then it would surely be extraordinary that he was not skilled in the arts of influence. As a staff officer, as he remained throughout the war, White could only gain his objectives by acting through and on his superiors. Birdwood's flaws were well known. He was skilled in projecting his personality both to superiors and to the dominion citizen soldiers whom he commanded for most of the war. But he also found administration uncongenial. In a further demonstration of the essentially complementary nature of successful staff-officer-and-commander partnerships, White supplied what Birdwood largely lacked. White's capacity for taking pains over administrative detail (the kind of work he had excelled in during the raising of the AIF, the evacuation of Anzac and the doubling of the AIF) balanced Birdwood's ability to project himself to both his superiors and to his subordinates.

To succeed, however, this relationship depended upon the seeming deference of the staff officer, White. However influential his memoranda, appreciations, plans and suggestions might be, they needed to be represented as Birdwood's. Indeed, the more White supplied Birdwood's ideas, orders, directions and intentions, the more carefully their origins needed to be concealed. (In an appreciation of White written after White's death, Birdwood confirmed that 'he kept himself entirely in the background'.[27]) The evidence is highly ambiguous – the more so because not only does all the official evidence conceal the join, but all involved in the command relationship had a vested interest in ensuring that the successful partnership should continue regardless of who was the brains behind the operation.

From early 1916 to May 1918 White served as Birdwood's chief of staff directing I Anzac Corps and latterly the Australian Corps on the Western Front. He was closely involved in every major operation in which the corps participated. In contrast to the eulogies his administrative work occasioned, no one has investigated in detail White's role in planning and implementing these operations. Indeed, so self-effacing was White, it is difficult now to determine exactly what he did or did not do to contribute to the sequence of mainly costly failures or at best qualified successes in which the Australian divisions were committed. There is a need for detailed studies of the planning and execution of Australian actions to establish the degree of White's involvement in devising and controlling battle plans. It would seem that admiration for White's qualities as an administrator may have obscured his complicity in some of the bloodier Great War battles. Some examples help to point to tentative conclusions.

Australian military history is punctuated by a number of renowned set-pieces: the conference on the beach at Anzac; the confrontation between Pompey Elliott and Haig's staff officer before Fromelles; the departure of Gordon Legge from Singapore; the argument between Morshead and Auchinleck at Alamein – and so on. One of the most celebrated – because it pits the young Australian Brudenell White against the patronising Douglas Haig – occurred at Birdwood's headquarters at Contay after Legge's 2nd Australian Division had failed at Pozières on 28 July 1916. It was at this meeting that Haig condescendingly told Birdwood and White that 'you're not fighting Bashi-Bazouks now', and when White, despite dark looks from Haig's staff, proceeded to correct Haig's mistakes by reference to a map. Haig singled out White as 'a very sound capable fellow'.[28] Was it a calculated demonstration by a supposedly modest man?

The episode is usually presented in Australian accounts to show how patronising and remote was Haig, but John Bentley astutely notes that it also discloses that White approved of the plan for his rival Major-General Gordon Legge's 2nd Division's attack (the failure of which led to Haig's visit) and did nothing to amend or revise it. Bentley even, interestingly for one of White's admirers, suggests that 'White set Legge up to fail and provide the mechanism for Legge's further marginalisation'.[29] Legge was in due course removed: but if Bentley's supposition is justifiable then his division incurred over 3000 casualties because White wished to take Legge down. Chris Clark documented White's role in Legge's dismissal. Later in 1916, though Legge appeared to have become more compliant (White told Ethel that

Legge had become 'so tame now he will almost eat out of my hand'), White (and Birdwood) used Legge's falling ill as an opportunity to have him replaced. White acknowledged to Ethel that he had played what Clark describes as 'an active role in bringing about the outcome'.[30]

White's ruthlessness contrasts markedly with Bean's benign picture of him. During the Somme fighting he described how White could be seen in his office in the château of Henencourt, 'and passers-by could see him through the window, pipe in mouth, quietly studying reports or drafting memoranda, or closeted with someone who sought his advice or help'.[31] Many of those memoranda would have determined the careers or even the lives of those whose fate White held in his hand. In her book *Attack on the Somme*, Meleah Hampton indicates that White allocated insufficient artillery to support the 2nd Division's attack on Mouquet Farm on 26 August.[32]

On 2 January 1917 White was promoted to temporary major-general, at just 40. The year 1917 was not only the hardest year of Australia's Great War, but also White's most exhausting. Though publicly amicable, the relationship between White and Birdwood remained uneasy. White felt that Birdwood was lazy and took him for granted. After Birdwood was awarded the KCB in 1917 White 'could not bring myself to congratulate him', feeling that Birdwood was 'a man of no quality'.[33] In June 1917 he confessed to being 'irritable', damning Birdwood's staff as 'a set of gibbering idiots'. He had snapped, it seems over some minor matter – possibly the appointment of an ADC. 'I vented my anger in rudeness to my Chief', he admitted, and repeated before an officer he knew would tell tales that 'I was fed up and the sooner I was allowed out of this job the better.'[34] (Typically, he reproached himself for 'cowardice' in relying on tittle-tattle rather than confronting Birdwood directly.)

While attempting to resist the unjustifiable hero-worship of Bean that has for so long clouded White's reputation, we need to remain sympathetic to his essential and long-standing predicament as the chief of staff to Birdwood. By June 1917 White had been effectively working without real respite for over a year. He had not only supported

Birdwood, a commander happy to leave the detail of administration and the more onerous aspects of command to him, but also had the heavy additional responsibility of advising Birdwood as administrative commander of the AIF in Europe. No wonder he confessed to Gellibrand (with whom he seems to have reached an accommodation after Gallipoli) that he was 'so tired' he 'could not follow the rhythm and . . . cannot hear the music', craving 'rest and freedom from responsibility'.[35] There was little respite for White: with what effect on his involvement in operational planning in I Anzac Corps? We need detailed studies before we can say.

The feasibility of this suggestion can be tested by reference to the Operations files for I Anzac Corps headquarters during the Bullecourt battles.[36] These files contain a selection of the surviving headquarters documentation, especially appreciations written in and messages emanating from Birdwood's headquarters, over which White exercised control. They demonstrate the problems which battlefield records present. While White's hand can be detected both in papers he wrote and those he directed be written, it is almost impossible to reconstruct the atmosphere in which they were written, or the verbal or informal instructions the writers received. It is easy to detect messages actually written (or rather dictated) by Birdwood; but much harder to discern White's role in responding to the German withdrawal and in planning the Australian part in the two attacks directed at the Hindenburg Line at Bullecourt. Crucially, though, nothing in the documents justifies the resumption of an attack on the position: was it considered? If so, where is the evidence? Dissecting out the individual contributions of various commanders, staff officers and formation commanders (and in turn their staffs) would require a minute reconstruction of the drafting and approval of orders, using complementary written evidence and perhaps techniques such as hand-writing analysis. Even then, so discreet was White, it is likely that at such a distance in time, and in the absence of definitive evidence, such an analysis is now impractical.

Bean asserted that 'the number of times during the war in which White acquiesced in a decision which he believed to be wrong was infinitesimal'.³⁷ The corollary of this assertion is that White agreed with decisions he implemented. This amounts to him accepting, for example, the pointless slaughter at the Nek, Quinn's Post or German Officers Trench, the disastrous sequence of futile attacks at Pozières, the folly of the second battle of Bullecourt (over the same ground as the first, but at twice the cost) and the bloody and unavailing continuation of attacks at Ypres. If White can be given credit for the AIF's successes, then equally he is implicated in the many occasions when the force became committed to operations that did not justify the cost in lives.

White's dealings with several of the AIF's most notable members also illuminates his willingness and capacity to handle subordinates and superiors. For example, his part in frustrating Pompey Elliott's ambition has been revealed in Ross McMullin's biography *Pompey Elliott*. The volatile Elliott could not offer more of a contrast to the cool, measured – not to say calculated – conduct of White. Elliott had little time for White, whom he saw as Birdwood's hatchet-man. Far from Bean's admiring portrayal of White doing Birdwood's job without credit, Elliott saw White as 'completely under General Birdwood's thumb' whose association with Birdwood had 'more than once led to the betrayal of Australia's interests'.³⁸

The cautious White and mercurial Elliott had long had an uneasy relationship. When Elliott was commanding one of the 'advance guards' pursuing the German retreat to the Hindenburg Line, for example, White condescendingly criticised Elliott's 'Napoleonic ideas'. In May 1918, in an echo of his handling of Colonel Monash in 1912, White told Elliott firmly that he would not be gaining the divisional command he coveted. In all this White acted not just as Birdwood's emissary, but also as a principal in the AIF's king-making, threatening Elliott with dismissal if he appealed to the Minister for Defence George Pearce. What McMullin describes as 'an acute blend of intimidation and inducement' rings truer than Bean's idealised portrait of a *gentilhomme sans reproche*.³⁹ White appears to have been an able politician, as canny as any back-room dealer. Faced with more able brigadiers than could be promoted in 1918, for example, he seems to have promised several first dibs on vacancies, unable to deliver on such implied undertakings. Charles Bean's official history rightly documented White's part as one of the dominant influences in the AIF. Bean regarded White as 'the greatest man it has been my fortune intimately to know', and he referred to White directly no fewer than 238 times across his six volumes.[40] Dermot Millar's critical study of Birdwood as commander takes an astringent view of this prominence, arguing that in the official history Bean 'magnified the role of White'.[41]

Their correspondence substantiates White's influence on Bean in great and small matters. The two corresponded often and Bean checked drafts of his typescripts with White and sought White's advice. His letters to Bean show how fully he exercised the power of comment and even veto that Bean accorded him. 'It might be well to alter your wording . . .', White would counsel – in that case over the question of whether Bean should disclose that Birdwood had destroyed Elliott's inflammatory account of Polygon Wood (which in fact Major John Treloar preserved).[42] In 1935, for example (after Bean had published four volumes), White suggested that Bean not use the colloquial expression 'they then let fly': the phrase did not appear in Volume V.[43] White's watchword post-war was caution. However outspoken he had been in confronting Douglas Haig as a brigadier-general, by the early 1930s he had become more circumspect. He counselled Bean against criticisms of 'GHQ' – that is, Haig – pointing out that 'you might destroy the world value of your work by allowing that criticism to be too didactic', praising Bean for having 'passed very skillfully over Elliott's operations'.[44] In short, White not only shaped the AIF's actions, but also the record of those actions.

But what influence did White wield over the AIF as a whole? His impact on the Western Front was limited to his immediate circle of Australian divisional commanders and their staffs, with whom he as chief of staff to I Anzac and then the Australian Corps dealt. That is not to say that his advice and orders did not affect every member of the formations under his command, but his influence did not arouse comment, at the time or since.[45]

Bean's bland portrait of his hero failed to capture White's depth. Rosemary Derham, though idolising her father, hinted at the deeper currents of his character. She wrote of the 'great deal of tension' under which he lived, wracked by 'sick-headaches', migraines that his wife, Ethel, was sworn not to reveal, and probably asthma that could have debilitated him except for his overpowering dedication.[46] His willpower was prodigious, impelling him to work however he felt; a clue, perhaps, to how he sustained the unremitting effort required of him, especially on the Western Front during 1916–18. His famous modesty was perhaps a reflection of his inner turmoil. William Hughes, fishing for possible commanders of the Australian Corps, asked White 'did you ever hear of a chap named White?' White merely laughed and shook his head.[47] Though a major-general and highly eligible for promotion, White perhaps preferred to exercise influence without the responsibility of formal command: but why?

We may never get to the heart of White's character. His papers, though voluminous, seem not to contain evidence that would enable the formation of a justifiable impression of the extent and nature of his influence, especially on his seniors. It is likely that he carefully winnowed them even before his daughter adopted the protective custodianship that preserved them from scholarly scrutiny for so long. White remained a man who gave away little of himself in the documents. His diaries record where he was and terse comments on the events in which he was involved, but nothing of his inner feelings or his actions. (For example, his diary during the second attack on Bullecourt is unreflective, merely reading 'We succeeded/ 62[nd British] Div failed/ Tough time …'.[48]) His letters to his wife describe his frustrations (especially in working under Birdwood) but nothing of his dealings with his superiors, little of his relations with his contemporaries; and nothing, of course, on the detail of operational planning. For a man with several dozen boxes of papers in two major archives, White's discretion survives long beyond the grave.

White became renowned as 'the maker of the A.I.F.' – though, again, the accolade is Bean's.[49] John Bentley's doctoral thesis, the most recent and detailed treatment of his career, argues that White contributed to what he calls an 'Australian military culture'. It becomes clear in his thesis, however, that Bentley did not actually mean the military culture of the AIF as a whole, but rather the organisational culture of the tiny coterie of senior commanding and staff officers responsible for brigade command and upwards, and not the attitudes, ideas, behaviour or actions of the great mass of the force. While Bentley is able to portray White justifiably as 'Australia's foremost soldier' (of the Great War anyway), he fails to argue convincingly that White established 'the beliefs, values and principles that ... became the foundations upon which Australian military culture later developed'.[50] Sadly, as mentioned earlier, Bentley's work is disfigured by his use of sociological language. For example, he describes White's time at Camberley as 'a form of enhancement rite in which the organisational values were reinforced and recognition was given to White's achievements by placing the letters psc (Passed Staff College) after his name'.[51] He should be commended for directing attention to the mechanics and dynamics of senior command in the AIF, but stretches a long bow in arguing that White decisively influenced the force's 'military culture'.

The AIF's members undeniably had characteristic ways of thinking, speaking and behaving, in and out of battle, regardless of their rank. Its military culture was a compound of the men who comprised it, their civilian habits and culture, the ideas with which they were imbued (as 'White men', subjects of the empire, Australians and as men), along with the training and experience they acquired, the circumstances in which they served and the formalities and expectations of both the AIF in particular and the armed forces of the British Empire in general at that time. The characteristics they collectively developed have been revealed and celebrated many times (such as their casual discipline, disinclination to salute, respect for merit rather than simply rank, etc.). White played a decisive part in the force's formal organisation and in devising its command and management structures and processes; he had almost nothing to do with what we might call its 'informal' manifestations.

As the subject of analytical biography White is fascinating (and, it must be said, frustrating). What judgment can we make on him and his contribution? The hagiography of his friend and admirer, Charles Bean, can no longer stand unchallenged; nor the encomiums of his family and scholars who have perhaps taken them as evidence rather than advocacy. Instead, we can conclude only that a man seemingly so familiar in Great War scholarship demands a closer scrutiny. Guy Verney endorsed the judgment of Sir Alfred Kemsley (who as a junior officer had known White). He cautioned that White had been 'no mere staff officer', but he was not actually a 'commander' either.[52] White's actual contribution remains curiously nebulous.

White's character, as it is apparent from the seemingly abundant but actually intractable sources, is contradictory. He is both the courtly gentleman sketched out by admirers but also seems scheming and manipulative. He affected modesty but admitted to ambition. The model of a deferential staff officer, he apparently resented his subordinate status, but also did nothing to be relieved of it. Regarded as a paragon of military talent, he was implicated in planning some of the AIF's most brutal and costly battles, for which he suffered no consequences, either at the time or in reputation. Hailed as the virtual creator of the AIF, he arguably influenced only its command stratum, not the great mass of its members. Lamented as 'forgotten', he figures in most studies of the AIF's war. But his presence so often seems to derive ultimately from Bean's encomiums rather than on fresh scrutiny of the documents available in overwhelming quantities. An examination of White drawing on the AIF's operational records and affording greater clarity is long overdue.

Further reading

C.E.W. Bean, *Two Men I Knew: William Bridges and Brudenell White Founders of the A.I.F.*, Angus & Robertson, Sydney, 1957

———, *Official History of Australia in the War of 1914–18*, Vols I–VI, Angus & Roberston, Sydney, 1921–42

J. Bentley, 'Champion of Anzac: General Sir Brudenell White, the First Australian Imperial Force and the Emergence of the Australian Military Culture 1914–18', PhD, University of Wollongong, 2003

C.D. (Coulthard-)Clark, *A Heritage of Spirit: A Biography of Major-General Sir William Throsby Bridges*, Melbourne University Press, Melbourne, 1979

———, *No Australian Need Apply: The Troubled Career of Lieutenant-General Gordon Legge*, Allen & Unwin, Sydney, 1988

M. Derham, *Brudenell White: An AIF Legend*, Oryx Publishing, Melbourne, 2015

R. Derham, *The Silence Ruse: Escape from Gallipoli*, Oryx Publishing, Melbourne, 2000

J. Grey, 'Sir Cyril Brudenell White (1876–1940)', *Australian Dictionary of Biography*, Vol. 12, <adb.anu.edu.au/biography/white-sir-cyril-brudenell-1032>, accessed 16 January 2016

M. Hampton, *Attack on the Somme: 1st Anzac Corps and the Battle of Pozières Ridge, 1916*, Helion, Solihull, 2016

A. Hill, *Chauvel of the Light Horse*, Melbourne University Press, Melbourne, 1979

R. McMullin, *Pompey Elliott*, Scribe, Melbourne, 2008

J.D. Millar, 'A Study in the Limitations of Command: General Sir William Birdwood and the AIF, 1914–1918', PhD thesis, UNSW, 1993

J. Mordike, *An Army for a Nation: A History of Australian Military Developments 1880–1914*, Allen & Unwin, Sydney, 1992

P. Pedersen, *Monash as Military Commander*, Melbourne University Press, Melbourne, 1985

P. Sadler, *The Paladin: A Life of Major General Sir John Gellibrand*, Allen & Unwin, Sydney, 2000

G. Verney, 'The Army High Command and Australian Defence Policy, 1901–1918', PhD thesis, University of Sydney, 1982

———, 'General Sir Brudenell White: The Staff Officer as Commander', D. Horner, (ed.), *The Commanders: Australian Military Leadership in the Twentieth Century*, Allen & Unwin, Sydney, 1984

4
NOT UP TO THE JOB?
Major-General Gordon Legge

CHRIS CLARK

IN THE HISTORICAL ACCOUNT of Australia's participation in the First World War, James Gordon Legge (1863–1947) is regarded as the spectacular failure among the divisional commanders of the Australian Imperial Force (AIF). Essentially, this is a perception based on the tragic events in France in late July and early August 1916, when Legge's 2nd Division struggled to seize German-held ground beyond Pozières after the village had been taken by the 1st Division, succeeding only at the second attempt with over 6800 casualties. As the biographer of another Australian who achieved senior command late in the war put matters in recent years, Legge was the 'unpopular' general who caused his division to be 'wrecked at Pozières'.[1] So comprehensively has Legge been airbrushed from the historical record that even recent commemorations of the story of the 2nd Division – which still exists today as the headquarters commanding all the reserve brigades of the Australian Army – pay relatively little attention to the man who raised the original AIF formation and led it both at Gallipoli as well as France, in preference to Charles Rosenthal, who led it with far greater success during the great battles of 1918.

Major-General James Gordon Legge, twice Chief of the General Staff (1914–15, 1917–20).
Australian War Memorial, AWM 100140

The key figure in the diminution of Legge's reputation and career was official historian Charles Bean, whose volumes often relied too unquestioningly on accounts, claims and opinions of certain of Legge's contemporaries who were themselves arguably motivated by personal and professional jealousies. As a consequence, the extent and significance of Legge's contributions to the development of Australia's military forces – both before and after the First World War – has never been properly recognised. Today Legge receives even less credit and acknowledgment than does William Bridges (see Chapter 2), a figure with whom he was frequently associated in the first decade after Federation and with whom he had a lot in common.

Like Bridges, Gordon Legge – he preferred to use his second given name – was not a native-born Australian, having been born in London in 1863 as the eldest of nine children (eight of them boys) of a bank clerk. In 1878 the Legge family moved to Australia, arriving in Sydney in December when Gordon was aged 15; Bridges did not arrive in New South Wales until nine months later, when he was 18. Unlike Bridges, however, Legge arrived in Australia having already spent four or five years in the British public education system as a boarder at Cranleigh School in Surrey, and had even achieved some distinction as a student of Classics.[2] The difference between the two young men may not have been fully pronounced at the time of their arrival at Sydney, but within a few short years afterwards there emerged a gulf of separation as Legge embraced the evolving form of colonial nationalism, which held that being Australian entailed a sense that was distinct if not entirely separate from counting oneself as British. Within a few years this form of nationalism would come to be termed 'Australianism', and Legge was later regarded as one of its leading exponents.

For two years after his family's arrival, Legge continued his schooling at Sydney Grammar before then entering Sydney University in 1881. His time at that institution of learning extended over the next decade, and saw him gain degrees in Arts (B.A. 1884, M.A. 1887) and Law (LL.B. 1890). Because of the family financial circumstances during this period, he had largely sustained himself by his own exertions – firstly through manual labouring jobs then, from May 1886, as a teacher at Sydney Boys High School, which post he only resigned in September 1890 to practise law. In March 1891 he was formally admitted to the New South Wales Bar as a barrister. While Bridges may have acquired the cachet of the scholar, without having done much to practically earn it, Legge was unquestionably the 'real thing' – at age 27 he was already a man of recognised intellectual ability, with the speaking skills to eloquently express his ideas and arguments.

It was during his university years that Legge first made his entry into the colony's military forces. The same international events that prompted Bridges' change of career in 1885 also triggered a response by Gordon Legge. The threat of war between Britain and Russia on the frontier of Afghanistan, at the very time that New South Wales had depleted its defensive resources by sending a contingent of troops to Sudan, caused a sudden expansion in the colony's militia and volunteer forces. In May, Legge became a first lieutenant (unpaid) in a volunteer infantry regiment based at Lithgow, a coal-mining town on the far side of the Great Dividing Range from Sydney. This first period in uniform, however, lasted barely a year, after the patriotic impulse that sparked it had duly waned. Only after Legge had completed the study requirements associated with his Masters degree in 1887 did he again entertain ideas of involving himself in part-time soldiering; in October 1887 he received a commission as second lieutenant in the 1st Infantry Regiment, a Sydney-based militia unit that was at least partially paid.

Legge's early military career thus had to be pursued in the background or as an adjunct to the effort he needed to commit towards establishing himself in the legal profession. By all accounts, his time at the New South Wales Bar was not particularly satisfying or lucrative, in part because the Australian colonies were in the midst of an economic recession in the early 1890s. On at least two occasions he was forced to accept part-time work as a science teacher (he reportedly had an expert knowledge of chemistry) back at Sydney Boys High School.

It seems that most of his time in chambers was spent in researching the legal precedents applied and judges' decisions reached in 300 notable legal cases heard in the Supreme Court between 1825 and 1862. When published in 1896 – in two volumes totalling 1600 pages – the product of his industry promptly became known in legal circles as *Legge's Reports* and for decades afterwards was constantly quoted in court arguments.[3]

Even before Legge's major accomplishment from his time at the Bar finally appeared in print, he had already decided on a career change. With his interest in military affairs still growing, he had decided to make the army his full-time occupation. By comparison with his experience in the law, his time with the militia had proved far more rewarding. In 1892 he was promoted lieutenant in the 1st Regiment, and two years later he was acting as the unit's adjutant. It was late in 1894 that he received an invitation – reportedly at the instigation of Major-General Edward Hutton (see Chapter 1), the colony's British commandant – to join the forces' small permanent administrative and instructional cadre. The offer of captain's rank, at an annual salary of £360 and nearly £155 in allowances, was almost certainly attractive to the 31-year-old Legge. Added to the appeal was the opportunity to immediately proceed on a training visit to British forces stationed in India for four months.[4] He was probably unaware until his return that the preferment he appeared to have received prompted jealous criticism from another officer in his former regiment that was expressed through hostile questions in the Legislative Assembly; it was not the last time that he was subjected to such treatment during his career. The financial security that Legge's new employment provided also enabled him to marry in October 1896.

On his return to New South Wales from India, Legge became adjutant of the 2nd Infantry Regiment, also headquartered in Sydney, and set about demonstrating his serious interest and growing competence in the military profession. He had already been expressing this through active participation in the affairs of the United Service Institution (USI), where he had been a member since 1889, and was elected to its council in 1892. After being re-elected to the USI's council in 1896, he used the institution's session in October 1897 to present a controversial paper calling for simplification of the British close order drill being taught to the colony's infantry – by eliminating and amalgamating the number of movements in squad drill from more than 70 to 32. Claiming that the training manual in use was unnecessarily complex and often irrelevant to the extended formations required in modern warfare, he argued that the present system reduced the amount of time that local militia troops could spend in mastering the infantry minor tactics they actually needed.[5]

Unfortunately for gaining acceptance of the case that Legge presented to the USI, he allowed his comments to adopt a distinctly Australianist edge when he observed that local military forces owed no duty of deference to imperial authorities, who were not paying to maintain them – 'it is ourselves we have to consider in the first place,' he said. Many in his audience were offended at this suggestion, while others took umbrage at remarks that were critical of the time Legge claimed to have seen wasted in British regiments with perfecting parade-ground polish. Legge was probably not deliberately setting out to be provocative, but the brash and tactless manner in which he advocated change within the Australian system was very much to become a hallmark of his later style.

Notwithstanding Legge's unconventional and challenging views, his career within the New South Wales forces continued to advance. In 1897 he became assistant commandant and instructor at the School of Infantry, and was also appointed to a committee set up by General Hutton's successor to consider how rifle shooting might be made a more effective form of military training by conducting it under active service conditions. Two years later he was also appointed to a board tasked with taking control of sourcing uniforms for the colony's military forces, after the previous system of contracting local suppliers was criticised on the grounds of cost and quality. Also in 1899 he delivered another address to the USI in Sydney in which he outlined his thoughts on creating an effective 'Australian Defence Force' once

Federation had been achieved. Concluding that voluntary enlistment had proved a failure, he argued that the only solution was a system of universal service – by which he meant a general obligation for men to join in defending the nation, as with the Swiss militia system, rather than using compulsion to fill the ranks of a permanent force.[6] Less than five years after embarking on a career as a full-time professional military officer, Legge was demonstrating a willingness to think critically and deeply about Australian defence problems and arrive at solutions that called for fundamental changes rather than merely adjustments at the margins.

Within days of the South African War breaking out in October 1899, Captain Legge was nominated to lead one of the first small units that New South Wales offered for service with British forces. Already considered 'the smartest officer of infantry in N.S. Wales',[7] he was appointed to command the only company of infantry the colony sent to the conflict before it became clear that mounted troops were much preferred. The contingent sailed from Sydney in November, and upon arrival in South Africa, local British authorities decided to combine Legge's troops with other company-sized units from other colonies to form an 'Australian Regiment' – an arrangement from which Legge was soon attempting to extract himself and his men. Although his action sits oddly with his Australianist outlook, Legge's opposition to being involved with such an entity which prefigured Federation was shaped by the discovery that the regiment's Victorian component had been 'outrageously favoured in everything', from regimental appointments to 'even rations'.[8]

After four months the Australian Regiment experiment was quietly dropped, though not before the unit had been converted to mounted infantry. It was in this capacity that Legge's company had begun to see action during skirmishing around Colesberg, and Legge himself gained his first taste of leading men under fire. If the letters home from one of his subordinate officers are to be believed, Legge's judgment in command during this period did not entirely shine, although his courage and ability were never in question.[9] On the Australian Regiment's disbandment in April, Legge's company was absorbed as a squadron of the 1st New South Wales Mounted Rifles (NSWMR) and he became adjutant for the remainder of the first contingent's 12-month 'tour' of service in South Africa. While his former squadron returned home in December, however, he chose to remain behind – but in a new post as intelligence officer of the British brigade-size 'column' in which the rest of the NSWMR continued to serve during the phase of fighting that involved pinning down and destroying enemy mobile commandos. As was later commented, this was 'an important job now that sniffing out Boer hiding places was so important but a surprising one to give to someone ignorant of local dialects' so necessary in collecting information from the African population.[10]

For the next 18 months before the war's termination, Legge continued to perform intelligence duties. This did not mean that he did only staff work at a headquarters. In August 1901 he was present with a force of South Australians who came upon dozens of Boers at a farm on the Vet River and routed them after a wild night-time melee. Unfortunately for the attackers, the notable Boer commander Jan Smuts was also nearby with a large force and at dawn he moved to surround the South Australians. It was at this juncture that Legge galloped with three others back through a gap in the Boer ring to where the rest of the column was approaching and urged them to hurry a gun forward. 'Somehow the four got through the [gauntlet of] rifle fire they attracted and evaded the thirty Boer horsemen sent after them.'[11] His British column leader, Lieutenant-Colonel Beauvoir de Lisle, was later reputed to have written that Legge was 'the most intrepid intelligence officer that I have ever been associated with'.[12] For all that, however, when Legge returned home in October 1902 after a three-month furlough in England (meaning he had been away from Australia for almost three years), he received no greater recognition of his service in South Africa than a grant of brevet rank of major in December.

By the time Legge arrived back in New South Wales, the Commonwealth of Australia had been in existence for nearly two years, although moves to bring the military forces of the former colonies under unified command and create a federal system of administration were still ongoing. He took up duty as staff officer to the 3rd and 4th Regiments of infantry outside Sydney and was simultaneously appointed chief instructor of short-term district schools for infantry training and topography. In September 1903, however, he became secretary to a committee at army headquarters in Melbourne that was responsible for drafting the first federal military regulations. Though he returned to Sydney in time for Christmas, by mid-January 1904 he was back in Melbourne on further duty. When the 1903 *Defence Act* was proclaimed in March he published a handbook on Australian military law, the Act and its regulations. That year he also wrote a booklet outlining rules for framing operation orders in the field.

The period of roughly a year that Legge spent in Melbourne had provided a tantalising glimpse of the currents and characters at the administrative heart of the nation's defence forces. It had also given others the opportunity to be favourably impressed by his knowledge, skills and ability – although that may not have been immediately apparent, since his next posting in September 1904 was back to the district headquarters in Sydney as Deputy Assistant Adjutant General. At least this brought with it substantive promotion to major. A year later, however, when a Department of Military Science was being set up at the University of Sydney, Legge's name suddenly came to the fore. When Lieutenant-Colonel Bridges, the Chief of Intelligence, was tasked by the Minister for Defence to provide army assistance in setting up the new department, he nominated Legge as lecturer in military administration and law – a post Legge formally received in November 1906, with a seat on the university's board of military studies. By March 1907 Legge was actively performing his new role, teaching military topography to students who had enrolled in the military science course.[13]

Legge's days as a university lecturer in uniform were to be cut short by subsequent developments, and had only been part-time in any event. In December 1905 he had been appointed to act as assistant adjutant and chief staff officer at the district headquarters, a duty he performed until a more senior officer was posted into the position in May 1906. It was back as Deputy Assistant Adjutant General that in September 1906 Legge was required to prepare the Defence Department's legal case in a New South Wales Supreme Court action for damages caused by stray bullets fired on the army rifle range at the Sydney suburb of Randwick. The evidence that Legge gave convinced a jury that the claim was without merit and delivered to the Commonwealth the win that the department was so anxious to achieve.[14]

Added to the prominence that Legge had been achieving in this period was a talk he gave at the USI in June 1905, on the subject of organising a military reserve for the defence of Australia. Arguing that Japan's naval defeat of Russia at Tsushima the previous month created new urgency for fixing existing deficiencies in Australia's defensive arrangements, he urged putting the rifle club system onto a basis where it could become an effective national reserve. Though introduction of universal service seemed a remote prospect at that time, he could not resist thinking that an element of compulsion might need to be applied to reforming the rifles clubs too.[15]

These lifts in Legge's public profile probably contributed to a perception that he was the right man to undertake special duty during 1907 at army headquarters, where Bridges had been seeking to obtain additional staff for his undermanned Intelligence Department. The new Minister for Defence in the second Deakin ministry, Thomas Ewing, had been unwilling to accede to Bridges' requests, but did agree to Legge being 'instructed to work with the C of I for three months' from June until September.[16] When this term had expired, however, Legge was not automatically returned to Sydney; instead he was 'detailed for duty at Head-Quarters until further orders'. This further period, which turned out to be nine months, involved working directly under Ewing on a scheme for introducing compulsory military training, including the preparation of a draft Bill.[17] On 13 December, Prime Minister Alfred Deakin unveiled to federal Parliament his government's plans to create an 80,000-strong national guard based on the principle of universal service for men aged between 19 and 21. This new scheme was, Deakin declared, to be the cornerstone of a complete military system that would include a 'military college' (which, as described, was actually more a mobile team of instructors) for training, and a cordite factory for producing ammunition.[18]

Although Legge had been publicly advocating universal service since at least 1899, the announcements of 1907 did not simply represent the government's eventual adoption of his ideas. There is no evidence that he had fully developed his proposals into a comprehensive scheme for political consideration at any stage. Rather, it seems likely that Ewing, who was the member for the New South Wales seat of Richmond in the House of Representatives, had identified Legge previously as a serving officer willing to consider and work with ideas that were then being discussed and debated around the country in such organisations as the Australian National Defence League. Legge was therefore seen as more in sympathy with the Deakin government's aims and aspirations of addressing Australia's home defence arrangements than were other, more senior, officers who were the minister's main advisers in the Defence Department – men such as Bridges, who remained fully committed to implementing the ideas of General Hutton which tied Australian defence to schemes for the greater defence of the empire.

The reality of what had occurred behind the scenes during 1907 was fully appreciated by Hutton's supporters in the Australian forces, though naturally there were few who accepted the changes that Deakin's government proposed making. Bridges observed in a letter to Hutton in London that: 'It is apparently intended to destroy the existing troops and replace them by men without votes. Where the officers and N.C.O. are to come from is not at all clear. Anyway, it cannot be claimed that the Government have adopted the Swiss system – whose keynote is efficiency.' He went on to complain that the Military Board had never been consulted about the new proposals: 'The suggestions are, I believe, due to Legge, who has been working directly under the Minister.'[19] The reaction of the imperialist faction at headquarters soon assumed a note of personal invective, with Legge being characterised by his opponents as an opportunist who was merely seeking advancement by currying the favour of politicians. Others portrayed him as 'a Fenian sort of person' bent on destroying the nation's existing military class in pursuit of some weird ideal of Australian egalitarianism.[20] From this point on, Legge had plainly made himself a host of enemies among his fellow officers, many of whom were merely jealous that he had been marked as the 'coming man', the rising star in the defence firmanent.[21]

That Ewing and Deakin were well pleased with Legge's work in helping to articulate the new direction the government wished to take in defence arrangements was clearly indicated when, in June 1908, he was appointed to the Military Board with temporary rank of lieutenant-colonel. Initially he assumed the post of Military Secretary, a new position responsible for a range of issues such as dress, equipment, rations, quarters and postal services; aspects of mobilisation regarding transport and routes; and miscellaneous legal questions not involving discipline. The prime focus of his role, however, continued to be arranging for the introduction of universal service, or what was equally referred to as universal training.[22] The Deakin government's Bill providing for the change was tabled in Parliament in September 1908, but the government lost office two months later and was replaced by a Labor ministry headed by Andrew Fisher. Though the Bill lapsed, this gave little satisfaction to opponents of what was widely regarded as Legge's scheme. A conference of the Labor Party held earlier in 1908 had also adopted the principle of compulsory military training, so there was actually no change in political will to implement the change.

On 1 January 1909 the effects of a major reorganisation of duties within the federal military headquarters came into force. At the same time as Bridges (now a colonel) became the first Chief of the General Staff (CGS), Legge assumed a new appointment on the Military Board as Quartermaster-General.[23] This was essentially a redesignation of his former duties – including responsibility for universal training

– but the position brought with it a greater role in providing for many of the elements intended to maintain and support the national guard once it was formed, chiefly factories to manufacture locally much of what the new force would need to sustain itself. Beginning with an expansion in small arms ammunition production at a leased site in Melbourne in 1910, Legge began planning a program that would eventually extend to creating factories to make harnesses, saddlery and leather goods (1911), uniforms and headgear (1912), small arms (1912), cordite propellant (1912) and woollen cloth (1914).[24] This program was undertaken to ensure that Australia became militarily self-reliant and nationally efficient, but it would also come to play a crucial part in supplying the defence forces after the First World War began. Several of those factories – ammunition, small arms and clothing – remained in the national inventory into the 1980s.

Much of Legge's work as Quartermaster-General needed to be progressed and signed off by the Military Board, which under the new general staff arrangements applying from January 1909 operated not merely as a committee but now effectively like a functional headquarters. When Bridges was supplanted as CGS by Major-General John Hoad in May, the tone of proceedings on the board underwent a dramatic change. By September the Adjutant-General, Colonel E.T. Wallack, wrote to Bridges in London remarking: 'You should hear Hoad and Legge fight on the Board!!!'[25] This disputation came at a time when Legge's workload had increased immensely as a consequence of another change of government, which saw Deakin back in office and determined to make a second attempt to introduce universal service. In late September the government tabled a heavily revised Defence Bill, which dispensed with the national guard concept in favour of retaining a militia fed by the youthful products of a cadet scheme based on compulsory training. By the time the Bill was passed in December, Legge felt he was close to the end of his tether, having endured months of strain that left him physically and mentally exhausted.[26]

To help ensure acceptance of the new defence arrangements, Deakin had already decided on the device of obtaining approval from some suitable imperial authority for what the government was doing. In June 1909 an invitation had been issued to Field Marshal Lord Kitchener to visit and carry out an inspection tour of Australia's defences and to advise on the best means of developing and perfecting them. The visit, which began with Kitchener's arrival at Darwin on 21 December, has been regarded ever since as a pivotal event in the history of Australian defence. By the time the field marshal handed in his report on departing for New Zealand on 12 February 1910, the government had the endorsement it wanted. Kitchener not only proposed a land force of 80,000 men – half earmarked for local defence of Australian ports and cities, the other half in a field force that could be deployed anywhere within the country (or overseas, though he did not say that) – he accepted compulsory training as the foundation of his scheme, and even extended the period of training to age 25. He also pointed to deficiencies in mobilisation plans, and recommended establishment of a military college to produce the junior officers needed to oversee training.[27]

Because of his close involvement in preparing government defence plans over the previous two years, Legge was detailed by the defence minister to supply Kitchener with all the information the field marshal needed and to work with him in developing the fine detail of his report. This put Legge in closer proximity to Kitchener than probably any other Australian officer for the duration of the visit and would have added to the impression that most of what appeared in the final report had its origins in Legge's brain. Legge himself seemed inclined to think the same thing, later making the claim that: 'Substantially the whole of Lord Kitchener's proposals for Universal Training had been recommended by me at earlier dates.'[28]

Despite the extraordinary burden that had been placed on him over a prolonged period, in March Legge learned that it was proposed that he fill the duties of Director of Defence Organisation (later changed to Director of Operations) in addition to his existing workload as Quartermaster-General. The position was a key appointment on the general staff, involving matters of organisation, war planning, defence schemes, and strategic and tactical reconnaissance. Believing that the change was a ploy by Hoad to bring the drafting of universal training regulations under his direct control, Legge was not pleased with the arrangement but acquiesced when formally appointed in August (backdated to March). When he found himself also called upon to explain and justify proposals related to universal training to the Inspector-General (Kitchener's former staff officer, Colonel George Kirkpatrick), he felt an impossible point had been reached and asked in November to be allowed to resign his duties as Director of Operations. The defence minister in the Labor government, Senator George Pearce, insisted that Legge withdraw his request, but he was allowed to retire in June 1911 while remaining as Quartermaster-General.[29]

Legge still had plenty to occupy his attention in establishing the defence factories, and creating a War Railway Council as recommended by Kitchener to assist with planning mobilisation measures in the event of war. He also took an interest in arrangements to establish the military college that Bridges was brought back from England in May 1910 to start. Over subsequent months he assisted Bridges with the drafting of regulations for the new institution. He was not successful in obtaining one of the two director positions working for Bridges at Duntroon, but nonetheless attended the college's official opening in June 1911 when he read the speech from the CGS (Hoad) who was absent through illness.

In January 1912 Legge was nominated to be Australia's representative on the Imperial General Staff, after the War Office requested a replacement for Bridges, who had vacated the post in April 1910. He sailed for London on 12 June, and two days later was appointed CMG in recognition of the important work he had accomplished as Quartermaster-General, both in setting the supply side of the army house in order and for bringing the compulsory training scheme to fruition. At Whitehall, Legge experienced many of the same frustrations that had irritated his predecessor, feeling that there was little interest shown at the War Office in the military affairs of the dominions and in practice he was little more than a junior observer of the British organisation. In January 1913 he published an account of Australia's universal training system in the prestigious British Army publication *Army Review*, this being followed by a second invitation to contribute another article on forest or bush fighting which appeared in print in July 1914.

From time to time Legge found matters in which he could deliver useful outcomes for the Australian forces. One of these was the Defence Department's decision to embrace aviation for military purposes by establishing a flying school, a proposal that he already knew about through his former position on the Military Board. After he visited one of the major British flying centres on Salisbury Plain in November 1912 he contacted Melbourne to pass on advice he had received that the first four aircraft ordered by Australia to equip its school were actually unsuitable for the initial training of pilots, and a slower type of machine was preferable. This advice was heeded and a Bristol Boxkite was added to Australia's order.[30] The interest thus shown by Legge in the emerging technology of flight would re-emerge five years later when he became a major figure in the debate about establishing a large-scale and permanent aviation branch within the Australian Army.

Possibly the most remarkable use made of Legge's presence in London occurred in July 1913, when he wrote to Melbourne to pass on assessments he had obtained regarding Japan's capacity to move three divisions by sea from Yokohama to Sydney in under four weeks from mobilisation, and without Australia receiving forewarning of the attack greater than seven to 14 days.[31] The naval and military staffs in Melbourne were known to periodically take an interest in the threat that Japan might potentially pose to Australian territory, but there is no known indication of action that might have resulted from the information received from Legge on this occasion. The greater significance of this incident may well be that it revealed a concern on Legge's part about Japan's strategic intentions towards Australia, a concern that he would again display during the First World War.

On 1 May 1914, as Legge was nearing the second anniversary of his arrival in London, he was promoted colonel and appointed CGS back in Australia with effect from 1 August. Boarding ship in London on 3 July, he was still at sea when war began in Europe and did not reach Melbourne until 9 August – four days after the news that the British Empire had joined the conflict was received in Australia. Press reports state that within hours of arrival he entered an interview with the Minister for Defence, Senator Edward Millen, in which he was offered command of the Australian Army 'so long as "a state of war" might continue'. This placed him in charge of the 'active military defence of the Commonwealth', while the Inspector-General, Brigadier-General Bridges, concentrated on raising a force of 20,000 men that Australia had offered to Britain for overseas service.[32]

Home defence was not Legge's sole priority, however, because on 6 August a request had been received from London asking the Australian government to take action against Germany's colonial territories in the Pacific. Special attention needed to be given to putting out of action radio stations at Yap in the Caroline Islands, Nauru, and near Rabaul in German New Guinea, which were fundamental to the enemy's naval operations across the Pacific region. This task also probably formed part of Legge's interview with the minister, because after the meeting Millen announced the government's decision 'to organise a small mixed naval and military force for service within or without Australia . . . quite distinct from that being organised for service in Great Britain', and recruitment for this force would begin immediately.[33] Thus Legge was placed in charge of raising what became the Australian Naval and Military Expeditionary Force – Australia's first contribution to the war effort – and despatching it into action from Sydney on 19 August.

Because the disposition of the powerful German naval squadron in the Pacific was not known during the first weeks of war, Legge also had the major responsibility of providing for the defence of Australian territory against attack. For this task there were 3000 permanent soldiers and 50,000 militia available, although these resources were also being heavily drawn on by Bridges and his staff in raising the force for overseas service, the AIF. To supplement the existing military organisation, Senator George Pearce, the Minister for Defence in the Labor government that came to power on 17 September 1914, announced – on the advice of Legge and the Military Board – the raising of an Australian Army Reserve to assist with home defence.[34] There was therefore the need for a large training organisation to be established and maintained, to meet home defence requirements as well as providing for subsequent AIF contingents and reinforcement drafts of 3000 men a month.

Although the destruction of the main German naval squadron off the Falkland Islands in December removed the threat of anything more than nuisance raids, Legge still kept in mind the possible threat that might arise from Japan – despite that power entering the war on the side of the Allies on 23 August. As Legge commented to the commander of the Australian Naval and Military Expeditionary Force in November: 'The end of the war is not in sight yet, and the settlement may mean another war with parties redivided – how? So we must push in Australia's preparation. We have the rifle, cordite, Ammunition and leather factories all working their hardest.'[35]

Underlining Legge's concerns about Japan's motives and intentions was the fact that Japanese marines had landed on the German island of Yap in October and effectively taken possesion of the Caroline Islands. The authorities in London believed that this occupation was intended as temporary, until an Australian force could be sent to relieve the Japanese, and it was on this basis that Legge began planning, in conjunction with the navy, for despatch of a further component of the Australian Naval and Military Expeditionary Force (to be known as 'Tropical Force') for service north of the Equator. It was only five days after this force sailed from Sydney on 28 November, intent on first dealing with a suspected enemy base on the Sepik River in New Guinea, that a further cable from London asking that the question of occupying the northern islands be left for settlement after the war. Although the Australian government acquiesced in this, there remained strong concern about Japan's strategic intentions. On 8 January 1915 Tokyo presented the Chinese government with the 'Twenty-one Demands' that aimed at expanding Japanese economic and political interests in China. The level of anxiety caused the Council of Defence (with Legge a member) to decide unanimously in February 1915 that new units raised for the war effort should be retained in Australia, 'at all events for present'. Even three months later the future of the northern islands remained a matter of ongoing concern in defence circles, and one to which Legge's attention would again return in later years.[36]

It was at this juncture that news was received from Egypt that Bridges, the commander of the AIF, had been fatally wounded during fighting on the Gallipoli peninsula. Legge was appointed to succeed him in command of the 1st Australian Division on 20 May and sailed from Melbourne that day. This selection of the Australian government was to trigger an extraordinary reaction from AIF brigadiers who considered they had been passed over, and many of whom were undoubtedly also venting their personal dislike of Legge based on jealousy at his rise to prominence in the years before the war. Representations made by these officers (Chauvel, McCay, Monash) to the British commander of the Australian and New Zealand Army Corps (ANZAC), led to protests against Legge's selection being passed up the command chain to Lord Kitchener, Secretary of War.[37] The Australian government was unwilling to revoke their choice, however, and Legge's appointment was let stand. Nonetheless, the spectre of his alleged 'unpopularity' was to follow him throughout his time with the AIF.

By the time that Legge actually reached the ANZAC position on 24 June – two days after he was promoted major-general – the worst of the crisis situation that existed after the corps' landing in late April had passed, and many of the first issues he needed to deal with were administrative rather than operational. He had also succeeded to Bridges' wide powers as commander of the AIF, in addition to 1st Division, and issues such as transfers, promotions and demotions of personnel, along with changes to units, all fell to him even though his decisions might cut across the authority of the ANZAC commander,

William Birdwood. After less than a month on Gallipoli, Legge was asked to form the mass of new Australian units arriving in Egypt into a 2nd Division and was sent to Cairo on 26 July to organise it. With his departure, Birdwood inquired about having Legge's AIF powers vested in himself and was rewarded with what he wanted in September (although the formal title of General Officer Commanding AIF did not follow for another year).

Legge subsequently brought the 2nd Division onto Gallipoli in late August – too late for all but a couple of his units to take part in the great August offensive, which represented the Allies' last chance to break the stalemate that had developed on the peninsula. He was sent away sick in late November and did not resume command of the division until it had been withdrawn to Egypt following the evacuation of Gallipoli. In March 1916 the 2nd Division sailed for France as part of a newly constituted I Anzac Corps under Birdwood. It was on the Western Front that Legge's military career hit a road-block at Pozières in July–August 1916, for reasons that will probably long be debated. Recent research has shed new light on the circumstances of the fighting at Pozières, and later at Mouquet Farm,[38] which prompted British commander-in-chief Douglas Haig to condemn in sweeping manner 'the ignorance of the 2nd Australian Division' and conclude that Legge 'was not much good'.[39] But analysis of this evidence does not make clear the extent to which Legge was personally to blame for what happened, so much as his divisional staff (for which he *did* bear ultimate responsibility), the peculiar and special conditions faced, and even the conduct of Birdwood and the commander of the army in which the division served, among others.

Regardless of the judgments that might be made with hindsight, the result of the events of 1916 was that Legge was evacuated to England at the end of January 1917 – ostensibly for health reasons, although he protested that he had never 'been sick for one day in France from arrival'.[40] Having informed Birdwood that if he was not to be again given an operational command he would prefer to return to duty in Australia, Legge was back in Melbourne by mid-April

1917. Still wearing honorary rank of major-general, he was appointed Inspector-General on 30 April, before resuming the post of CGS on 1 October. In this capacity he again became a significant figure in administering war arrangements on the home front. One of the major issues confronting him was the problem of maintaining the number of reinforcements sent for the AIF, which the government, led by William Hughes, attempted to resolve through the introduction of conscription. As CGS, Legge could hardly avoid being caught up in the government's efforts to justify the move during a bitter referendum in December, which was as unsuccessful as an earlier referendum in October 1916.[41]

Over the course of 1918 Legge revealed himself to be a strong advocate of air power for the Australian forces and was appointed to a committee which put forward a plan in January 1919 that, two years later, led to the formation of the Royal Australian Air Force.[42] During 1919 he joined a committee to consider a scheme for remodelling Australia's post-war citizen forces, and was also appointed to an expanded conference of senior officers which was held in January 1920 to consider the same matters. By then he knew that his departure from the CGS position was imminent; although he and three other officers were made substantive major-generals in the permanent forces early in 1920, in recognition of their war service, two of the three (H.G. Chauvel and C.B.B. White) were given seniority above him, so his supersession was only a matter of time. The inevitable occurred on 1 April, when it was announced that Legge would become commandant of the Royal Military College (RMC) in June, his place as CGS being taken by White.[43]

On taking up his new post at Duntroon, Legge found the college in a crisis because of the scarcity of applicants for a military career and severe reductions in funds. Constant pressures to find economies at RMC made his time there difficult and frustrating, with little opportunity to make changes that would be beneficial to the life or future of the institution. After two years it was announced by the defence minister that Legge was among officers to be retrenched for reasons of economy.⁴⁴ He was placed on the unattached list in August 1922 and, with financial assistance from the soldier settlement scheme, moved onto a farm within the Australian Capital Territory where he spent the rest of his life.⁴⁵ Transferred to the army retired list with honorary rank of lieutenant-general in January 1924,⁴⁶ he became a rural recluse and little was heard of him within military circles again.

Although Legge's record between mid-1915 and the end of 1916 while at the head of Australian divisions on Gallipoli and at the Western Front can never be described as impressive, it has not been convincingly demonstrated that his performance failings were as obvious or as terrible as his many detractors have maintained in opinions offered primarily to blacken his name. A major difficulty also arises in attempting to fairly weigh the worth of assessments from individuals who were themselves notably imperialist in outlook, or Australianists only until their personal ambitions came into play. Regardless of the view taken of Legge's war service, he remains a figure of major importance on the Australian defence scene before the First World War, with his work in helping to shape the scheme of universal training – the first distinctly Australian initiative ever taken in national defence matters – being his major contribution. Had the war not intervened, the system for training militia members from secondary school onwards would probably have remained in force beyond 1929 when it was finally abandoned for ideological reasons opposed to conscription as much as on cost grounds.⁴⁷ In addition to this, the work Legge undertook to create the means for supplying the army with *matériel* placed Australia in far better shape for coping with wartime demands than it would have been otherwise.

Further reading

C.E.W. Bean, *The Story of Anzac: From 4 May, 1915, to the Evacuation of the Gallipoli Peninsula*, vol. 2 of *The Official History of Australia in the War of 1914–1918*, 11th ed., Angus & Robertson, Sydney, 1941

———, *The Australian Imperial Force in France, 1916*, vol. 3 of *The Official History of Australia in the War of 1914–1918*, 12th ed., Angus & Robertson, Sydney, 1941

C.D. (Coulthard-)Clark, *Duntroon: The Royal Military College of Australia, 1911–1986*, Allen & Unwin Australia, North Sydney, 1986

———, *No Australian Need Apply: The Troubled Career of Lieutenant-General Gordon Legge*, Allen & Unwin, Sydney, 1988

———, *The Third Brother: the Royal Australian Air Force 1921–39*, Allen & Unwin, North Sydney, 1991

J. Grey, *The War with the Ottoman Empire*, vol. 2 of *The Centenary History of Australia and the Great War*, Oxford University Press, South Melbourne, 2015

M. Hampton, *Attack on the Somme: 1st Anzac Corps and the Battle of Pozières Ridge, 1916*, Helion Publishing, Solihull, 2016

A.J. Hill, *Chauvel of the Light Horse: A Biography of General Sir Harry Chauvel, GCMG, KCB*, Melbourne University Press, Melbourne, 1978

S.S. Mackenzie, *The Australians at Rabaul: The Capture and Administration of the German Possessions in the Southern Pacific*, vol. 10 of *The Official History of Australia in the War of 1914–1918*, 10th ed., Angus & Robertson, Sydney, 1941

R. McMullin, *Pompey Elliott*, Scribe Publications, Carlton North, 2002

J. Mordike, *An Army for a Nation: A History of Australian Military Developments 1880–1914*, Allen & Unwin, North Sydney, 1992

P.A. Pedersen, *Monash as Military Commander*, Melbourne University Press, Melbourne, 1985

P.S. Sadler, *The Paladin: A Life of Major-General Sir John Gellibrand*, Oxford University Press, South Melbourne, 2000

G. Serle, *John Monash*, Melbourne University Press, Carlton, 1982

B.H. Travers, *William Holmes: Secretary and Soldier*, Echo Books, Canberra, 2016

C. Wilcox, *Australia's Boer War: The War in South Africa 1899–1902*, Oxford University Press, South Melbourne, 2002

C. Wray, *Sir James Whiteside McCay: A Turbulent Life*, Oxford University Press, South Melbourne, 2002

5

THE SOLDIER AS TECHNOCRAT
Brigadier John William Alexander O'Brien

JEFFREY GREY

THE SECOND WORLD WAR laid the foundations for modern Australia. For all the rhetoric surrounding Anzac, Gallipoli and the formative experiences of the Great War, it was the great national trial of 1939–45 and its consequences that established the basis of the Australia we now live in, and which is now undergoing similarly fundamental changes whose consequences we can only dimly perceive. The creation of a multinational society, rather than a remorselessly Anglo-Celtic one, is the product of the massive schemes of post-war, non-British migration which are, in turn, a direct consequence of the Second World War. The American alliance that has underpinned virtually every aspect of foreign and defence policy for more than 60 years is a product of Britain's decline as a global power which, itself, is a direct consequence of the Second World War. The diversification of the economy away from reliance on agriculture and extractive industries to embrace heavy industry and secondary manufacturing – a trend now coming to an end – flowed directly from the need during the Second World War for the nation to make what we did not have and could not procure from

Brigadier J.W.A. O'Brien, Deputy Master-General of the Ordnance (Equipment Division) and chairman of the Army Inventions Directorate.
Australian War Memorial, AWM 126234

external sources. The jobs that flowed from these activities helped to underpin the long period of post-war prosperity, in marked contrast to the experience of the 1920s and 1930s.

There was some heavy industrial capacity in Australia before the war – steel-making, for example – but the Depression was particularly hard on the manufacturing sector, while the nucleus of government munitions factories, intended to preserve core capabilities on which to expand and equip the armed forces in the event of war, were forced to engage in manufacturing civilian items in the 1930s since there was little or no work of a military nature to be had until the government made decisions about rearmament from 1937.[1] For the first few months of the war, the government establishments moved their production up but there was little attempt made to mobilise and organise the commercial industrial sector. The fall of France in May 1940 reinforced the fact that the war was likely to be a long one and resulted in a rapid drying up of British sources of supply for Australia and the other dominions while the British Army scrambled to make good the massive losses in arms and equipment at Dunkirk.

The machinery for the mobilisation, expansion and management of the economy and industry developed over the first half of the war, receiving a considerable additional fillip of urgency and purpose after Japan's entry in December 1941. As in Britain, the United States and elsewhere among the combatant powers, industrialists, businessmen, scientists and civil and military officials found themselves in positions of authority and overseeing production enterprises in a manner they could not have imagined before the war.

One such individual was John William Alexander O'Brien. He was born in Collingwood, Melbourne, on 13 June 1908, the son of a policeman who had served in South Africa in the 2nd Battalion, Australian Commonwealth Horse and thereafter had been in the militia. A Catholic family of modest means had little to spare for higher education, and O'Brien attended the Working Men's College (subsequently Royal Melbourne Institute of Technology) to study civil engineering while working for Dorman Long and Company, the British firm that would build the Sydney Harbour Bridge. He joined the militia in 1926 and was commissioned in the 2nd Artillery Survey Company in August 1928. He did extremely well in both civil and military spheres, and in May 1930 he embarked on a world trip, taking in the United States and Britain, working in both countries and studying techniques for artillery survey while also visiting the battlefields of the American Civil War and the Great War.[2]

In 1938 O'Brien went into business for himself and acquired a closer acquaintance with defence contracting through work for the Royal Australian Navy. He also gained valuable experience in managing a large and growing skilled workforce as the pace of work increased with the outbreak of war in 1939. Nor had his militia career slowed. He was acting adjutant of the 10th Field Artillery Brigade between 1932 and 1936, and served subsequently as a battery commander.[3] When the war came he was transferred to army headquarters in Melbourne as a major in the role of Deputy Assistant Director of Artillery to Major C.E.M. 'Gaffer' Lloyd, for whom he had worked previously. One of the first tasks they faced was the motorisation of the field and medium artillery. He was young for his rank (certainly by comparison with his regular army counterparts), made the most of his connections and was uncommonly well qualified for his role at the beginning of the war, matching extensive knowledge and experience as an engineer and manager with a wide range of both staff and regimental experience.

O'Brien decided to enlist in the 2nd Australian Imperial Force (AIF) when the government announced in February 1940 that it was raising the 7th Division for overseas service. There were many more applicants for positions than there were vacancies to be filled, especially among officers, and O'Brien's application was supported by Lloyd, E.J. Milford and C.A. Clowes, all of whom were regulars, all of whom would be generals by mid-war, all of whom went to posts in the 7th Division and for all of whom he had worked previously. He was appointed second-in-command of the 2/7th Field Regiment and played a large part in training its two constituent batteries – the 12th and 13th – which were spread between South and Western

Australia. Having arrived in the Middle East, he was soon promoted to lieutenant-colonel and given command of the 2/5th Field Regiment, making him the youngest regimental commander in the 2nd AIF. He commanded the regiment through the short but intense Syrian campaign in June–July 1941, in which he earned a Distinguished Service Order and was mentioned in despatches. He had also acquired combat experience and impressed those around him – below as well as above – with his abilities.

The 7th Division returned to Australia in early March 1942, and within weeks O'Brien found himself promoted to brigadier and was appointed as the Director of Artillery in army headquarters. He was, again, the youngest occupant for his rank in the army and his recent active service experience, obvious engineering and organisational talents, and connections with industry made him a natural choice, especially since his predecessor had evinced a strong preference for British sources of supply over local products, seemingly oblivious as well to the political ramifications. This attitude was untenable given the turn in the war's fortunes in the first months of 1942.[4] O'Brien himself was aware that his appointment was unusual and recalled subsequently that it was 'remarkable that I broke through the barrier to what was a plum staff corps appointment. The urgency of war and the non-availability of a suitable officer had much to do with it, but I had luck', while he also recognised that his wide-ranging interests and reading, combined with his engineering experience, also played an important part.[5]

O'Brien headed the Directorate of Artillery for eight months, and was influential in a major development in artillery fire support which emphasised the need for the army to think more adaptively in the conditions of the Pacific war. The standard field gun-howitzer in the British and empire armies was the 25-pounder, a quick-firing and flexible field piece that was developed before the war to replace the obsolescent 18-pounder gun and 4.5-inch howitzer that had been the standard field pieces during the Great War. It was an adaptable and dependable gun well suited to the conditions for which it was designed – which did not include the rugged jungles of New Guinea. The solution was to redesign the gun, cut down the barrel and recuperator, make the trail lighter and remove the gun shield. The result was a weapon that could be broken down into ten lighter-weight components able to be air dropped or packed into a jeep for quick reassembly. It was easier to deliver, easier to manhandle and gave the tactical commanders a heavier firepower option well forward. Designated the 'Short 25' or colloquially as the 'Baby 25', 213 were manufactured in Australia during the war, as against 1527 of the standard model.

In his biography of O'Brien, Gordon Rimmer states that the Short 25 'was one of the three important innovations made by Australian designers during the Second World War', and there is no question that O'Brien was its initiator and did the early design modification drafts himself.[6] It was not a perfect weapon, but a compromise born of an urgent situation. Although it had some critics given its limitations, the official history was doubtless fair to conclude that whatever 'the gun's shortcomings may have been they appear to have been outweighed by its good points'.[7] O'Brien's role perfectly exemplified his approach to finding suitable staff for the various organisations he headed in the second half of the war: 'young officers with Middle East experience and at least some professional knowledge of artillery, weapons and associated equipment, preferably with some engineering knowledge'.[8] He acknowledged that such paragons were 'very rare birds' and that in consequence much of what the directorate did comprised 'learning by doing'.

In January 1943 he became Deputy Master-General of the Ordnance (Equipment), a position that gave him primary responsibility for the management of testing and then acquiring a wide range of equipment to meet the army's evolving needs. In this position he dealt regularly with the dedicated and long-serving Secretary of the Department of the Army, Frank Sinclair, with whom he quickly developed a strong relationship. Personalities and personal ties were important, and a small but formidable group consisting of Sinclair, O'Brien himself, Sydney Menzies, a businessman recruited to become

Director of Production Orders in the Ministry of Munitions (and brother of former and future Prime Minister, Robert), and 'Gaffer' Lloyd who became Adjutant-General in early 1943, coalesced in order to streamline procedures and actually get things done. For O'Brien this meant a great increase in committee work and higher-level administration, and less 'hands-on' technical work of the kind that he knew and at which he excelled.

This role was a crucial one, placing O'Brien as the pivot between the army and its needs on the one hand, and, on the other, the manufacturers who could meet the army's material needs, and the rest of the army and, by extension, the wider economy, which were in competition for resources. In modern parlance he had to manage below, above and laterally. He found it especially frustrating getting feedback from the 'end users' in the field concerning inadequacies in equipment, and to this end he travelled widely both in Australia and north to the theatre of the campaign in New Guinea. On one such visit he came to appreciate that an occasional, random visit to forward areas by staff officers – no matter how senior – was a fairly fruitless approach, and in response created a network of ordnance officers in the field who could gather information and act as regular conduits between the units and formations in the field and the various staff divisions in Melbourne. He also regularly visited factories of all types, often trying to find solutions to production delays and short-comings in the face of the acute scarcity of skilled male labour. As the war entered its final stages and the Japanese threat receded ever more clearly, he also found delays in procedures and attempts to restrict the financing of new projects, and countered with the observation that no one could predict when the war would end and that it was therefore foolish to restrict production in anticipation of a point which no one could accurately foresee.

His job involved the trial and acquisition of numerous items and platforms, not all of which necessarily proved suitable for issue and use in the field – that was part of the point of the work he and his staff undertook. D.P. Mellor's volume of the official history discusses the wide rank of industrial and scientific activity pursued as part of the war effort, only parts of which concerned O'Brien and the army, but which nonetheless gives an excellent and quite detailed overview of the scale of the national endeavour. We have noted O'Brien's direct contribution to the modification of the 25-pounder. The only items outside his portfolio essentially were rations, stationery, engineering stores and medical supplies. Some of the problems were critical but unglamorous, such as the need to 'tropic proof' equipment, rations, ammunition and even clothing against the rigours of operating in a hot, humid climate and mountainous terrain.[9] Others were problems that he inherited.

One such was the rancorous dispute over whether the army should adopt the Australian-designed Owen submachine-gun, or a modified British design – the Austen, based on the British Sten gun – or cut its losses and adopt an American weapon. It will be remembered that his predecessor as Director of Artillery had been moved on because of his opposition to acquiring Australian designs, and this had given O'Brien his opportunity. He sought to be even-handed on the issue, although he personally believed the Owen was the superior weapon on the basis of field trials. When the views of units on operations showed a clear preference for the Owen based on performance, he did not hesitate to recommend its adoption. Unlike some of those around him, O'Brien understood both the manufacturing issues that arose from equipping a large army for the first time as well as the political imperatives that were in play.

Another legacy project was the Cruiser, an Australian-made armoured fighting vehicle or tank. This project truly was a bold move, since in 1939 Australia did not possess the industrial base to manufacture automobiles, much less armoured vehicles. The design was always a compromise reflecting Australia's limited industrial base and capabilities, and the first tanks, the AC1s, were completed in October 1942. From initiation to completion in 22 months was a remarkable achievement, but this remained the only truly impressive aspect of the project. Its main armament was the British 2-pounder gun, by then obsolete in that role and described by O'Brien (who, it will be remembered, knew a thing or two about guns) as 'pip squeaks'. In any case, he was underwhelmed by the prototypes and believed, with some justification, that the resources in both materials and skilled manpower would be much better used in other areas of production. He informed Blamey that 'the Australian tank will never be a real success although it will eventually become a runner'.[10] In June 1943 Prime Minister John Curtin made the decision that production of the Cruiser prototypes should cease (though not until after the federal election in September), while the need for tank capability in the army was to be met with the American M4, the Sherman. No Cruiser tank ever saw service in an army unit.

One of the arguments in favour of scrapping tank development was the need to construct small watercraft for the army and maintain and repair existing ones. With the war at a distance from Australia's shores and main centres of population, the need for watercraft of all kinds increased – not just the obvious, such as landing craft, but also pontoons, trawlers, tugs and other in-shore vessels. So important was this issue that, as Rimmer notes, between May 1943 and the end of the war in August 1945 'there are more entries on small craft in O'Brien's journals than on any other matter'.[11] This was not only an argument about resources but about priorities and allocations, since the Americans were also voracious consumers of locally constructed shipping and also had a pressing need for expanded maintenance facilities. In late 1942 the Americans had placed extensive orders with the Australian shipbuilding industry, pretty much swamping capacity, and leaving nothing over for the Australian Army. Appeals to the Americans to share some of the allocations they had swept up in this manner were rebuffed.

For whatever reason, O'Brien believed that the Australian Shipbuilding Board favoured American orders over those originating with the army. To compound the difficulties, the small shipyards involved in construction were manpower intensive, worked on a small scale and used old-fashioned and often outdated methods, such as riveting rather than welding. 'This is an interesting antiquarian project', he wrote, 'and unlike other projects we have struck, we have not applied much of the methods developed overseas to Australian conditions but have tried to tackle the task by obsolete methods borrowed from other countries.'[12] The issue became easier from late 1944 when the Americans began to cancel existing orders as no longer needed, but it took the provision of American-built landing craft to the Australian forces to ensure that the amphibious assault operations in Borneo went ahead. The fundamental problem was the refusal by the Americans to share production, a product of the War Cabinet's decision that General MacArthur should be the deciding authority in all such matters. The biggest problem, about which O'Brien individually could do little, was structural – as Mellor notes, when war came in 1939 'the country was without any worthwhile merchant shipbuilding industry'.[13] All the main players in the issue, the Americans, the Directorate of Water Transport, the navy and the army, faced the same range of problems, and they were unable to create a successful framework or set of procedures either separately or in concert. As Rimmer notes, 'Despite O'Brien's grasp of the issues, it was only the end of hostilities that really closed the file on the saga of the small craft'.[14]

As the war ended, he, like other thinking senior officers, turned his mind to post-war arrangements in those areas with which he had close familiarity – in his case equipment and design or what would, in time, come to be called development and acquisition. 'The principal lesson that I have learned during my association with the Army', he wrote, is:

> How quickly we ignore what we have learned, and how glibly we endeavour to get by with makeshifts already proved to result in disastrous consequences . . . We cannot guarantee that our possible future enemies will not on their part learn something from the lessons of this war, and furthermore that they will not endeavour to apply those lessons. The present proposals for the design and development of equipment for

> the post-war Australian Army provide approximately the same resources as were available to us in 1939, whilst on the other hand developments in engineering and science now require far greater resources than those proposed even to maintain a standard relative to the very low one reached in 1939.[15]

It would be difficult to find a more clear-eyed and succinct encapsulation of the problems faced by small- and medium-power armies in the acquisition of platforms and systems.

As a militia officer, even a reasonably senior one who was well connected and enjoyed a high profile within the army by virtue of his years at army headquarters, O'Brien faced a problematic future in the post-war army. Once again, his network of connections in high places and a fortunate combination of qualifications and good timing worked in his favour. The Commonwealth government decided to send a small team of experts to Japan to obtain 'scientific and industrial data that might prove of use', and O'Brien was selected to lead it when the original choice became unavailable.

Almost as soon as he arrived in Tokyo he was approached by an American senior officer to head up one of the staff divisions of the Economic and Science Section in the US occupation authority's civil administration. He quickly found himself heading the Science and Technology Division (S&T Division), 'an important but lesser-known' part of the occupation administration tasked with overseeing the dismantling of scientific research with military applications, but also with playing 'a constructive role in helping Japanese scientists and engineers recover from defeat and contribute effectively to economic recovery'.[16] O'Brien was the only non-American in uniform at MacArthur's headquarters and one of very few non-Americans at any level. Although he would find much of his time in Japan personally frustrating and encountered considerable opposition to his ideas and proposals on economic and scientific policy, especially where they ran counter to MacArthur's policies or US interests (not always or necessarily the same thing), he nonetheless played an important role in the establishment of the Science Council of Japan and the reconstruction of Japanese scientific and research institutions in the aftermath of the destruction of the war.[17]

In late 1948, with the work of his division starting to wind down, he was tapped to sit as president of the military court convened to try Admiral Soemu Toyoda, the last chief of staff of the Imperial Japanese Navy and Commander-in-Chief of the Combined Fleet. This was a trial on the principle of 'command responsibility', the notion that a senior officer was responsible for the actions of those nominally under his command even though he might not be in the same region physically when war crimes were committed. This principle had seen General Yamashita hanged for war crimes in what some, even at the time, thought was a kangaroo court. Unlike his hapless army counterpart, Toyoda was found not guilty on all counts in a trial that lasted ten months. O'Brien enjoyed the trial work, but when it was over returned to the S&T Division where there was, in truth, increasingly little for him to do. Although he enjoyed the relative opulence of the occupation's lifestyle, he needed another job and, once again, his network in Australia found something apparently suited to his skills: Senior Supply Representative in the United States, in the rank of honorary major-general. He answered to the Department of Defence Production and had a shifting set of responsibilities for strategic materials and procurement from US sources. Although he would spend three years in Washington DC in the role, he once again found the restrictions and pettiness of peacetime public administration and embassy politics frustrating, and he returned to Australia and the private sector in Sydney towards the end of 1954. After a few years working for others he founded his own precision tools manufacturing company. He died after a period of ill-health on 27 May 1980.

O'Brien's most important contribution came during the Pacific war and in the unglamorous role of the senior staff officer. It is the nature of staff work and administration that it attracts little obvious attention, as he himself acknowledged: 'there is little honour or glory working in the MGO [Master-General of the Ordnance] Branch, the main reward is one's own satisfaction of a job well done'.[18] For a man in his 30s, his achievement was considerable, forecasting the army's requirements across a wide range of equipment types and then ensuring that these were met. To be sure, the final decisions lay with the Cabinet, but the advice that guided them in taking those decisions came from the MGO Branch.

His mix of skills and experience was quite possibly unique in the army of his time, and would be hard to replicate even today. His engineering experience and wide-ranging interest in military equipment, acquired as a young officer before the war, were allied to his undoubted capacity as an artillery officer demonstrated on active service. His knowledge of, and contacts within, industry and his growing flair for administration were the final elements in the mix. He had impressed his contemporaries and seniors in uniform and this, together with a number of lucky breaks and a knack for being in the right place at the right time gave him opportunities that would likely have come to him in no other way and, as his less happy post-war career suggested, at no other time. A great global conflict in which, for a time, the future security of the country seemed at stake and under threat, called for measures out of the ordinary, and O'Brien was always eager to avail himself of these. As his biographer describes it:

> [i]t was as if he sat at the centre of an enormous web that covered businessmen, public servants and politicians . . . Not many people could match the knowledge of manufacturing industry that he had accumulated . . . [He] impressed many of those in high places with his businesslike but cautious approach to administration, his grasp of detail combined with an appreciation of broader issues, his balanced judgement and confident forthright manner.[19]

It was in the nature of modern industrial warfare in the 20th century that victory was as dependent on industrial managers as much as it was on armed forces fighting a campaign. O'Brien's career and contribution to victory perfectly exemplify this fact.

Further reading

In addition to the works below, O'Brien's journals, correspondence and other papers and photographs are held by the Australian Army Museum New South Wales at Victoria Barracks in Paddington, Sydney.

B.C. Dees, *The Allied Occupation and Japan's Economic Miracle: Building the Foundations of Japan's Science and Technology, 1945–1952*, Routledge, New York, 2013

D.P. Mellor, *The Role of Science and Industry*, G. Long (ed.), *Australia in the War of 1939–1945, Series 4: Civil*, Vol. 5, Australian War Memorial, Canberra, 1958

J. O'Brien, *Guns and Gunners: The Story of the 2/5th Australian Field Regiment in World War II*, Angus & Robertson, Sydney, 1950

G. Rimmer, *In Time for War: Pages from the Life of the Boy Brigadier*, Mulavon, West Ryde, 1991

A.J. Sweeting, 'O'Brien, John William Alexander', *Australian Dictionary of Biography*, Vol. 15, Melbourne University Press, Melbourne, 2000

6
THE QUIET ACHIEVER
Lieutenant-General Sir John Northcott

ROBERT STEVENSON

THIS CHAPTER BRIEFLY ADDRESSES the military career and attainments of one of Australia's forgotten soldiers, and highlights the service of a long-serving professional who, in spite of his personal ambitions, had no occasion to command Australian soldiers overseas and so was deprived the opportunity to win the accolades that might have elevated his reputation and earned him a seat in Australia's Valhalla. Instead he served quietly, in whatever capacity the government and his military superiors thought best for the country and the army. Without men of his calibre and talents, however, it is doubtful if Australia could have mobilised and sustained the forces it did during the Second World War, and their combat performance would have been much diminished; without the efforts of Northcott, Australia's soldiers would have entered battle less well prepared and the campaigns they fought might well have been lost for the want of a nail or a tank.

Following the cessation of hostilities in 1945 there were four substantive Australian lieutenant-generals on the army list who, under Sir Thomas Blamey, formed the army's senior tier and were the leaders and

Lieutenant-General Sir John Northcott, who raised and commanded Australia's first armoured division in 1941, was Chief of the General Staff from 1942 to 1945 and the first Commander-in-Chief of the British Commonwealth Occupation Force in Japan.
Australian War Memorial, AWM 107728

shapers of the Australian Military Forces (AMF) during the Second World War: John Lavarack, Iven Mackay, Vernon Sturdee and John Northcott.[1] While Blamey, Lavarack, Mackay and Sturdee have all been the subject of biographical scrutiny, Northcott remains a relative unknown and his military service is unchronicled.[2] If this leading soldier is remembered at all, it is more likely for his selection as the first Australian-born Governor of New South Wales, a position he held for 11 years and one in which he came to be both admired and respected. Few people recall his influential role in establishing a home-grown armoured corps, his pivotal position as Blamey's chief administrative subordinate during the Second World War, and his appointment as the first Commander-in-Chief (C-in-C) of the British Commonwealth Occupation Force in Japan in 1946. While all the officers treated in this volume march in the ranks of Australia's forgotten soldiers, none perhaps more than Northcott is literally a 'shadow man'.[3]

Northcott, despite rising to the pinnacle of his profession, served for most of his career in the background, out of the limelight, often in positions of great influence though rarely in the headlines. This occurred not by choice, rather the conditions were created mainly by circumstances beyond his control. Serving briefly during the First World War, his frontline service was cut short by severe wounds he suffered at the Gallipoli landings. In the bleak interwar years he chose to remain a professional soldier at a time when defence was a low government priority and the army was struggling to survive in the face of severe economic austerity and public apathy. During the Second World War he was again denied the opportunity of an overseas field command, this time because his services were deemed indispensable at home. Lacking an opportunity to lead soldiers in battle deprived Northcott of that essential credential for joining the pantheon of Australian battlefield heroes. Instead he served as a strategic fighter; his weapons were his powers of persuasion and motivation rather than firepower and manoeuvre, his enemies were political ignorance and bureaucratic arrogance, and his battles were waged over the allocation of resources in the committee room rather than over foreign terrain. Little in Northcott's early life pointed to such latent talents.

John Northcott was born in 1890 in the Victorian country town of Creswick, the eldest son of English-born parents. Young Northcott received his education at Dean State School and Grenville College, Ballarat, where he displayed an early interest in the military as a keen member of the school cadets. After leaving school he briefly attended Melbourne University and joined the militia to be commissioned in 1908. Two years later he was promoted and appointed adjutant of his unit.[4] With solid secondary schooling and some tertiary education (not common at that time), a fine physique, and a clear aptitude for military service, he applied for an appointment in the permanent forces, being commissioned in 1912.[5] As a member of the small Administrative and Instructional (A&I) Staff he was posted for duties in Tasmania. Within two years the outbreak of war in August 1914 saw Northcott volunteer for transfer to the Australian Imperial Force (AIF).[6]

On 25 April 1915 Northcott's 12th Battalion (AIF) landed as part of the covering force for the Australian and New Zealand Army Corps (ANZAC) landings at what became known as Anzac Cove. Early in the day, 'almost as soon as he got on to the beach', Northcott was severely wounded in the chest by a rifle bullet.[7] Lucky to survive, he was evacuated to Egypt and thence to Britain. His wounds required extensive convalescence and eventually an army medical board assessed that the young officer was no longer fit for active service and he was invalided to Australia in December 1915.[8] Back home, his AIF appointment was terminated, though the demands of maintaining an expanded overseas force and the home-defence militia saw Northcott posted to Perth as General Staff Officer (GSO) Grade Three.[9]

With the end of the war in Europe, Northcott, unlike many of his peers, chose to remain in the post-war regular army, joining the newly organised Staff Corps as a major in 1920.[10] Despite his war service being cut short, his potential for higher appointments was reinforced when he passed the competitive examination for the British Staff

College and in 1923 was selected to attend the two-year staff course at Camberley commencing the following year. At the time the commandant was none other than Major-General Edmund Ironside (later Field-Marshal 1st Baron Ironside) and the staff included Colonel J.F.C. Fuller and Lieutenant-Colonel Alan Brooke (later Field-Marshal 1st Viscount Alanbrooke) and Lieutenant-Colonel Bernard Montgomery (later Field-Marshal 1st Viscount Montgomery of Alamein).[11] Having 'passed staff college' Northcott was awarded the prestigious postnominal 'psc' and was rated as:

> A good type of officer who has shown power of command and decision. He possesses a strong character and is unassuming and modest. He has proved himself a keen and intelligent worker and has been of great assistance to his Division. I have no hesitation in recommending him for Command or Staff.[12]

Returning to Australia at the beginning of 1926, Northcott joined army headquarters in Melbourne. He served as Staff Officer Supply and Transport (S&T) and then as Director S&T from 1926 to 1931. As part of his duties Northcott was Chairman of the Commonwealth Transport Committee and Secretary of the War Railway Council. In his capacity as Director S&T he was intimately involved in the development of Australia's armoured forces. During the interwar years the Australian Army was kept regularly informed of wider British developments through periodic correspondence between the Australian Chief of the General Staff (CGS) and the Chief of the Imperial General Staff (CIGS) in London.[13] It is likely that this was a source of advice to Australia on British trials with the Experimental Mechanised Force in 1926–27, prompting the formation of a nascent Australian Tank Corps and an order for British-manufactured tanks. While awaiting the arrival of these machines and the training of Australian staff in Britain, the army's governing Military Board appointed a committee to report on the mechanisation of the AMF as a whole. Chaired by Brigadier Charles Brand, the four-man committee, which included Northcott, reported back to the Military Board in June 1928.[14] Although it made a number of sensible and modest recommendations, government financial stringency undermined the army's plans and delayed most of their suggestions.[15] Despite this, Northcott's involvement was the beginning of a long association with mechanisation.[16]

In the meantime Northcott finished his tenure with army headquarters and in 1931 began a series of staff appointments with Citizen Military Forces' (CMF) formations until 1933 when he returned to Britain as an exchange officer. He first served a three-month attachment with the War Office and then nine months as an exchange officer with the 44th (Home Counties) Division, headquartered in the Royal Artillery Barracks at Woolwich. Here Northcott was exposed to the challenges of operating with the British part-time Territorial Force. In 1935 Northcott attended the Imperial Defence College (IDC) in London during which time he was promoted to lieutenant-colonel.[17] Northcott's selection for IDC was a clear indication that he was being groomed for a senior rank, as only five other Australian Army officers attended the prestigious course up until the Second World War.[18]

The establishment of the IDC in 1927 added a new dimension to British defence education, concentrating on a broader range of subjects and pitched at a higher level than those covered at Staff College. The course was concerned with strategy rather than tactics. Major-General Leslie Beavis later recalled Northcott reflecting on his time at IDC.[19] Northcott recounted how 55 minutes of a lecture delivered by Sir Robert Vansittart, the civil head of the Foreign Office, was devoted to European affairs and only five minutes to the rest of the world. During the ensuing question time Northcott queried this ratio, to which Vansittart replied that this was roughly the ratio of time given to day-to-day problems in the Foreign Office.[20] The marked 'Eurocentric' approach of British policy-makers led Northcott to reflect in one of his papers that the absence of any principle of cooperation or mutual support across the empire meant that 'at present we are rather like a team which has no captain and is not sure which of its members will play'.[21]

Following IDC, Northcott attended the Senior Officers' School at Sheerness, a course designed for officers earmarked for unit command. His secondment to Britain was rounded out with a four-month attachment to the Committee of Imperial Defence (CID), but as Beavis recalled such an assignment 'was not viewed kindly in some official civil circles'.[22] In fact, Northcott's attachment was engineered by the CGS, John Lavarack, who was eager for a direct source of information about imperial defence policy and discussions of policy affecting Australian defence. The proposal immediately earned the ire of Frederick Shedden, Secretary of the Defence Committee.[23] Shedden jealously guarded his position as gate-keeper of defence policy advice to the Australian government and warned the Minister for Defence, Sir Robert Parkhill, against the proposal.[24] When queried on the reasons for the attachment, Lavarack advised that Northcott was to be attached to study air-raid precautions and for general purposes. Parkhill, his suspicions raised, approved the attachment but only to the CID sub-committee dealing with air-raid precautions and he stymied the attempt to have Northcott gain a broader knowledge of the workings of the CID. Having been exposed to the machinations of the defence bureaucracy, Northcott rounded out his diplomatic and political education with a ten-month attachment to Australian missions in the United States and Canada for the Australian government in connection with coordination of transport services.[25]

In June 1937 Northcott returned home and took up an appointment as GSO Grade One with the 4th Division and was promoted to colonel.[26] In the following year he moved back to army headquarters and in September 1938 became Director of Military Operations and Intelligence, at the time of the Munich crisis, holding this appointment until October 1939. Northcott's predecessor was Sturdee, who had held the appointment since 1933 and who during his tenure was vitally concerned with the development of the Plan of Concentration for the defence of Australia, detailing how the country was to meet the threat of a Japanese invasion. Northcott's broad staff experience and formal education gave him an unrivalled knowledge for such work, particularly logistics, important to any plan for mobilisation. His assiduity in making contact with leaders in industry, including influential figures such as Essington Lewis, Managing Director of BHP and future Director-General of Munitions, made him as well known outside the army as within.

One of the earliest decisions by the Australian government following the declaration of war in 1939 was the matter of an expeditionary force to support Britain in Europe. Northcott became responsible for planning what form this force might take. Following the precedent set in 1914 and based on contingency plans held at army headquarters, the Australian offer was for an initial infantry division with a proportion of ancillary troops. The plan and detailed composition was produced at an early Joint Planning Committee meeting under the chairmanship of Northcott, which decided the Order of Battle (list of units) to be included. Once the plan was settled, his recommendations went directly to the Military Board.[27]

In October 1939 Northcott was promoted to major-general and appointed Deputy Chief of the General Staff (DCGS).[28] Northcott's responsibilities in this period embraced the sweeping tasks of:

> organising and training new formations, providing staffs, planning accommodation, obtaining weapons and all that went with them, and getting financial approval from a Treasury which did not always at that time readily open the coffers for projects approved as Government policy. Not least of his responsibilities was that of giving advice in the formulation of policy and the making of major decisions.[29]

Given his position and extensive contacts in Britain, Northcott was the ideal choice to accompany Richard Casey, the Minister for Supply and Development, to attend the Dominions Conference in

London as chief military adviser.[30] From October to December, as the 2nd AIF was raised and prepared for overseas service in Australia, Northcott and Casey served as the Commonwealth's advisers to the British government and operated as the conduits of information to the Australian government and the service chiefs.[31]

On 3 November Casey and Northcott met with British Prime Minister Neville Chamberlain seeking assurances that Australia would be safe from Japanese attack if it were to send forces to Europe. This was a contentious issue, as the Australian High Commissioner to Britain, Stanley Bruce, knew that before joining the British government Winston Churchill had written a paper that 'amounted to letting the Far East go until the allies had established an overwhelming position at this end of the world'.[32] Three days after their meeting, Casey advised that the British were pressing for the 6th Australian Division to be sent overseas. Their assessment at this time was that the immediate danger to Australia from Japan was 'remote' and it recommended that the Australian division should be despatched to the Middle East.[33] Next day Northcott, who had been busy visiting the War Office, cabled the acting Australian CGS, Lieutenant-General Ernest Squires, that the Germans would be likely to have a numerical superiority of two-to-one on the Western Front. His recommendation was for Australia to send troops as a 'counter to enemy propaganda regarding half-hearted Dominions cooperation'.[34] Northcott's advice was based not solely on War Office assessments: he took the opportunity to visit the British Expeditionary Force in France and the Maginot Line during the 'Phoney War' interval, and his advice that there was no general reserve behind the British and French armies informed Australian assessments on the European situation.[35]

On 13 November the Australian Defence Committee met to consider the advice from Casey and Northcott.[36] Given the strong recommendation from Northcott, the committee recommended that the 6th Division be despatched to complete its training in the Middle East and that a second division be sent overseas as soon as it could be raised and organised, completing an Australian corps of two divisions. The War Cabinet met in Canberra to consider the issue but given its importance the matter was deferred for consideration by the full Cabinet.[37] A vacillating Cabinet met without reaching a definitive conclusion on 20 November, although the CGS was authorised to conduct preliminary planning for the despatch of the first division, if authorisation was later forthcoming.[38]

With the likelihood of the 6th Division deploying, Northcott now became involved in rectifying the Australian formation's drastic equipment shortages. On the day after Cabinet gave the go ahead to plan for a possible deployment, Squires cabled Northcott a long list of equipment deficiencies, inquiring as to what items Britain could supply. Squires detailed that if the division was to sail in a timely manner, it would do so without approximately two-thirds of its motor transport and none of its Universal (Bren) carriers. As for weapons, the division had no modern 25-pounder field artillery, 2-pounder anti-tank guns, anti-tank rifles, 2-inch mortars, or Bren light machine-guns. Even its First World War vintage Lewis guns would have to be sent back to the militia once the formation arrived and replacement weapons were issued. Furthermore, the division lacked much of its signal equipment, engineer stores and even basic items such as field tenting.[39] Such was the parlous state of the army following the neglect of the interwar years and the government's misguided faith in the Singapore strategy.[40] On 28 November the full Cabinet agreed to send the first contingent of the 2nd AIF abroad, a decision announced in Parliament the next day by Prime Minister Robert Menzies.[41]

On their return journey the Australian delegation visited the Middle East where it was expected the Australian forces would soon complete their training, as they had during the Great War. Northcott, negotiating on behalf of the Australian government, discussed that matter with General Sir Archibald Wavell, the British C-in-C Middle East. Wavell, who had seen the problems created by ill-disciplined Australian troops in 1914, was concerned that they might repeat their performance.[42] Northcott countered:

> When we came here then ... not a single amenity of any kind was provided by the Egyptian command (which was then British) for the 20,000 Australians camped on the desert outside Cairo. This time we are coming fully provided with amenities, and I don't want to go near Cairo at any price.[43]

When asked where he thought the Australians should train, Northcott suggested southern Palestine; Wavell agreed.

Following the return of the delegation, Northcott continued as DCGS but he soon had the added responsibility of acting as CGS. In the New Year of 1940 Squires' health failed, forcing Northcott to step-up for two months. Then on 2 March, just six months after the declaration of war, Squires died. In seeking a suitable replacement, Menzies discussed the matter with the Minister for the Army, Geoffrey Street. After deciding on General Sir Cyril Brudenell Bingham White (see Chapter 3), Street despatched Northcott to sound out the old general's willingness to come out of retirement. Despite some personal reluctance, White accepted and took up his appointment on 18 March. Northcott became White's indispensable 'right-hand man'.[44]

Northcott was thrown into the work of mobilisation and preparing the home army for war. At this time the government believed its main task was to build up the 2nd AIF in the Middle East, a decision that Northcott had influenced, but as a result few resources were left for the defence of Australia. White and the other service chiefs agreed with this plan, but by August 1940 there was mounting concern that the British forces in Malaya were inadequate for the task of defending Singapore. On 6 August Northcott, who headed the Joint Planning Committee, sent a note to the Chiefs of Staff advising that the plan to defend Australia against a 'minor' or 'raid' scale attack should be changed to the heaviest scale of attack.[45]

Before the Chiefs of Staff could consider this advice, the defence community was struck a cruel blow when White, Street and a number of other senior staff were killed in an air crash on the outskirts of

Canberra on 13 August. To fill the void Northcott was once again appointed acting CGS, although not all appear to have supported this choice. George Vasey, a fellow regular officer who knew Northcott well from their service together at army headquarters, wrote on receiving the news: 'What a terrible disaster it was in Canberra ... I see Northcott is acting CGS. Lord what we are reduced to.'[46] Whether Vasey was being flippant is not clear but whatever Vasey's misgivings the government moved quickly to replace White, selecting Sturdee as the new CGS.

In October, as the decision was made to raise a third AIF division for overseas service, Northcott was considered for command.[47] Unfortunately the deaths of Squires, White and Street had created such turmoil in the army's senior command structure that it restricted Northcott's options for employment. Although Sturdee recommended his subordinate for command of the 8th Division he was excluded from serious consideration because his knowledge and experience were vital to the smooth transition of a new senior leadership group.[48] As a result command of the ill-fated division passed to Major-General Henry Gordon Bennett.[49]

By the time Sturdee had taken over as CGS, the British government was beginning discussions with the US about a coalition approach to a possible war with Japan. As a result a conference was held in Singapore in late October 1940 to consider defence of the region. Once again Northcott was the senior Australian military representative. On his return Northcott was involved in the resulting high-level deliberations, and in mid-November the Australian Chiefs of Staff presented their report. They concluded that 'in the absence of a Main Fleet in the Far East, the forces and equipment at present available in this area for the defence of Malaya are totally inadequate to meet a major attack by Japan'. Therefore, the 'first and immediate consideration must be to ensure the security of Malaya against direct attack'. They recommended a brigade from the 8th Division should be located as a temporary measure in Malaya until such time as it could be relieved by Indian troops.[50]

The matter was considered first by the Advisory War Council and then by the War Cabinet, after which Britain was asked if it needed an Australian brigade to bolster the defences of Malaya.[51] On 23 December a grateful Churchill accepted the offer.[52] An Australian brigade was despatched in early February 1941, although it was never replaced, indeed the deteriorating situation in the Pacific led to its reinforcement. Northcott was once again in the strategic forefront, providing advice to the government and shaping the future direction of Australia's war effort. His next task was more 'hands-on'.

One of the early lessons derived from the remarkable success of Germany's panzer forces in Europe was the need for an equivalent Australian body. On 14 December 1940 Percy Spender, the new Minister for the Army, presented the Military Board's proposal for the creation of an Australian armoured division. Briefed by Northcott and discussed by the War Cabinet on 8 January 1941, the proposal received endorsement confirming the constitution of an Australian Armoured Corps, the raising of an AIF armoured division, and the establishment of an armoured fighting vehicles school and two armoured training regiments.[53] The War Cabinet also acknowledged the progress being made in local tank production:

> It was noted that arrangements had been made to provide for the supply of the armoured fighting vehicles, consisting of 660 cruiser tanks and 240 universal carriers, and for the necessary armament for an armoured division as approved in War Cabinet minutes 375 and 407. The Deputy Chief of the General Staff [Northcott] stated that the local provision of tanks was proceeding satisfactorily. The design of the tank had been decided upon, and a wooden 'mock-up' was now being made.[54]

While Northcott was optimistic in his assessment of the progress towards a home-grown tank (designated the Armoured Cruiser Number 1, or AC1), he was operating on advice given from subject-matter experts. In February 1941 Cabinet was informed that the first Australian tank was expected to be available in November of that year.[55] In fact, the designers of the tank were plagued with every kind of problem.

Four months after Northcott's brief to the War Cabinet, Spender chaired a meeting in late April to discuss munitions production generally and tank production in particular. Northcott was in attendance and this meeting, according to one historian, 'is a very important element of the story of Australian tank production'.[56] While there was general agreement on the development of the Armoured Cruiser tank, it was clear that despite optimistic assessments by the designers, those responsible for its manufacture realistically saw the many challenges in bringing such a project to a successful conclusion. At the end of the meeting both Spender and Northcott supported the proposal to order 200 American M3 light tanks (designated the Stuart) as a stopgap solution to the inevitable delays in producing the Australian tank.[57] In fact, the first production of the Australian Cruiser program did not make its appearance until August 1942, and the Australian tank was destined never to see operational service.[58]

Northcott's influence in the command structure is difficult to discern because he served as Sturdee's deputy. What can be surmised is that Sturdee relied on Northcott and considered him indispensable in the early period of his tenure as CGS. Northcott's name is sprinkled liberally in correspondence between army headquarters and the Minister for the Army often pointing out that the neglect of the army along with the shortage of equipment and the government's economic priorities was hindering the army's ability to prepare for war.[59] Sturdee certainly thought highly enough of him to recommend him for the appointment of C-in-C AMF and when Major-General Henry Wynter fell ill, Blamey specifically asked for Northcott to command the 9th Division in the Middle East. Once again Sturdee was not willing to release his deputy, but as the situation in the Pacific continued to deteriorate it appeared that Northcott might finally be given his chance.[60]

Northcott's opportunity to command came in July 1941. With his intimate involvement in the creation of an Australian armoured force, Northcott was the logical choice to be appointed General Officer Commanding (GOC) 1st Australian Armoured Division. He did this initially as DCGS, while waiting the return from the Middle East of Lieutenant-General Sydney Rowell, but as Rowell later observed, Northcott was given 'an impossible task' in attempting to juggle two demanding appointments simultaneously.[61] The creation of the armoured division was a proposal 'of such magnitude as to surpass, in the effort required, any previous wartime military project' as Lieutenant-Colonel Ronald Hopkins observed.[62] The army possessed negligible numbers of personnel trained on armoured vehicle systems, lacked appropriate training equipment and had little experience in armoured warfare. Raising an entire division was more complex and expensive than raising an equivalent infantry formation because of the much larger numbers of skilled personnel required, together with much greater quantities of equipment. The situation Northcott faced was exacerbated by the fact that many of the staff in the small pre-war militia armoured units were already serving overseas with the 2nd AIF.[63]

As Northcott grappled with his dual responsibilities, the selection of divisional staff was his first task. Hopkins, who had had a long association with the general and was experienced in armoured matters, was chosen as the senior operations officer, and Colonel W.M. Anderson, who knew the general from their service together at army headquarters, became the senior administrative staff officer. Although Hopkins was Northcott's selection, he apparently harboured strong reservations over the suitability of his commander. Writing a dozen years after Northcott's death, Hopkins recalled how he 'was seriously concerned when it was confided to him that Northcott was to command the armoured division . . . However fitted General Northcott may have been for the projected command of an infantry division, he was not quick enough at grasping the essentials of a situation nor at decision making for the direction of such a highly mobile force.'[64]

Hopkins obviously kept these views to himself at the time because if Northcott had known of his subordinate's lack of confidence in him he would likely have replaced him. Instead Northcott despatched Hopkins to the Middle East to gain first-hand experience and gather information on the latest British tactical and organisational developments. After Hopkins returned to Australia, Northcott was able to hand over his duties as DCGS to Rowell, and on 1 September 1941 he joined the 2nd AIF.[65] Wishing to see matters for himself, Northcott with Anderson set off on a tour of inspection of the Middle East. Northcott served a ten-day period attached to the British 7th Armoured Division before joining Headquarters Australian Corps for nearly a month. Departing the Middle East in mid-December, Northcott transited through Singapore where he was alarmed at the deteriorating British position, and cabled Australia recommending reinforcement.[66]

Northcott formally commanded the division for just seven months from early September 1941 to early April 1942. Throughout his tenure he faced serious challenges attempting to raise and prepare his division for battle, most notably the lack of equipment and shifting manpower priorities. It was a difficult and frustrating time as he had a constant battle to get the right equipment while fending off attempts to poach his high-quality officers and non-commissioned officers (NCOs). In a letter to Headquarters Home Forces four months into his command, he observed that 'the two most recently formed Regiments in each Brigade were required to select the best-trained officers, N.C.O's. and other ranks to make up the two Independent Squadrons for immediate service overseas'.[67] The disruption caused by this 'milking' was significant. Even more frustrating, the personnel chosen for the independent squadrons were informed on the eve of their departure for Malaya that they would not be deploying and were returned to the division. This had a long-term negative effect on morale in the division. Much to Northcott's frustration, just as matters were improving, he was superseded.

At the end of March 1942 the first pilot model of the Australian Cruiser tank was due to commence trials at Puckapunyal under

Northcott's watchful eye. On the due day the general was standing on the roadside awaiting the vehicle's arrival. A staff car pulled up and Northcott was joined by Colonel W.D. Watson, the British officer responsible for much of the AC1's design. Watson carried with him a copy of the *Melbourne Herald* and addressing Northcott expressed his regret that the general was leaving the division. The newspaper headline announced that Northcott was to be succeeded the following day by the flamboyant Major-General Horace 'Red Robbie' Robertson.[68] According to a witness: 'The general looked at the newspaper and turned white' and commented, 'This is what they do to me just as my first tank is coming down the road.'[69] On 5 April Northcott handed over the division to Robertson. Northcott's pivotal role in raising Australia's first armoured formation has received scant recognition. Despite this, the evidence suggests that he played close attention to the building of his subordinate formations and visited training frequently, speaking to his officers and men.[70] Even after leaving the division he continued to champion the use of tanks, including his former 2/6th Armoured Regiment, which was the first Australian tank unit to see battle at Buna, New Guinea, in December 1942.[71]

Although Northcott was initially unsure of what lay ahead, his herculean administrative and organisational efforts in raising the 1st Armoured Division were recognised by his promotion to lieutenant-general and command of II Australian Corps on 6 April 1942.[72] Northcott's elevation was part of a sweeping reorganisation of the Australian land forces initiated by Blamey in mid-April. At this time the territorial military districts were abolished, and Iven Mackay's Home Forces Command was replaced by three major field formations: the First Army, covering Queensland and New South Wales; the Second Army, covering Victoria, Tasmania and South Australia; and III Corps, covering Western Australia. Lavarack's First Army consisted of two corps, the first went to Rowell, the second to Northcott. Once again Northcott was catapulted into an organisation that barely existed and at the time was purely a training and holding headquarters being established near Sydney. Despite this turn of events, II Corps would soon be responsible for the defence of the Newcastle–Sydney–Port Kembla area of New South Wales against the threat of Japanese attack. Later in August II Corps shifted north to be headquartered at Esk in southern Queensland and took over responsibility for the defence of the eastern seaboard.[73]

But Northcott's chance to show his merits as a field commander were again cut short when he was recalled to Melbourne after just six months in command, and replaced by Major-General Edmund Herring. The change of appointment was one of several in senior army commands made by the War Cabinet on Blamey's advice, when he was appointed C-in-C AMF. Sturdee, who had been CGS since Northcott's time as DCGS, was named Head of the Australian Mission to Washington, and with his departure the post of CGS became vacant.[74]

On 10 September 1942 Northcott was appointed CGS. He would hold the appointment for the rest of the war, not standing down until 30 November 1945.[75] As Blamey's principal non-operational subordinate, Northcott was responsible for administration of the army and according to Blamey he 'served with distinction as the army's principal representative and as principal staff officer to the C-in-C on the Committee of Defence and at War Council and War Cabinet meetings, which he attended regularly'.[76] Beavis recalled how 'General Blamey had complete confidence in Northcott's wisdom, tact and loyalty and relied on him increasingly to present the army's problems and proposals to the War Cabinet, and to maintain a friendly liaison with the rear echelons of G[eneral]H[ead]Q[uarters].'[77] Northcott also managed to develop excellent relations with key officers at General Douglas MacArthur's headquarters and Blamey's Advanced Land Force Headquarters, and he worked harmoniously with members of the Royal Australian Navy and the Royal Australian Air Force.[78]

Northcott's challenges were further complicated by the difficult position in which Blamey found himself. As C-in-C AMF and Commander Land Forces South-West Pacific Area (SWPA) Blamey answered to two masters. His dual lines of responsibility both to John

Curtin, the Australian Prime Minster, and MacArthur, the Supreme Commander SWPA, placed Blamey in a precarious position. When the fighting in New Guinea created a crisis in Australian senior command, Blamey sought to shore up his position and ease his burden by having Northcott appointed as his permanent deputy. In September 1942 Blamey wrote to Curtin recommending that Northcott be appointed Deputy C-in-C as well as CGS, so he could take over additional administrative responsibility.[79] The government was unwilling to take this step and the matter was never resolved, though in reality Northcott did function as Blamey's deputy in effect if not in name.[80] In late 1942, during the leadership crisis that resulted in the sacking of Rowell, Blamey advised Northcott that while he was in New Guinea he:

> authorised me [Northcott] to approve of all matters on his behalf concerning policy generally, except in the case of major movements of troops, when I was to refer to him before giving direction, and similarly to L[ieutenant-]G[eneral] A[dministration] [Wynter] in regard to actual delegation of authority for expenditure and administrative details.[81]

Later in the war when Blamey was absent from Australia for lengthy periods, such as his three-month tour accompanying the Prime Minister to Britain and the US in mid-1944, he left Northcott in command.[82]

Northcott's position was a delicate one but he excelled. It was greatly to his credit that he carried out his duties as a trusted and loyal lieutenant without the problems that characterised a similar command arrangement in the Royal Australian Air Force between Air Vice-Marshals George Jones and William Bostock. This was mostly due to Northcott's personality and, while Blamey recognised that his subordinate was an exceptional soldier, there were four essential elements that cemented their relationship, 'loyalty, skill, tact, and devotion to duty'.[83] The first, at least in the eyes of Blamey, was probably

Northcott's strongest characteristic. He served all of his superiors loyally, even at times when it did not serve his personal interests. Certainly this loyalty was not blind, but when it came to his relationship with Blamey, as Sir Frank Berryman suggested: 'If you serve him [Blamey] loyally you got back one hundredfold.'[84] It was for this reason that both Berryman and Northcott survived and even thrived under Blamey's command, unlike others who were sacked or sidelined.[85]

Blamey's confidence in and close relationship with Northcott and Berryman is apparent in their correspondence. Blamey confided in his two key subordinates when he wanted discretion and information treated confidentially. In a letter to Northcott in late 1942 discussing current operations and future troop movements, he concluded, 'I am sending a copy of this letter direct to Major-General Berryman and I hope it will not be necessary to discuss it with anyone else for the present. As you know, the moment any matter of this kind is announced in Australia, it immediately gives rise to a crop of rumours.'[86]

Blamey's appointment as C-in-C AMF was far from unanimous among the military and political hierarchy. There were a small number of senior officers who clumsily attempted to influence the Minister for the Army, Frank Forde, in the appointment of the C-in-C AMF. Nothing came of this so-called 'revolt of the generals', but it did little to cement Blamey's position. Later in September 1942 William Dunstan, the general manager of the *Melbourne Herald*, told Rowell that John Curtin at one stage was not entirely satisfied with Blamey and that there 'has been a canvas of names. You, Northcott, Herring, Morshead'.[87] Again nothing came of this. There is no doubt that Northcott had his own ambitions; however, in his relationship with Blamey and his peers this was never a problem as it was for others, notably Gordon Bennett, Lavarack and Rowell. Although Northcott's name might have been mooted as a possible replacement for Blamey, Northcott probably never contemplated himself as a candidate. His unswerving loyalty in accepting whatever job he was given demonstrated that he was a subordinate who could be trusted above most others.

In terms of skill Blamey was not referring to Northcott's tactical abilities since he had no opportunity to display them. Rather the C-in-C recognised that his subordinate's thoroughness, friendly persona and his 'capacity to express himself lucidly and convincingly even in circumstances when the facts at his command might have been more extensive', were attributes that made Northcott such a formidable advocate for army in the committee room.[88] When coupled with tact and a refusal to be dissuaded or browbeaten by superiors, Northcott became the ideal foil to the politically unpopular Blamey.

The close relationship between Blamey and Northcott was not completely smooth or without its challenges. Northcott observed that although Blamey delegated considerable authority to him during the C-in-C's absences in New Guinea this system 'has not in fact operated as we find that many of our most normal staff decisions have been peremptorily cancelled without reference to us and usually without a knowledge of the facts concerning them. Most of these decisions, of course, have to be subsequently amended when the full facts have been reported.'[89] The particular incident to which Northcott was referring was the case of Blamey's sudden and unexplained decision to stop the issue of the Australian-made Owen submachine-gun. The development and production of this weapon is clouded in controversy, which it is not necessary to fully explain here; however, in late 1942, while Blamey was still in New Guinea, he decided that the weapon could not be adopted while the troops were still actively engaged in operations. Northcott wrote a respectful but forcefully worded personal letter explaining the full situation, which had apparently occurred because Blamey was not aware of requests from New Guinea Force for the rapid introduction of the Owen and the dire lack of ammunition for the American-made Thompson submachine-gun. Northcott wrote:

> Quite frankly, I must say that I feel you are on the wrong foot over this matter and, instead of a preremptory [sic] wire of

> cancellation, and in view of our difficulty in consulting you, in fairness to the Staff, I would suggest that you might give them the credit for having thoroughly considered the matter, particularly in view of N[ew]G[uinea] Force Signal SD 6 of 28 Oct . . . [He concluded] Action regarding the despatch of Owen guns to New Guinea has now been cancelled in accordance with your instructions, but I strongly urge, in view of the whole of the circumstances, that you re-consider this decision.[90]

Blamey, who was probably uncomfortable with being wrong and anxious over any criticism, especially following his recent sacking of several senior officers, responded quickly in threatening terms, demanding Northcott withdraw his letter.[91] On the same day, however, Blamey wrote another, more consolatory letter to Northcott acknowledging that the Owen had been pushed into service because it was not possible to sustain the Thompson and it was 'apparent that there have been crossed communications in relation to the utilization of the Owen Gun in New Guinea of which I was not aware'.[92] Northcott, having made his point and achieved his aim, tactfully complied with Blamey's direction to withdraw the offending correspondence.[93] Rather than simply seeking to ingratiate himself with Blamey, Northcott consistently displayed behaviours that demonstrated irrevocably that he set devotion to duty and the army above personal ambition.

Major-General Ronald Hopkins left an interesting pen portrait of Northcott in which he identifies some of his perceived limitations as well as those characteristics that made him so well suited to his duties as CGS:

> Northcott was pleasant to deal with, very patient and had a reputation for thoroughness. He was considered astute and he was good at running a team. In fact, he possessed the attributes of a staff officer but lacked some of the important ones necessary to be an armoured commander. Many of his

contemporaries in the Regular army shared these views, and independent confirmation has been given by British officers who worked closely with him both at Staff College and the Imperial Defence College.[94]

It would be ungenerous to leave the matter there. In the later years he was undoubtedly well placed in the post of Chief of the General Staff where he dealt diplomatically on behalf of his Commander-in-Chief with members of the War Cabinet, the War Advisory Council and the other Services. He was strongly built and gave a solid, confident, feet-on-the-ground impression to all who met him. A pleasant, hearty manner and plenty of assurance inspired a warm respect and appreciation on the part of his political and civilian associates as well as many army officers who served or had contact with him throughout the war.[95]

Hopkins' post-war reminiscences, influenced by his relationship with Northcott early in the war, provide a partial portrait of his work as CGS, but they give no inkling of the complexity of the work he undertook.

Northcott's tasks as CGS embraced the strategic direction of the war and the army's place in the national war effort, which mostly occurred away from public scrutiny. His was a 'raise, train and sustain' function, albeit always under the direction of Blamey. The matters that occupied most of his attention during his tenure as CGS included the rapid adjustment of the army to the peculiarities of tropical warfare. This involved a fundamental, micro-level restructure of all divisions.[96] To equip these forces for the task of defeating the Japanese required a range of new equipment, from Owen submachine-guns and jeeps to short 25-pounder field howitzers and tanks.[97] These decisions were not made in splendid isolation from the realities of the front, and throughout his tenure Northcott regularly visited New Guinea and the islands. At the end of 1943 he wrote to Sturdee advising his old chief, 'I have just returned from a visit to NG, where I spent some two weeks with 7 & 9 Divs during the current fighting. It was of course most valuable to me to be able to see forward Bdes [Brigades] and learn of their condition and experiences at first hand.'[98]

The significance of Northcott's task of equipping the army may be gauged from the fact that in the financial year 1942–43 the expenditure on arms and equipment was £125 million, then equal to one-third of federal revenue. In the following year it was still over £80 million. The periodic schedules for warlike stores went to the War Cabinet for approval and more often than not Northcott was the army's representative to state the case and provide the answers. These material requirements included the extensive Lease Lend program with the US.[99]

When it came to manpower, the war effort demanded high-quality personnel for war industries, primary production and the three uniformed services. Competition was always fierce and Northcott carried the burden of arguing the army's case for its fair share in accordance with government priorities.[100] The army was always the largest of the three services and so often it appeared to be the government's biggest target. With the fading Japanese threat by mid-1943 the government turned its attention to the use of the nation's finite manpower and the redistribution of labour to the civilian economy. To determine the army's future personnel requirements defence planners sought clarification from the government on the nature of Australia's future participation in the war. In September 1943 the Defence Committee presented its findings.[101] Consequently in October the government informed the army that it would have to discharge 20,000 soldiers to industry by the following June. This was the first of a series of reductions to remove over 100,000 men from the army.[102]

Manpower problems continued to cause Northcott concern and in May 1944 he wrote to the Australian Army Representative in London:

> the shortage of manpower for the Army is causing us very grave concern at present; and, on the C-in-C's behalf, I have to keep it almost continuously under review. The present

situation is far from satisfactory; and the indications are that, towards the end of this year, it will be very difficult to maintain, in re-inforcements, either the offensive formations or any less active troops, such as those in captured areas outside the mainland.[103]

Based on the agreement of the Americans and the British, the War Cabinet decided upon a further cull. On 23 August 1944 the government ordered the army to reduce its establishment by a further 30,000 men, over and above normal discharges, in order to increase the labour pool in agriculture and other areas of the economy. The government ordered the final wartime reductions in June 1945, when it commanded the release of 50,000 personnel, a figure later raised to 64,000.[104]

It was Northcott who had to cope with the War Cabinet's decisions, but he was no 'yes man'. In May 1945 the government decided that 'all members of the Army and Air Force with operational service overseas and who have over five years' war service are to be given the option of taking their discharge'. Blamey suggested that this drastic decision, which could have deprived the army, including formations then in action, of a great number of its key personnel, should be modified by restricting discharges to men who had enlisted in 1939 and adding the proviso 'when the present operations permit'. Senator James Fraser, the acting minister, instructed Northcott that his view was that 'full, immediate effect' should be given to the decision and that no troops affected by it should thenceforth leave Australia. Northcott explained the impracticability of the decision and declined to carry it out. The minister insisted, but Northcott stood firm. On 18 June he stated his case before the War Cabinet, which on the strength of his arguments found a compromise solution.[105]

Northcott's efforts in shaping the army have gone largely unnoticed. However, by the time it faced its final tests in the Pacific the official historian of the Second World War, Gavin Long, made the following assessment of the army in 1944:

> The army which had now entered upon its final campaigns, and whose leadership and equipment were the subject of such keen debate at home, was at this time, in many respects, at the peak of its efficiency. More than two years earlier, it had established a tactical superiority over the Japanese, and since then it had gained in skill and confidence, and, in particular, in the art of living healthily and cheerfully in tropical bush. Its experience included warfare in many kinds of terrain and climate, and in Africa, Europe and the South Seas. Its system of training and schools was comprehensive and their methods severe.[106]

This was an army that at the end of hostilities on 15 August 1945 had a strength of 383,000, with some 177,000 troops outside Australia.[107] Much of the credit for the performance of the army in the Pacific is owed to Northcott. While he may not have led his troops in battle he was instrumental in shaping their efficiency, equipping them and supervising the many training schools that prepared the officers and soldiers.

Following the dropping of the two atomic bombs, Japan agreed to surrender. While Blamey proceeded to Tokyo for the surrender ceremony, arguments continued between Australia, Britain and the United States over the composition of the occupation force to demilitarise Japan. Australian Prime Minister Ben Chifley wanted Australia to have a separate force reflecting the role Australia had played in the defeat of Japan. In contrast both Dr H.V. Evatt, Australian Minister for External Affairs, and Northcott were against Chifley's proposal, Evatt believing it was politically important to have a combined British Commonwealth force with an Australian in overall command, while Northcott saw the practical problems of a small, independent Australian force dependent on American and British shipping and base supplies.[108] As a result of their efforts, on 18 September the War Cabinet approved a proposal by which Australia would join a Commonwealth force under an Australian C-in-C who would be responsible directly to General Douglas MacArthur for operational matters and to a body known as the Joint Chiefs of Staff in Australia, comprising the Australian Chiefs of Staff and a representative of the British Chiefs of Staff, for all administrative matters.[109] The British accepted the proposal but it took two months before a satisfactory arrangement could be negotiated with the Americans. Northcott played a key role in bringing about this outcome, and he would soon be rewarded for his efforts.[110]

With the end of the war, Sturdee was again invited by the government to become CGS. His acceptance of the post was made conditional on Northcott being given the appointment of C-in-C of the British Commonwealth Occupation Force (BCOF). This was eventually agreed and announced on 31 October.[111] The Australian government formally sent the BCOF proposals, on behalf of the governments of Australia, Britain, India and New Zealand, to the US Chiefs of Staff on 20 October. The Americans agreed in principle to employ this force in Japan but delayed final approval until objections by MacArthur and the Soviet Union were overcome. These differences were eventually resolved by negotiations between Australian and US officials in November, and between MacArthur's staff and Northcott in December.[112]

Northcott's command comprised six discrete organisations: a British naval port party; the British–Indian Division of two brigades and divisional troops; an Australian brigade group; a New Zealand brigade group; a separate combined headquarters commanding the air assets including seven Australian, British, Indian and New Zealand squadrons; and the Headquarters British Commonwealth Base. In all, the force comprised 37,000 troops of whom about 12,000 were Australian.[113] Northcott's appointment was well deserved, but it did meet with opposition, and not just from MacArthur. The senior British commander initially refused to serve under Northcott and others felt it was Britain's right to command BCOF.[114]

Given the complexity of his command it was essential that Northcott visit the troop-contributing countries to discuss with the various national staffs the command and administrative arrangements for BCOF and to visit Japan to see first hand their future operating environment. On 8 December he left Australia for Japan, not returning home until Christmas Eve. In the New Year he flew to India on a two-week visit, returning home on Australia Day 1946. Only on 20 February did Northcott arrive in Japan to take command of BCOF, and on 7 March he formally accepted responsibility for an area centred on Hiroshima Prefecture, garrisoned by the US 24th Infantry Division.[115]

Nothcott's task was a delicate one and the ambiguity of his position was not enhanced by the directive he received from the Joint Chiefs of Staff in Australia. Essentially they tasked Northcott with three broad objectives, all related to representation of the British Commonwealth, enhancing prestige and impressing the Japanese.[116] The directive was later amended, but BCOF's loose objectives remained unchanged. The actual plan for the force was not issued by the Joint Chiefs of Staff until May 1946 at the end of the concentration of BCOF and exactly one month before Northcott relinquished command.[117]

Among the greatest challenges Northcott faced initially was integrating a command composed of officers and staff from different nationalities and different services. It was, in his words, 'in many ways a unique experience'.[118] Among BCOF's first tasks was to deploy 45 observer teams to ensure free and fair local elections. At the same time some 7000 Japanese employees had to be screened and issued passes. This allowed the work of restoration of accommodation to begin. Initially Northcott concentrated the BCOF engineering effort on ensuring an initial minimum standard for all headquarters, formations and units to enable them to function. Priority was given to hospitals, medical centres and troop accommodation. Most of the work was directed at rehabilitation of existing accommodation rather than attempting to build new facilities, while fire hazards and the Japanese sewage system posed particular challenges. The initial surge in effort was hampered by a shortage of shipping and the lack of cement, bitumen and timber.[119]

Northcott faced an unenviable task from the very beginning, and his achievements in raising and commanding BCOF have been overshadowed by his more flamboyant successor. Typical of the contemporary judgments passed on Northcott's tenure in Japan are those found in recollections by Rowell:

> BCOF was put in a devastated area and it really had to face a battle situation, although there was no enemy shooting at it. The troops came from several countries, with differing needs and supplies coming from widely separated sources, so the chance of administrative breakdown was not unlikely. It appeared to us in Melbourne in the winter of 1946 that the situation was becoming desperate. Without being critical of Lieutenant-General John Northcott, the commander, who faced a dreadfully difficult task in a devastated area with a staff and multi-national force hastily put together and in no way 'run in', it is true to say that his successor, Horace Robertson, was able to correct the situation and establish this force firmly.[120]

While Rowell is correct in his judgment of BCOF's initial difficulties, he fails to give Northcott the credit he deserves for improving conditions.

When BCOF arrived in Japan there is no doubt that conditions were severe; it could not have been expected otherwise. The US Navy's wartime blockade of the Japanese home islands had caused widespread shortages of every commodity and forced urban Japanese onto starvation rations, while the US Air Force had conducted a ruthless aerial bombing campaign of Japan's major cities, causing widespread devastation even before the virtual destruction of Nagasaki and Hiroshima. Rowell was correct in that BCOF found a war zone – and reports of the poor conditions were quickly and widely reported in the Australian press and elsewhere – but Northcott moved quickly to improve matters for his soldiers, and the success of his efforts are supported by later accounts given by BCOF soldiers.[121]

Northcott relinquished command of BCOF on 15 June 1946. Undoubtedly the charismatic Robertson was able to regularise arrangements, although even he could not fix the difficult command relationships, especially with the British and Indians.[122] What few have conceded are the unprecedented challenges Northcott faced, not only in occupying a devastated country but having the unique challenge of creating the first British force of its kind, in that it was integrated on a national and on a service basis and controlled by a Joint Chiefs of Staff organisation from Australia.[123] It is always easier to improve an organisation once it is up and running than being the first incumbent who has to create the organisation from the ground up under the most austere conditions. Furthermore, Northcott achieved his task with little assistance from the contributing nations, including Australia since Rowell and the other army staff in Melbourne were thoroughly distracted by domestic issues such as demobilisation and the reordering of the post-war army.

Northcott's appointment as Governor of New South Wales was announced on 1 April 1946. Returning home to Melbourne in July, Northcott was duly sworn in on 1 August.[124] He became the thirtieth Governor of New South Wales and its first Australian-born incumbent. Northcott brought to his new role the same 'qualities of correctness, competence and dedication' that he had displayed in his long military career.[125] He retired in July 1957 and died, aged 76, on 4 August 1966 at his home in Wahroonga, Sydney.[126]

Sir John Northcott's military service displays many of the hallmarks of missed chances and thwarted ambition. Badly wounded on the day of the Gallipoli landings, he missed the opportunity afforded many of his peers to gain experience and recognition on the bloody battlefields of the Western Front. Unlike others, however, he did not become disillusioned in the bitter winter of the interwar period, and perhaps his lack of combat experience drove him to excel. Northcott became one of the most qualified and connected officers in the small regular army. Certainly by the outbreak of war in 1939 he was among the most experienced senior professional servicemen in Australia. His qualifications and connections nevertheless proved to be both a boon and a millstone. Deemed too important to be released, he missed the opportunity to gain early field command experience and so was destined to spend most of his second war desk-bound.

Throughout his career Northcott was a highly regarded staff officer. In a series of important positions he played a pivotal role behind the scenes shaping and preparing the army in peace and war. During the Second World War, as DCGS, he was instrumental in raising Australia's overseas army and influencing where and when it trained and fought. As CGS he served as Blamey's chief administrative subordinate, shaping and equipping the army others led on the battlefield. Northcott's skills by training, education and inclination were best exploited in the national interest at the politico-strategic level where it is harder to win public acclaim and recognition. Northcott served his country in a modest, steady and professional manner, like the man he was.

In contrast, Northcott's periods in command were uninspiringly brief. His time with the 1st Armoured Division, II Corps and BCOF are seldom applauded and many of his contemporaries damn him with faint praise. On the other hand it is difficult for a commander to stamp his personality on a formation when that organisation is in a state of flux and when the commander's tenure is limited, as were Northcott's three appointments. BCOF, Northcott's most important and certainly his most complex command, is typical. Appointed commander on 1 December 1945, he arrived at his extemporised headquarters in Japan on 4 February 1946 and relinquished command on 15 June.[127] His command of a combined, joint task force would have been daunting under any circumstances, but Northcott had just four and a half months in which to set up a completely new organisation, based on contingents drawn from four different nations, while garrisoning a country devastated by four years of war. Perhaps for these reasons even those who imply criticism of his performance also note that the tasks he was given were 'impossible' or 'dreadfully difficult'.[128] It is also noteworthy that on two occasions Northcott was followed by 'Red Robbie' Robertson, an officer who possessed the personal ebullience and flair that Northcott lacked. It should be acknowledged, without in any way denigrating Robertson's achievements, that much of the hard work for which Robertson garnered high praise was expended more quietly by his predecessor.

The qualities Northcott brought to the various positions he held are not those popularly associated with military high command. Northcott's knowledge, dependability, calmness and loyalty are four traits that stand out. Blamey clearly recognised his subordinate's talents, but he appreciated more the unswerving loyalty Northcott brought to the position of CGS. Nothcott displayed an aura of unassuming and self-effacing dependability among civilian and military peers often noted for their personal ambitions and Byzantine behaviour. While it is difficult to discern from dry cables and minutes of committee deliberations what influence Northcott exerted on his peers and superiors, it is clear that his quiet professionalism and breadth of knowledge had a steadying effect on a raw and often vacillating War Cabinet in times of high stress. Northcott brought to the table professional knowledge accrued over a lifetime of service and education, and a physical presence and quiet natural authority cloaked in the uniform he wore. As one of his peers wrote, 'Northcott's experience, calm temperament and logical and forceful exposition made him an advocate for army of exceptional ability.'[129]

In Australia's national capital there is a minor road that tracks the short distance from the rear of Defence Headquarters at Russell Offices, along the western boundary of the Australian Defence Force Academy, and culminates at the outlying defence directorates housed at Campbell Park. In a city where most suburbs pay passing homage to national notables, long-forgotten politicians and dead military heroes, this particular avenue is named in honour of Sir John Northcott. Northcott Drive passes below a lookout atop Mount Pleasant. On 23 November 1963 Sir John unveiled a Royal Australian

Armoured Corps memorial on the mount and appropriately the memorial took the form of the Australian-built AC3 'Thunderbolt' tank.[130] The selection of Northcott to dedicate this memorial was an interesting choice since today it is widely held that Major-General Ronald Hopkins is the 'Father of the Royal Australian Armoured Corps'.[131] But Northcott has an equally strong claim to that sobriquet due to his championing of the creation of a home-grown armoured corps, his foundation command of Australia's first armoured division and his post-war support for a regular tank unit (later the 1st Armoured Regiment) as part of the Interim Army, which became the Australian Regular Army.

Whatever the merits of various claimants it is fair to say that victory often has many fathers but not all get the credit they deserve. Ironically the memorial Northcott unveiled is no more, replaced in 1977 to make way for the Royal Regiment of Australian Artillery national memorial dedicated by Queen Elizabeth II during her Silver Jubilee visit.[132] The only remnant of the Northcott memorial is an anonymous, concrete foundation upon which the vehicle once rested. In its own way this forgotten memorial is an appropriate metaphor for one of Australia's least known, historically important soldiers.

Further reading

L.E. Beavis, 'General Northcott: A Wartime Chief of Staff', *Australian Army Journal*, No. 215, April 1967, pp. 3–11

H.J. Coates, 'Northcott, Sir John (1890–1966)', *Australian Dictionary of Biography*, Vol. 15, Melbourne University Press, Melbourne, 2000, pp. 493–4

R.N.L. Hopkins, *Australian Armour: A History of the Royal Australian Armoured Corps 1927–1972*, Royal Armoured Corps Tank Museum, Puckapunyal, 1993

D.M. Horner, *Inside the War Cabinet: Directing Australia's War Effort 1939–45*, Allen & Unwin, St Leonards, 1996

———, *High Command: Australia and Allied Strategy 1939–1945*, Australian War Memorial and George Allen & Unwin, Canberra/Sydney/London/Boston, 1982

J. Wood, *The Forgotten Force: The Australian Military Contribution to the Occupation of Japan 1945–1952*, Allen & Unwin, St Leonards, 1998

7
FALL AND RISE
Lieutenant-General Sir Sydney Rowell

KARL JAMES

AT 9 AM ON 28 September 1942 General Sir Thomas Blamey sacked Lieutenant-General Sydney Rowell from command of New Guinea Force (NGF). In a cable to the Australian Prime Minister, John Curtin, and the American theatre commander, General Douglas MacArthur, Blamey stated that Rowell was 'competent but of a temperament that harbours imaginary grievances'.[1]

Blamey, who was both Commander-in-Chief, Australian Military Forces and Commander, Allied Land Forces, South-West Pacific Area, had been sent to Port Moresby to 'energise the situation' in the territories of Papua and New Guinea. Earlier in September, the Australians had defeated the Japanese amphibious landing at Milne Bay at the eastern tip of Papua, and the enemy were withdrawing northwards across the Owen Stanley Range. In New Guinea, a small Australian force was raiding and observing the Japanese occupying the Lae–Salamaua area.

Lieutenant-General Sir Sydney Rowell, Chief of the General Staff 1950–54 and, prior to this, Vice Chief of the General Staff 1946–50, where he played a key role in the post-war military reorganisation.
Australian War Memorial, AWM 026582

Blamey had arrived in Port Moresby on the afternoon of 23 September, and, after what Rowell described as 'three very big discussions', Blamey concluded that he had to relieve his corps commander. Rowell returned to Australia. On 1 October Blamey elaborated to Curtin that, apart from Rowell's 'insubordinate attitude', it had been his lack of energy in seeking opportunities for aggressive action that had been Blamey's principal reason for dismissing Rowell. This, Blamey concluded, was owing to Rowell's 'limited' command experience.[2]

One would assume that such actions and remarks would have ended Rowell's military career; they nearly did. Blamey refused to accept Rowell for a field command, and wanted him retired. He even went so far as to describe Rowell as a 'source of evil' and intrigue for factions within the army.[3] Curtin's government, however, wanting to avoid a potential public controversy or inquest, shielded Rowell from the worst excesses of the Commander-in-Chief's wrath.

The circumstances surrounding Rowell's dismissal were indeed extraordinary. His command experience was limited but he was also one of the army's most significant officers. He was a master of his profession. Tall with a trim build, the general was intelligent, austere, quiet yet forceful, and highly principled. A fellow officer remarked, 'the trouble with Syd is that he expects everyone to act like a saint'.[4] War correspondent and Blamey biographer John Hetherington described Rowell as detached, scholarly and a paradox: highly strung yet he never displayed excitement.[5]

Rowell had been among the first cadets to enter the Royal Military College (RMC), Duntroon, in Canberra, and had served in the Gallipoli campaign. During the interwar period he devoted himself to his professional study, attending Staff College and the Imperial Defence College in Britain, and serving on exchange with the British Army. In the Second World War Rowell held key senior staff appointments with the Australian forces in the Middle East in 1941. Following his dismissal from NGF in September 1942, Rowell was banished to Egypt and Britain for the rest of the war. After Blamey was retired from the army in November 1945, the new Chief of the General Staff (CGS), Lieutenant-General Vernon Sturdee revived Rowell's career by appointing him Vice Chief of the General Staff (VCGS). Rowell would succeed Sturdee as CGS in 1950, and he remained Australia's top soldier until his retirement in 1954.

In partnership with Sturdee, Rowell did much to shape Australia's post-war army. At a time when recruits and resources were limited, Rowell was a strong advocate for the new Australian Regular Army. With the onset of the Cold War he oversaw the army's expansion, the deployment of Australian forces to the Korean War, and the introduction of compulsory military service under the National Service scheme in 1951. Rowell believed in the continued importance of the British Empire, and saw the spread of communism in South-East Asia as a direct threat to Australia.

Despite his long service, Rowell is best known for his clash with Blamey in Papua. David Horner, building on earlier works by historians such as Dudley McCarthy and John Hetherington, has written the most comprehensive study of this episode.[6] Yet beyond Rowell's own memoir, *Full Circle* (1974), a measured and considered monograph that at times reads like a manual for senior officers, his broader career has received little popular or scholarly attention. This chapter will examine Rowell's contribution to the Australian Army by concentrating on his relationships with the three men who most shaped his career: Lieutenant-General Ernest Squires, Blamey – who even Rowell acknowledged helped in his 'earlier days' – and Sturdee.[7]

Sydney Fairbairn Rowell was born on 15 December 1894, the fourth son of James and Zella Rowell, at Lockleys, South Australia, into a family with a strong military tradition. His father, James Rowell, had migrated to Adelaide as a boy with his family from England in the mid-1850s. The family became orchardists, and the future CGS's father and uncle served in the colony's volunteer military forces for many years. During the Boer War, Lieutenant-Colonel James Rowell raised the 4th Imperial Bushmen's Contingent and successfully commanded it in South Africa in 1900–01. Colonel Rowell later served in the Great War.

Sydney Rowell attended Adelaide High School and, after sitting a competitive entrance examination, he entered the first class at Duntroon on the academy's opening in June 1911. Already living in a 'semi-military atmosphere', including acting as his father's 'unofficial batman', it was the chance for further study that appealed to Rowell.[8] Duntroon was established to train Australian officers through academic studies in staff duties. At a time when the army was based on the part-time soldiers of the Citizen Military Forces (CMF), on graduation Rowell would join the small number of permanent officers. Rivalries between CMF and permanent staff officers remained an ever-present undercurrent within the army for decades.

Following the British declaration of war on 4 August 1914, Rowell and his fellow classmates were commissioned as lieutenants and allotted to the embryonic Australian Imperial Force (AIF). Rowell secured an appointment in the South Australian–raised 3rd Light Horse Regiment, initially commanded by a cousin. Through illness and a broken leg from a horse fall, his time with the regiment was brief. In May 1915 the 20-year-old joined the regiment on Gallipoli. He commanded a troop for a few weeks before being medically evacuated. He returned to the peninsula in August. Promoted to temporary captain, he fleetingly commanded a squadron before being appointed to adjutant. In November he was evacuated with typhoid fever, first to Egypt and then to Australia in early 1916. In August 1919 Rowell married Blanche 'Peggy' Murison, an army nurse, in Adelaide. The couple later had a daughter. Rowell survived the Great War, but his service had been less than remarkable. Beyond brief periods commanding a troop and a squadron, he did not hold a field command again until 1942.

In October 1920 all permanent army officers, such as Rowell, were transferred to the newly created Australian Staff Corps. The interwar period was typically a time of frustration and disappointment for the Staff Corps with slow promotion, reduced pay and limited prospects.

Staff Corps officers typically held staff positions within CMF battalions or regiments, while CMF officers held command and leadership appointments. This practice helped fuel the rivalry between the two groups of officers. In 1925 Rowell went to Britain for a year to attend Staff College at Camberley, in Surrey, where he was promoted to major. A decade later he returned to Britain as an exchange staff officer with a Territorial division. In 1937, now a lieutenant-colonel, he was selected to attend the Imperial Defence College in London. He returned to Australia after three years in Britain, and became staff officer to the British Lieutenant-General Ernest Squires, the newly appointed Inspector-General of the army.

Squires was the son of a British clergyman, born in British India and commissioned in the Royal Engineers in 1903. He served in India, and during the Great War served on the Western Front and in Mesopotamia. During the 1920s and 1930s Squires held a series of significant staff and instructional appointments. In June 1938 Squires accepted the Australian government's invitation to become the Australian Military Forces' Inspector-General. His first task was to investigate the army's readiness for war. In preparing the report, Squires and Rowell toured facilities around the country. When the British officer questioned Rowell on various Australian officers, the latter asked to what extent was he able to speak at liberty. 'If you don't,' replied Squires, 'who on earth will?' Rowell later adopted the same approach.[9]

Squires submitted his report in December 1938. He was critical of the army's ability to defend the Australian mainland from raids and attacks, and the army's capacity to mobilise and expand to resist a large-scale assault. He thought the CMF's training was poor; its units under strength; and their weapons and equipment lacking. He recommended expanding the CMF and creating a permanent field force consisting of nine rifle battalions, a machine-gun battalion, two field artillery brigades, anti-tank batteries and engineer field companies.[10] The government approved many of Squires' proposals, and while Prime Minister Robert Menzies did not implement Squires' permanent field force, the Darwin Mobile Force, the first field force raised in the Permanent Military Force, was established. Squires became acting CGS in May 1939 and helped oversee the formation of the 2nd AIF following the British declaration of war on 3 September before his death in March 1940 following surgery for cancer.

The first AIF formation formed in the Second World War was the 6th Division, commanded by Lieutenant-General Sir Thomas Blamey. In January 1940 the division began sailing from Australia for the Middle East. The AIF was subsequently expanded to a corps, under Blamey's command, and three additional infantry divisions were raised. The 7th and 9th Divisions joined the 6th Division in the Middle East while elements of the 8th Division were sent to Singapore and initially northern Australia.

Intelligent and brusque, Blamey was a skilled staff officer with a cutting intellect and forceful personality. The rotund general was also tactless, attracted controversy and took a combative approach to the press. Robert Menzies, the Prime Minister who appointed the general, thought Blamey's 'toughness' was his most valuable quality: 'He will take on anything or anybody.'[11] In the Great War, Blamey had landed at Gallipoli on 25 April 1915, and served with distinction as Lieutenant-General Sir John Monash's chief of staff in 1918. Blamey soldiered on during the interwar period with the CMF, but his time as Victorian Police Commissioner during the 1930s attracted scandal. When appointed to command the 6th Division, Blamey chose Rowell for his chief of staff, General Staff Officer I (GSOI). Blamey subsequently promoted Rowell to Brigadier, General Staff (BGS), the chief operations staff for the I Australian Corps headquarters, when the former was appointed to corps command.

Rowell was Blamey's right-hand man. A corps commander dealt directly with his two principal staff officers: the BGS, who handled the corps' artillery and engineer commanders, the chief signal officer, and other senior officers, and the Deputy Adjutant and Quartermaster General (DA&QMG), who dealt with administration and logistics.

In early 1941 the 6th Division and the I Australian Corps headquarters attacked the Italians in Libya before moving to Greece in March. The Australians joined New Zealand and British troops sent to honour a British pledge to defend Greece against unprovoked aggression. The Greeks had defeated an Italian incursion from Albania that had begun on 28 October 1940, but on 6 April 1941 Germany invaded northern Greece. The ill-fated British Commonwealth campaign quickly became a series of delaying actions and withdrawals that ended in defeat and evacuation. The seaborne evacuation began during the night of 24/25 April.

The Australian Corps headquarters had maintained control of the 6th and the New Zealand Divisions during the disastrous campaign. But in the crucible of war the differences in personality and temperament strained relationships. Rowell thought Blamey had been found wanting. He had not set a physical example and was 'quite incompetent as a field commander'. Rowell later alleged that prior to the evacuation Blamey was 'physically and mentally broken', 'almost in tears' and on one occasion gave such a 'garbled' verbal order that the BGS had to intervene and give the order himself.[12] Tension between Blamey and Rowell came to a head on the eve of the evacuation with the two disagreeing over who would be flown out to Egypt. Rowell wanted the corps' DA&QMG, Duntroon graduate Brigadier William Bridgeford, to join Blamey's party being flown out by air but was overruled by Blamey. Rowell eventually said: 'Well, even if you go, I'm stopping here' to carry on the fight. Blamey replied: 'I order you [Rowell] to come with me.' Blamey, Rowell and a handful of officers left Greece aboard a flying boat. Blamey included his son, who was a major, on the flight.[13]

Rowell was so distressed after Greece that he took the unusual measure of writing directly to the Australian CGS, Sturdee, to state Blamey was 'unfit to command troops in the field'. Rowell 'was not prepared' to serve with Blamey in the field again and would go to 'drastic extremes to avoid doing so'. Rowell attributed this letter to his subsequent recall to Australia.[14] Blamey too wrote to Sturdee, though the former was far more generous, commenting: 'Rowell has very great ability; is quick in decision and sound in judgement ... but he lacks the reserves of nervous energy over a period of long strain.' Towards the campaign's end, Blamey felt he needed to exercise 'considerable tact' with Rowell.[15]

Despite this personal friction, Rowell came out of Greece with his reputation enhanced. Many officers commented favourably on his coolness and professionalism. Lieutenant-General Sir Henry Wilson, the British commander in Greece, observed that while the Australian corps fought well, it was Blamey's 'chief of staff Rowell – a very brilliant staff officer who carried Blamey'.[16] Blamey was subsequently appointed Deputy Commander-in-Chief Middle East and made full general. In June Rowell and I Australian Corps, commanded by Lieutenant-General John Lavarack, participated in the successful six-week Syrian campaign alongside British, Indian and Free French troops against the Vichy French. Rowell was afterwards recalled home to become Deputy Chief of the General Staff (DCGS).

Rowell resumed work in army headquarters in Melbourne in early September 1941 with the rank of major-general. He worked directly with Sturdee in what Rowell considered was the most 'profitable partnership' of his service. There was little they did not discuss.[17] Rowell and Sturdee had first met in 1915 in Malta when convalescing from Gallipoli, and first worked together in 1933. Sturdee had joined the Australian Engineers in 1908, and had considerable command and combat experience in the Great War. He subsequently attended Staff College at Quetta in British India (now Pakistan) and the Imperial Defence College in London, and became CGS in 1940. Rowell described Sturdee as having a precise mind with a great sense for priorities. He was humble and kind and constructive in his criticism, though he did not suffer fools gladly. Sturdee above all knew how to laugh.[18] Together, Sturdee and Rowell would see off a series of potential crises as Australia confronted the gravest months in its history.

Japan's entry into the war on 7 December 1941 changed Australia's war overnight. Australia was not prepared for a conflict fought close to home. Naval and air forces in Australia were minimal. The only trained soldiers were the AIF's 1st Armoured Division (not yet equipped with tanks), and the 8th Division's 23rd Brigade. A battalion from the 23rd Brigade had already been sent to Rabaul, New Britain. The CMF, known as the militia, was weak, with its soldiers, many of whom were conscripts, called up for training periods of only three months. Weapons and equipment were equally limited. The CMF's permanent call-up would not fill its ranks until February 1942. The AIF was recalled from the Middle East, though this too would take time. With such threadbare resources, Sturdee and the other service chiefs decided to concentrate on defending vital areas in eastern Australia and Port Moresby, and to not reinforce Rabaul.[19] The commitment to support the Dutch in the Netherlands East Indies was honoured, however, with the 23rd Brigade's two remaining battalions being deployed to Ambon and Timor in December 1941.

It was a time for ruthless decisions. Sturdee knew those soldiers at Rabaul, and on Ambon and Timor, would likely be swept up by the enemy. But the Royal Australian Air Force (RAAF) would not commit aircraft to the islands to provide an early warning against the Japanese if ground forces were not sent to defend the airfields. The CGS and DCGS were unflinching. The commanders on Timor and Rabaul accepted their roles, but Sturdee labelled Lieutenant-Colonel L.N. Roach, battalion commander on Ambon, a 'squealer'.[20] Rowell explicitly told Roach 'to put up the best defence possible' on Ambon with the resources available, but after a series of messages requesting reinforcements, heavy weapons, and eventually evacuation to avoid 'purposeless sacrifice', in mid-January 1942 Rowell sacked Roach for accepting 'defeat as inevitable even before being attacked'.[21]

The Japanese captured Rabaul, Timor and Ambon soon afterwards. Singapore fell on 15 February 1942. These rapid disasters shocked many, especially in the government. Sturdee's most fateful recommendation was his insistence that the I Australian Corps (the 6th and 7th Divisions), then at sea on route for Java, be diverted to Australia. With the support of the navy and air chiefs, on 18 February Sturdee told the War Cabinet he would resign if the AIF did not return. Curtin agreed with his service chiefs, and after intense correspondence between Canberra and London, the corps returned to Australia. As David Horner has shown, during the weeks of panic in early 1942 Sturdee had been the government's rock.[22] While Sturdee was heavily engaged with strategic-political decisions at the highest level, Rowell dealt with many of the issues and requests that arose from other quarters. This included quelling the so-called revolt of the generals, a proposal from several officers that all officers over the age of 50 be retired, and the Staff Corps' Major-General Horace 'Red Robbie' Robertson be appointed Commander-in-Chief of the army.

In late March Blamey arrived in Australia, and was made Commander-in-Chief. The flamboyant General MacArthur arrived in Australia too, having being recalled by the United States President from the forlorn fighting in the Philippines. The American general's arrival was a tonic to the Australian government. MacArthur was appointed Supreme Allied Commander for the South-West Pacific Area, while Blamey was appointed Commander, Allied Land Forces. At the end of March Rowell was promoted lieutenant-general to command the I Australian Corps. He was not yet 48 years old. Blamey told him he had earned the appointment.[23]

The Japanese landed around the Buna–Gona area on Papua's north coast on 21 July and began moving inland. They had intended to capture Port Moresby in an amphibious landing, but following their defeats in the naval battles of the Coral Sea and at Midway in May and June, they attempted to take Moresby by land, advancing along the Kokoda Trail across the Owen Stanley Range. As the Japanese began to push southwards, Rowell was sent by air from Brisbane to Papua to assume command of NGF. He arrived in Moresby on 11 August with the nucleus of his corps headquarters staff.

Rowell's 49 days in Moresby from 11 August to 28 September 1942 is the most discussed period of his military life. In addition to

McCarthy, Hetherington and Horner, many other historians and authors have described Rowell's command during the crisis weeks in Papua, and his controversial sacking by Blamey. Opinions on the fairness of Rowell's removal and the intensity of the vilification of Blamey vary, though few dispute the basic chronology of events.

NGF's operations covered a vast geographic area, the resources initially available were modest, and the initiative everywhere seemingly lay with the Japanese. Rowell had overall responsibility for a small number of soldiers, codenamed 'Kanga Force', based around Wau and operating towards Lae and Salamaua in New Guinea; the hard-pressed 'Maroubra Force' desperately fighting along the Kokoda Trail; and 'Milne Force' developing and defending the airfields at Milne Bay. Moresby and its coastline also had to be defended against air attack and potential amphibious landings. Infiltrating Japanese raiding parties coming down from the mountains were also a possible risk. Rowell's ground forces consisted of inexperienced CMF troops, although during August and into September NGF was being reinforced by the veteran 7th Division.

On assuming command of NGF, Rowell was cautioned by the outgoing commander: 'The mountains will beat the Nips and we must be careful they don't beat us'.[24] Rowell's immediate objective was to recapture Kokoda for further operations against the Japanese at Buna. The forces he could deploy on the Kokoda Trail were limited by the number of Papuan carriers for logistic support and the number of troops available in Moresby. An attempt was made to hold the Japanese at Isurava by aggressive patrolling, while a reserve of supplies were dropped by air further back along the track at Myola.[25] But by late August the Japanese were pushing the Australians back along the Kokoda Trail.

During the night of 25/26 August the Japanese made an amphibious landing at Milne Bay. The ensuing battle between Japanese and the Australian soldiers, crucially supported by RAAF aircraft, was a hard-fought slogging match characterised by all-pervading mud, rain, poor communications, vague maps and confusion. Milne Force's commander, Major-General Cyril Clowes, was uncertain as to the actual strength and intentions of the Japanese. He also realised that the enemy could land another force on the bay's southern or western coastline. Clowes was fighting blind. On 30 August he wrote to Rowell, his old Duntroon classmate, commenting that he 'never quite realised how dense the fog of war could be!'[26]

Clowes was considered rather than cautious. In the rain and muddy tracks, he could not deploy his troops quickly by vehicle, nor did he have barges to move them by sea. In Australia, however, MacArthur's GHQ, ignorant of local conditions on the Kokoda Trail, perceiving hesitancy in Clowes' response, and lacking of information from Milne Bay, was overly critical of the Australians. Writing privately to Rowell, the DCGS, Major General George Vasey, warned his old friend that the atmosphere at MacArthur's GHQ was 'like a bloody barometer in a cyclone – up and down every two minutes'. GHQ was 'nervous and dwelling' on messages from the front.[27] Rowell did his best to shield his local commanders from the mounting pressure and growing scrutiny. 'I wish Chamberlain & Co. [MacArthur's senior staff officers] could visit the jungle and see what conditions are,' Rowell replied to Vasey, 'instead of sitting back and criticizing.'[28]

By early September Clowes had won a decisive victory against the Japanese. Yet, even as the surviving enemy troops were being evacuated by sea from Milne Bay, the Japanese on the Kokoda Trail pushed the battered remnants of Maroubra Force back towards Port Moresby. On 8 September Rowell decided to relieve the brigadier commanding Maroubra Force, just as it engaged in the desperate action at Efogi (known as the battle of Brigade Hill). The burden of battling GHQ as well as the Japanese weighed heavily on Rowell. 'Today', he admitted, 'has been my blackest since we came & none of the 28 days I've spent here has been free from worry.'[29] Just over a week later, on 17 September, the Australians on the Kokoda Trail withdrew to Imita Ridge. It would be their final withdrawal.

When Blamey and a small staff arrived in Papua on 23 September the Kokoda front had stabilised, and Port Moresby was increasingly strengthened with reinforcing Australian and American forces. Kanga Force, meanwhile, was continuing its guerrilla campaign against the Japanese around Salamaua and Lae. All eyes were focused on Port Moresby and Papua. Rowell's public profile was never higher. Only a few days earlier he was celebrated in the press as an able and outspoken officer, 'one of the outstanding soldiers of his generation' and predicted to be a future CGS. His wife and daughter similarly featured in *The Australian Women's Weekly*.[30] On 15 September Blamey delivered a national broadcast on the situation in Papua and New Guinea, and stated publicly he had been impressed with the troops' confidence in Rowell.[31]

Blamey arrived in Port Moresby just over a week later. He had been sent north to reinvigorate the situation because MacArthur and several senior parliamentarians were nervous, if not panicky, on the outcome of the fighting. Knowing Rowell would resent this move, Blamey wrote to NGF's commander stating openly that it had been 'the powers that be' that had decided he would go to New Guinea. 'I hope you will not be upset at his decision', Blamey continued, 'and will not think that it implies any lack of confidence in yourself.'[32] His appeal failed. A proud man, Rowell saw Blamey's arrival as a sign that he had either lost the government's confidence or he had lost Blamey's confidence.[33] Rowell could not check himself. The two generals alone know verbatim what was said, but after several frank and possibly aggressive conversations, by 28 September Blamey had sacked Rowell.

The difference in temperaments, personalities and, on Rowell's part at least, grievances that dated back nearly 18 months to Greece, proved too much.[34] In the heat of the moment, Rowell likely came close to insubordination and he irrevocably destroyed his relationship with the Commander-in-Chief. Blamey afterwards stated categorically to General Lavarack that he could never again entertain any esteem for Rowell, who 'really believed that I [Blamey] was lying'.[35] As Horner has shown, Rowell did not fail as a military commander, but he did fail to appreciate the external political pressures and interference that could be exercised on his campaigns. He also failed to establish a working relationship with a man whom he disliked.[36] Years later, Rowell would admit to his own 'stupid pride' in the affair.[37] This self-realisation, however, was in the future. He was furious when he wrote to his close friend Clowes, only an hour after his dismissal: 'I am sacked. So the fight is one & one of us will go down. I pray that I am successful & that this bad man & his rotten influence will be put out of public life forever.'[38]

Rowell left for Australia that evening. Flying overnight to Brisbane, he pleaded his case in person to MacArthur, and in early October had an interview with Curtin in Canberra. Rowell had been spoiling for a confrontation, but his temper was cooled when MacArthur made a veiled threat that any inquiry would likely end Rowell's military career. The American also made it clear that, if asked, he would state that he thought Rowell was more suited for staff work than command, and would absolutely oppose the Australian's return to Papua.[39] During their interview in Canberra, Curtin similarly explained he had sent Blamey to Port Moresby and that Rowell's assumptions had been wrong. The Prime Minister also emphasised that any questioning of Blamey's authority as Commander-in-Chief 'could not be permitted'. Curtin then granted Rowell three weeks' leave; Rowell, in turn, promised not to embarrass the politician. The general also had a series of interviews with the influential Secretary of the Department of Defence, Frederick Shedden.

Rowell had returned to Australia ready for a showdown, only to be put firmly in his place by the Prime Minister and the supreme commander. There would be no inquest, no court of inquiry into the defence of New Guinea. Curtin told a secret session of Parliament that Rowell's dismissal was due to 'personal incompatibilities' not 'operational considerations'. 'I am quite sure there will be no desire,' he concluded, 'on the part of anyone, to interfere in what is essentially an army matter.'[40]

Having avoided an embarrassing and likely sensationalist inquiry, the next issue was Rowell's future employment. Blamey did all he could to discourage a suggestion from Curtin and MacArthur that Rowell accompany a proposed military mission to the Soviet Union. Blamey's attitude hardened over time. He considered his salutary treatment was necessary, not only to discipline Rowell for his 'insubordinate attitude', but also to set an example to the 'critical and intriguing' Staff Corps officers and others, such as the war correspondent Chester Wilmot, who were openly critical of Blamey.[41] The Commander-in-Chief cynically divided the army's senior officers into two groups: the first were excellent fighting commanders, the second were ambitious elements within the Staff Corps who were only interested in higher appointments. Blamey wanted Rowell retired, or at the least have him revert to his permanent rank of colonel, rather than his temporary wartime rank of lieutenant-general.[42] Blamey recognised the pre-war tensions between some Staff Corps and CMF officers had only grown stronger during the war. He did not want the Rowell matter to further galvanise this factionalism, or for discontented senior Staff Corps officers to rally around Rowell.

Curtin, however, was adamant Rowell would not be dismissed from the service. Shedden similarly advised the Prime Minister of the importance of not overdoing Rowell's censure.[43] Rowell was eventually appointed to command the AIF Detail in the Middle East with the rank of major-general.

Rowell left for Egypt in early February 1943, and arrived in Cairo at the end of the month. Although the AIF's 9th Division had already returned home, Rowell took charge of the few remaining Australian personnel. He also acted as a liaison officer to the British GHQ and made arrangements for the repatriation of Australian prisoners of war from Europe. (His own nephew was a prisoner in Italy.) Rowell knew he had been banished. Little real preparations had been made for his arrival, and he was responsible for generating much of his work, such as providing army headquarters with reports on the Anglo-American operations in North Africa and Italy. But with many familiar British faces in Cairo, Rowell confided to Shedden: 'It would be perilously easy to sit back, drink gin, and do practically nothing.'[44]

Rowell also initiated an ongoing correspondence with Gavin Long, following the latter's appointment as official historian of Australia in the war. Rowell was among the first to offer Long assistance with information and material for the histories.[45] Mindful of his reputation, he was not prepared to leave history's judgment to chance. Rowell was for many years particularly forthright in providing comments and personal insights for the official histories.

Blamey's punishment of Rowell, meanwhile, continued. In August 1943 the Commander-in-Chief, India, Field Marshal Sir Claude Auchinleck, made an overture for Rowell to command a division in the British Army. Blamey, however, vehemently opposed such a move, not only because he considered Rowell had failed as a commander, but also because the offer originated 'entirely through his [Rowell] working amongst old friends'.[46] The personal network served Rowell more successfully later in the year. Partly through the influence of the Minister Resident in the Middle East, the Australian Richard Casey, and Chief of the Imperial General Staff, Field Marshal Sir Alan Brooke, Rowell was loaned to the War Office in London to become Director, Tactical Investigation. Brooke, along with General Sir Bernard Montgomery, had been two of Rowell's instructors at Camberley.

Rowell arrived in London on New Year's Eve 1943, and started at once in his new appointment. His directorate conducted field tests of new theories and weapons, and modifications of existing weapons. The office also collected tactical and technical information from senior officers returned from the Continent and from Allied and enemy intelligence reports. Innovations supported by Rowell included employing the total use of air power, including heavy bombers, in direct tactical support of land actions. In mid-July 1944 he briefly visited Normandy, where he observed a bomber raid flown to support Commonwealth ground forces engaged in heavy fighting. Despite the distance, Rowell keenly followed Australia's progress in the Pacific, and made astute observations on the AIF's future operations. With accurate foresight, in late August he commented to Shedden:

> I do hope that the AIF is used in a decisive role, such as the Philippines, and is not merely employed in 'mopping up'. We played a big part in the decision in 1918 and all the other Dominions are doing the same to-day. I'm sure we have lost politically and militarily by not having some token [AIF] force in Europe at this stage.[47]

Rowell worked in Whitehall amid the second Blitz from Hitler's terror weapons, the V1 'Doodle bug' flying bombs and V2 rockets. He was a member of a scientific committee tasked with deducing the V2's size, warhead load, propulsion method and guidance system. In February 1945 his wife and daughter joined him in London, a sure sign he would not be recalled to Australia anytime soon. His last major project was a study of the future organisation of the British Army.

Rowell later described his time in Cairo and London as his 'years in exile'.[48] Yet these appointments set him apart from his contemporary officers in Australia, and would contribute to his promotion to VCGS.

With the war over and victory won for the Allies, and with Ben Chifley now Prime Minister following Curtin's death, Blamey was quietly retired from the army in January 1946 with little fanfare or reward. Chifley believed Blamey's treatment of Rowell had been unjust.[49] Rowell's exile would soon be over. While Blamey finalised his affairs, the government appointed Sturdee as acting Commander-in-Chief. Following his time as CGS he had led the Australian Military Mission to Washington DC before returning to command the First Australian Army in New Guinea and the Solomon Islands in 1944–45. Sturdee faced many challenges in his new role. These included reconstituting the Military Board to administer the army and consider military matters for the government. He also needed to oversee both the demobilisation of Australia's large wartime army; the creation of a small interim army; and support the troops in Japan with the British Commonwealth Occupation Force (BCOF).

Sturdee viewed his appointment as acting Commander-in-Chief as temporary. In late November 1945 he had recommended Rowell, over Major-Generals Frank Berryman and Robertson, to become CGS. In addition to his seniority, Sturdee considered that Rowell's training, pre-war contribution to General Squires' report, and time with the British Army and in the War Office gave him an appreciation of the Allies' wider strategic conduct of the war, and an awareness of the latest scientific and technological developments that would likely dominate any future conflicts. Rowell's previous experience also showed him to be a skilled army administrator. These skills and background put him ahead of Berryman, whose wartime experience was limited to the Americans in the Pacific, whereas Sturdee assessed Robertson's talent lay commanding troops rather than in a headquarters. In Sturdee's opinion Rowell alone had the temperament, personality and ability to run an efficient army with 'loyal and efficient service'.[50] The government, though, decided on Sturdee as CGS. Rowell was instead appointed VCGS, a new position established to produce plans for the post-war army and with the view of him becoming CGS in the future.[51] Sturdee also made the case for his vice-chief to be reinstated with the rank of lieutenant-general.

The government did not dismiss Sturdee's original recommendation; Chifley was hesitant to appoint Rowell as CGS lest he publicly criticise Blamey. The year 1946 was an election year, and such remarks could easily be construed as a criticism of the Labor government. Chifley's personal sympathy lay with Rowell, and he commented forthrightly on the latter's treatment by Blamey: 'I hate bloody injustice.'[52] Rowell returned to Australia by air in early 1946, taking up his duties at army headquarters in Melbourne on 8 January. His family followed by sea two months later.

Sturdee and Rowell worked together on the composition of the reconstituted Military Board, which Blamey had abolished in March 1942, and the appointments and retirements of senior Staff Corps officers. In recommending officers for the board, the acting Commander-in-Chief sought people who would work together as a team rather than as a collection of individuals trying to promote their own theories.[53] In addition to himself as CGS (as of 1 March), Sturdee recommended Rowell as VCGS to become a board member along with Major-Generals Clowes, as the Adjutant-General; Bridgeford as the Quartermaster-General; and Leslie Beavis as Master-General of the Ordnance. The DCGS could also attend board meetings, but could only vote if the CGS or VCGS was absent. The board also included civilian finance and business members. The Minister for the Army was the board's president. The Military Board met for the first time at the end of February 1946.

Another priority was the raising of a regular Australian army and the re-establishment of CMF. Planning for the post-war army and defence policy had begun during the war. Australia's active cooperation in the collective defence of the British Empire remained the unshakable bedrock of this policy.[54] In late 1944 the Post War Army Planning Committee was established, and Major-General Vasey was commissioned to prepare a report on the future direction of Duntroon and the training of staff officers. Vasey's report assumed that the post-war regular army would have 20,000 men (as recommended by the Squires report). By June 1945, the army was planning to maintain a permanent division of 27,000 personnel. The navy and air force were also planning the scope of their post-war forces. This work was to be done irrespective of cost.[55]

Planning for the post-war army was pushed further along in March 1946, when Rowell circulated a policy paper surveying Australia's future strategic interests and threats, and possible force structure. This paper was Rowell's first major task as VCGS, and in many ways a continuation of his work with Squires a decade earlier. The VCGS identified the Soviet Union as Australia's only threat, particularly if it was able to influence or control China or Japan. Australia could not rely on its geographic isolation for its defence, but had to be ready to help friendly powers, such as the British Empire and the United States, to deter or defeat the Soviets. The pre-war army of 1939, Rowell wrote, had been based on the idea of local defence against raids or an invasion but had no consideration to any wider strategic sphere and proved to be woefully inadequate. Rowell believed the army needed to maintain a peacetime force of three divisions: a permanent division available for deployment overseas in three months, and two CMF divisions ready for deployment in nine to 12 months. Rowell also believed universal training was essential to the scheme. This would allow the army to draw on a pool of experienced men for future deployments.[56]

Rowell's paper was theoretical and made without any consideration of budget. He realised that any threat to Australia's security was unlikely to originate in the Pacific. He rightly predicted the government would not accept the costs associated with his proposed structure.[57] Rowell did identify some of the key ideas for the post-war army. These included the need for standing combat formations, the necessity for greater numbers of regular soldiers, the need for conscription, and a realisation that the army would serve again overseas. As historian Albert Palazzo points out, although the government rebuffed Rowell's paper, his ideas eventually came to pass.[58]

Ultimately it was fiscal rather than strategic considerations that decided Australia's future army. Chifley's peacetime government had priorities beyond the military. The total defence budget for the three post-war services (excluding BCOF) was capped at £50 million per annum. Less than a third, £12.5 million, was allocated to the army. In June 1947 the government approved plans for a permanent field force of a brigade group of three infantry battalions, plus an armoured unit and supporting artillery, engineer, signal and administrative units. The army would also consist of two CMF infantry divisions, an infantry brigade and armoured brigade groups as well as command, training and administrative troops. The army would number some 19,000 permanent soldiers and 50,000 members of the CMF. The forces serving in Japan with BCOF would constitute most of this new permanent force.[59]

With the structure and size approved, the next challenge facing the fledgling Australian Regular Army was recruiting. Australia's economy was strong and the country had just emerged from a costly world war. The army had to become an attractive employer. Trade apprenticeships were promoted, pay rates were eventually increased, so as to be more comparable with civilian wages, married quarters for soldiers' families were built, and a new Commonwealth superannuation scheme was introduced. The CMF was similarly reactivated in 1948, and a CMF officer was appointed to the Military Board.

The CGS had divided much of his duties between the DCGS and the VCGS. Sturdee concentrated on major matters of army policy as well as chairing the Defence Committee and the Chiefs of Staff Committee. The DCGS became responsible for BCOF, the Interim Army, and coordinating staff procedures at army headquarters in Melbourne. This left Rowell, as VCGS, to consider the future of the armed services and he additionally briefed the CGS on inter-service issues. Vacancies in the appointment of DCGS, however, meant that in reality Rowell covered both positions for much of the late 1940s. He also acted for the CGS when Sturdee was on leave or abroad. Rowell was acting CGS when Chifley ordered the army into the mines in mid-1949 to end a long-running dispute with coal-miners. At the height of the strike, some 4000 soldiers worked in open-cut mines at Muswellbrook and Lithgow in New South Wales. Rowell considered it 'a distasteful task', though he complied with the government's decision.[60] When Sturdee retired in April 1950 aged 60, Rowell became his successor.

When Lieutenant-General Rowell became CGS on 17 April 1950, he became the first Duntroon graduate to achieve this most senior position. Few would have foreseen this possibility seven or eight years earlier. The secretary of the Department of Defence had recognised Rowell's potential. The two had corresponded regularly since the general's time in exile. 'For many years I have considered you destined for this position', congratulated Shedden.[61]

As CGS Rowell was, in effect, the Commander-in-Chief. The members of the Military Board were his principal staff officers. The CGS advised the government on policy relating to the army, and he represented the service on the Defence Committee that advised the government on strategic matters. Due to Rowell's seniority in rank, he also became the chairman of the Chiefs of Staff Committee that looked at non-political service matters. In Rowell's view, the CGS had to avoid 'playing politics'. Advice or information given to the government had to be frank, accurate and complete. He saw his business as implementing government policy.[62] In addition to board and committee work in Melbourne and calls to the government in Canberra, he also toured military camps across the country, trying to see each National Service scheme intake, and represented Australia at imperial defence conferences in Britain, and at ANZUS meetings in the United States.

Soon after Rowell became CGS, Australia was again at war. In June 1950 communist North Korean forces invaded South Korea. A month later, Prime Minister Robert Menzies' government announced Australia would contribute forces to the United States–led United Nations coalition to defend South Korea. Australia's initial contribution included the 3rd Battalion, Royal Australian Regiment (3RAR), sent from occupation duties in Japan. Strengthened with reinforcements from the regiment's 1st and 2nd Battalions (1RAR and 2RAR) in Australia, 3RAR arrived in Korea in September where it formed part of a British Commonwealth brigade. The regiment fought in Korea for the duration of the war. 1RAR also deployed to Korea for a period before being relieved by 2RAR. The CGS twice visited Australian troops in Korea, but beyond personally selecting Colonel Thomas Daly – a future CGS – to command the 28th British Commonwealth Brigade in 1952, Rowell had little direct involvement with the conflict.

The limited forces Australia contributed to Korea were deployed as part of a larger international allied coalition where Australians once again served alongside British and American soldiers, sailors and airmen. This involvement was consistent with the earlier Chifley government's approach to post-war defence policy that was committed to the collective defence of the British Commonwealth with the view that Australia's contribution was best done in the Pacific in cooperation with the United States.[63] This approach suited Rowell's personal predilections, as he believed in the unity of the British

Commonwealth as an agent for world peace. His personal preference was for the 'old-fashioned' term 'empire'.[64]

Prior to the outbreak of war on the Korean peninsula, Rowell had chosen Major-General Bridgeford to lead a military mission to Malaya where British forces were fighting an insurgency by what the British labelled 'Communist Terrorists'. On his return to Australia in August 1950, Bridgeford's report described the struggle in Malaya as part of the global Cold War in a region 'particularly sensitive' to the spread of communism in Korea, China, Indochina and Burma. If the French fighting against the Viet Minh in Indochina failed, Bridgeford argued communist power and influence would penetrate through Thailand to Malaya.[65] Beyond a small contingent of aircraft, the Australian service chiefs realised they could not provide forces for both Korea and Malaya. Rowell, for example, thought the army could only offer the British in Malaya a few officers and technicians, and 2000 Owen submachine-guns.[66]

Rowell was very much a Cold War warrior. He saw communism as an ideology that challenged Western values of individual liberty and dignity, and a threat to the Australian way of life. As the country was geographically part of Asia, he warned in the press, a communist victory in Malaya, Indochina or Korea would be disastrous for Australia. A lesson from the Korean War was the sobering realisation that, having been encouraged by the Soviets, Communist China had become a great military power.[67] Rowell perceptively foresaw China dominating and influencing South-East Asia for years to come.

The spectre of the Cold War was ever present. With commitments to Korea, the regional and global menace from Communist China and the Soviets, and low enlistment for the regulars and CMF, in September 1950 Prime Minister Menzies announced the introduction of a National Service scheme. Compulsory military training was not a new idea in Australia. Training and service in school cadets and the CMF had been requirements during different periods since Federation, and men had been conscripted into the army during the Second World War.

As VCGS, Rowell had called for the reintroduction of compulsory training; now, as CGS, most of his work related to the National Service scheme. Under the scheme, all male British subjects aged 18 were required to register for National Service. Those who were called up underwent 98 days' continuous training in the first year, followed by 14 days' camp and 12 days' home training with the CMF for another three years. This provided a total of 176 days of training. Thereafter soldiers passed into the reserves for another five years. Menzies originally intended to call up 15,000 conscripts in three intakes of 5000, but in March 1951 the quota was upped to 29,250 in three tranches of 9750. (National servicemen were also allotted to the Royal Australian Navy and RAAF.) The scheme began in August 1951. Although cuts to the army's budget later saw the training obligation dropped to 140 days. Implementing and administering the National Service scheme stretched the army to the limit. Rowell later likened it to a 'shoe' that pinched 'severely'.[68]

Rowell's period as CGS also saw the re-creation of a women's army service, and he pushed for allowing the recruitment of non-British migrants. The Australian Women's Army Service had been disbanded at the end of the Second World War, yet a lack of manpower prompted calls from within the military for the enlistment of female personnel. In February 1950 Rowell, as VCGS, advised the government that the Military Board favoured recruiting women for a range of duties across the regular army. In July Menzies approved the creation of what became the Royal Women's Australian Army Corps. In September Rowell similarly requested approval to enlist 'New Australians' in the regular army. So long as non-British migrants could demonstrate an adequate knowledge of English and pass a security screening, the CGS felt they should be able to enlist in the same way as any other Australian. The government approved the request in November, although migrants needed to be of European descent and had to apply for a certificate of naturalisation on enlistment.[69]

After a lifetime of service, Rowell was knighted in June 1953 and retired on his sixtieth birthday on 15 December 1954. His final official act was to take the Graduation Parade at RMC the day before his retirement. In this way, both the first and final acts of Rowell's long military career were at Duntroon.

In his farewell message Rowell highlighted the army's achievements during his time as CGS, including its service in the Korean War, the regular army's ability to instruct, accommodate and equip the National Service scheme, and the reorganisation of the CMF, with national servicemen boosting it to a strength of 75,000. His final remarks were: 'Fear God. Honour the Queen.'[70]

Rowell served Australia for 43 years in war and peace, from Gallipoli to the atomic age. His history mirrored that of the Australian Army's during the first half of the 20th century. By heritage, professional training, and service he was also an officer of the British Empire. Studying Rowell's relationships with Squires, Sturdee, Blamey and others demonstrates clearly that the army was a social organisation where one's interpersonal relations with superiors and peers could help as much as hinder one's performance and success in the service.

One of Rowell's most influential contributions to the shaping of the Australian Army was the policy paper he tabled in 1946. The assumptions and philosophy of this paper were reflected in the government's eventual plans for the army, accepted in March 1947. The post-war army, led by Sturdee and then Rowell, saw regular infantry battalions win battle honours in Korea and create their own traditions. To a great extent, however, during the 1950s the Australian Regular Army existed to administer and train national servicemen and the CMF. National Service continued for the rest of the decade, and Australia remained reliant upon its citizen soldiers. In March 1954 Rowell told the government that the regular army was suffering because of the country's tradition of large citizen forces. Given the ongoing Cold War tensions across South-East Asia, he stated frankly that the question was not 'Can we afford considerable Regular Forces?', but 'Can we afford to be without them?'[71] It was his successors who finally convinced the government and the wider community that it was the regular soldier, not the citizen soldier, who was the bulwark of Australia's defence.

Lieutenant-General Sir Sydney Rowell died in his South Yarra home on 12 April 1975, a few days before his wife. His career cannot be defined by his personal clash with Blamey in September 1942; rather, Rowell's legacy remains his role as one of the principal shapers of Australia's post-war regular army. He was, inarguably, one of the most outstanding officers of his generation.

Further reading

J. Grey, *The Australian Army*, Oxford University Press, South Melbourne, 2001

D. Horner, *Crisis of Command: Australian Generalship and the Japanese Threat, 1941–1943*, Australian University Press, Canberra, 1978

———, 'Lieutenant-General Sir Sydney Rowell: Dismissal of a Corps Commander', in David Horner (ed.), *The Commanders: Australian Military Leadership in the Twentieth Century*, Allen & Unwin, Sydney, 1984

D. McCarthy, *South-West Pacific Area First Year: Kokoda to Wau*, Australian War Memorial, Canberra, 1959

A. Palazzo, *The Australian Army: A History of its Organisation 1901–2001*, Oxford University Press, Melbourne, 2002

S.F. Rowell, *Full Circle*, Melbourne University Press, Melbourne, 1974

G. Sligo, 'The Development of the Australian Regular Army, 1944–1952', in Peter Dennis and Jeffrey Grey (eds), *The Second Fifty Years: The Australian Army 1947–1997*, Australian Defence Force Academy, Canberra, 1997, pp. 22–47

8
A MILITARY INTELLECTUAL
Colonel E.G. Keogh

JEFFREY GREY

THE ARMY, LIKE AUSTRALIAN society generally, is usually mistrustful of intellectuals and uncomfortable in dealing with them. This may be because, in both cases, they encounter the genuine article but rarely. In the course of its history the army has produced thinking soldiers, well-educated soldiers and well-read soldiers as well as plenty of capable practical ones who were good at their core business – the management of organised violence. It is most unlikely ever to produce a major theoretician of war – an antipodean Clausewitz – but equally it only rarely produces someone capable of prolonged and sustained thinking and writing about the business of soldiering and the art of war.

While the army has generally been very proficient at training (defined as the development of responses to predictable circumstances, or the ability to act), historically it has been much less good at or certain about education (defined as the conditioning of responses in unpredictable circumstances, or the ability to think). Institutionally it has perceived a need for better and more rigorous education, at least for officers, since the establishment of RMC Duntroon in 1911

Colonel E.G. Keogh was a key figure within the Directorate of Military Training and had an enormous influence in the development of army training and doctrine.
Australian War Memorial, AWM 120551

and the recommendations of the review into extending tertiary qualifications to the service colleges led by Sir Edgeworth David in the early 1920s. Military education is, of necessity, generally aimed at instilling certain practical skill sets at different rank levels and ensuring that officers who complete, for example, Staff College have the requisite knowledge to function as staff officers at the appropriate levels for which they are being prepared. As in many other things, the Australian Army is a derivative organisation, patterned on its British progenitor and exhibiting many of that organisation's cultural behaviours overlain with more specifically Australian features. The British Army long professed a disdain for education and professionalism, and it is unsurprising that there is a legacy of such attitudes in its local progeny.

Two former army officers have identified the defining intellectual characteristics of the Australian Army as an institution clearly and in entertaining manner:

> If it were a person, the Australian Army would be a house builder. Pragmatic, practical, mistrustful of abstractions, questioning of government and not much interested in living in the realm of ideas. Like the builder, the Army applies its skills well in practical situations and is able to develop and apply innovative solutions to practical problems. Like the builder it doesn't see the need to apply much effort to developing possible solutions to prospective problems. The Australian Army is not stupid but nor is it curious. Its confidence in its ability to apply its well-developed common sense to real situations can make it appear arrogant. The Army reads newspapers but not books, it's good at suburban house building but hates dealing with 'creative' architects whom it sees as unnecessarily complicating what it perceives as a pretty simple activity. The Australian Army is unlikely ever to get a contract to build a shopping mall or office tower – if it did it would not know how to proceed.[1]

Although the observation is of more recent vintage, many of the characteristics identified in it apply to earlier periods in the army's history as well. Whatever its virtues, and it has a number, it is not an environment generally conducive to encouraging strong intellectual or scholarly activity among its members.

One of the early exceptions to this general observation was Eustace Graham Keogh. In a succession of roles as a staff officer, author and editor he established the foundations of military professionalism in the post-war Australian Army and especially in its new iteration, the Australian Regular Army. He was not the first army officer to recognise the importance of education and serious and sustained study in the development of the officer corps. He was not the first army officer to write serious history, although he was probably the most prolific to his time. The journal of the profession of arms that he established and edited for nearly two decades was not the first such publication to appear in Australia, although it was easily the most sustained and wide-ranging. What makes Keogh worthy of note and explains his influence within the army of his day is that he did *all* of these things and did so for an extended period of time.

Keogh was born in Rutherglen in Victoria on 24 April 1899. He enlisted conditionally with his parent's permission, since he was underage for both service and service overseas, just after his seventeenth birthday on 13 May 1916.[2] His father was a medical practitioner and young Keogh gave his occupation as 'student' since he was attending Christian Brothers, East Melbourne.[3] He saw service with the 1st Australian and New Zealand Wireless Signal Squadron as a driver in the Mesopotamian campaign. He was discharged in May 1919 but was commissioned in the militia as a lieutenant in November 1924, having qualified as a civil engineer and surveyor. His interwar career was generally uneventful, although it is worth noting that as a captain he won the AMF Gold Medal Essay prize in 1931, the first of three occasions on which he would do so.

He re-enlisted in the Australian Imperial Force (AIF) in April 1940, aged 40. Although his militia service had been with infantry battalions, he was very quickly seconded to the staff at the headquarters of the 7th Infantry Division, bound for service in the Mediterranean. He embarked for overseas service in October 1940 as a senior liaison officer, completed the Middle East Liaison Staff Course (graded 'distinguished') and served in this capacity at divisional headquarters, at headquarters, 1st Australian Corps, and subsequently at headquarters, AIF Middle East. He returned to Australia at the end of September 1942. He was promoted to lieutenant-colonel the following month, and thereafter he held a succession of increasingly senior staff positions concerned with logistics, movements control and liaison tasks. His final posting, back in Australia by this stage of the war, came in January 1945 when he took up duties in the Directorate of Military Training at headquarters, Allied Land Forces, in Melbourne. In this posting, his last before the war ended and he was demobilised, he had responsibilities for, among other things, policy for reinforcements training and the acquisition of training publications from a variety of sources. At a fundamental level this meant some involvement in matters of army doctrine.

Australian Army doctrine exhibited a similar pattern to education, noted earlier. An army that inherited its structure and weapons from the British and that expected to fight as a component (however large) within imperial forces naturally trained along British lines and thought and educated itself in line with British practices and assumptions. In the Great War and during the interwar period the army's tactical doctrine consisted of the British Army's *Field Service Regulations* (*FSR*), first published in 1909 and regularly updated and reprinted. By the 1930 edition, volume I (*FSRI*) dealt with 'Organisation and Administration', volume II (*FSRII*) focused on 'Operations – General' and was essentially concerned with tactics and some tactical-level administrative matters, while volume III (*FSRIII*) laid out the approaches to 'Operations – Higher Formations'. None of these treated what we would now call the operational level of war, a term not then in use in British-pattern armies and which described a concept with which the senior officers of those forces would probably not have been familiar. As the introduction to the 1935 edition of *FSRIII* stated, it dealt with 'war from the point of view of the superior commander and with the tactical handling of formations of all arms'.[4] Editions issued for Australian use were not modified for local use in any way, right down to retaining the endorsement of the Army Council (the British equivalent of the Military Board) and the notices advertising the purveyors of uniforms and other kit, all United Kingdom based.

In the European phase of Australia's Second World War effort, nothing much changed and for perfectly good reasons. The AIF remained organised and equipped along British lines, fought under British high command and in cooperation with British (and other empire) formations. It was heavily dependent on British resources for logistics, intelligence and much else besides. Cosmetic differences in uniform aside, the 2nd AIF in this stage of the war looked, sounded and behaved like its British counterpart.

This changed, sometimes dramatically, with the Pacific War. Faced with a new and threatening environment in which to operate against an enemy whose characteristics were both mysterious and tapped the racial fears of several generations of Australians, allied with the rapid recognition that neither the British nor the newly involved Americans were in a position to offer much by way of support, government and people were forced to draw some sobering conclusions. One of these was the recognition that even simple things like the dissemination of doctrine and instructional material to support training would have to be produced locally, and indeed even derived locally. Thus was born the series of doctrinal publications known as the *Army Training Memorandums* (ATMs).

The introduction to the first memorandum issued laid out the issue clearly.

> We are now face to face with the possibility that the AMF
> may be called on to fight in defence of our hearths and
> homes, our own people and our own ideals. Against an enemy
> equipped and trained as we know him to be, and waging war

in a ruthless manner there can be no place for half-hearted measures in training or operations.⁵

The ATMs gradually came to reflect training requirements and tactical doctrine specific to the needs of the Australian Army and the challenges it faced fighting in its own region, and thus represent the first sustained body of distinctly Australian doctrine produced. Much of it was pretty low-level stuff, and not all of it was useful. In May 1942 the Directorate released ATM 10, 'Notes on Japanese tactics in Malaya and elsewhere', written by the recently returned Lieutenant-General Henry Gordon Bennett. He had justified his abandonment of his command of the 8th Division in Singapore and thus his escape from the threat of Japanese captivity in terms of the intelligence about Japanese methods that he brought back with him, and this publication was, in a sense, the first exhibit in his defence. Bennett's careful biographer has concluded, however, that 'Bennett overestimated the value of his information', and that 'his information was not essential'.⁶ The ATMs overall were an important sign of the maturing of the army as an organisation, especially when seen in the context of other changes in mid-war such as the reorganisation of September 1943 and the replacement of the standard British infantry division organisation with smaller, lighter 'jungle' divisions for service in New Guinea.

Following his demobilisation, Keogh was soon back in the Directorate of Military Training, in a civilian capacity, having been suggested by the Vice Chief of the General Staff, Major-General S.F. Rowell (see Chapter 7). He quickly acquired responsibility for the new iteration of ATMs, which the army regarded as so useful that they were to continue in the peacetime era. Keogh later described their function in wartime as being 'to keep all concerned up to date on all aspects of training activities', but equally that 'in peacetime there was clearly not enough of this kind to produce a publication on a monthly or even quarterly basis'.⁷ They had already been reduced to six issues a year from the wartime monthly format, and Keogh oversaw a move away from the standard ATM appearance to a sort of hybrid journal 'of general military interest'. This did not enjoy much success, and it was discontinued in early 1948.

Keogh thought this first attempt at a journal for the Australian profession of arms 'uninspiring' and dull in format; 'It looked like a half-hearted attempt to pursue some ill-defined object.' He believed firmly in the necessity for an effective publication, however, as he made clear in a submission to the Chief of the General Staff, Lieutenant-General Vernon Sturdee. He argued for the importance of a means through which to keep army officers abreast of military developments, assist them with training and education, encourage the broader study of their profession (what we would now call 'professional mastery'), and create a body of professional literature 'equal in diversity and dignity [to] the military literature of other countries'. As noted in his inaugural editorial in the first issue, the conversion of the old ATMs into the *Australian Army Journal* (*AAJ*) represented 'another step in the reorganization of Australia's post war Army'. The funding environment was tight, however, and until June 1950 the journal appeared every two months. Thereafter it appeared monthly, and its distribution was restricted to within the army.

An accomplished writer, Keogh regularly produced copy for the pages of the journal, and it is a reasonable assumption that the items which appeared regularly under the attribution 'Directorate of Military Training, AHQ' came from his pen. The first (and only previous) military periodical produced in Australia, the *Commonwealth Military Journal*, had been established in 1911 and ceased to appear at the beginning of 1916. Like its later successor, it had been produced through army headquarters in Melbourne, but at least half (and often more) of each issue contained material reprinted from British Army publications or otherwise written by British Army officers. While the *AAJ* continued the practice of reprinting relevant material sourced elsewhere, and while in its early years a substantial number of articles were written by Keogh or his small editorial staff, it was never the intention that it should be an 'in-house' publication in that sense and over time the very great majority of articles appearing between its covers were written by members of the army itself.

Promotion examinations were reintroduced for officers of the regular army in June 1949. Promotion in the ranks from lieutenant to major was governed by a series of examinations in a variety of subjects, such as tactics, administration, current affairs and military history. In those days, selection for attendance at the Staff College was also subject to competitive examination. Extensive formal examinations formed a natural and common part of the civilian education system at all levels, and undertaking them was much less daunting than current generations find them when faced with something similar. That is not to suggest that they were a mere formality, and officers sitting them could and did fail, with a limited number of options to re-sit them depending on their rank.

Successful completion involved considerable preparation in the year of eligibility. An article in the first issue warned potential examinees that with the re-raising of the Citizen Military Forces (CMF) then underway 'the increase in training activity generally, will throw a heavy burden on formation staffs. Time simply will not permit them to run comprehensive and lengthy examination classes covering all the subjects in the syllabus.'[8] The 'considerable amount of self-study' which the examinations necessitated was supported in those days by the network of district base libraries, the Army Education Service and the United Service Institutions based in most state capital cities, but these were stretched and not necessarily easily or readily available to all. Some officers bought their own copies of relevant texts of course, but this was an expensive option at a time when pay and conditions were generally poor. In the years immediately after 1945 the recent war – or aspects of its conduct by the British Empire armies – was the subject of the military history examination, but in 1952 it was decreed that the subject would be the Shenandoah campaign of 1862 during the American Civil War. Suitable books to support this were scarce, and the Military Board ordered the Directorate of Military Training to produce a volume accordingly. Keogh and his staff stepped into the breach and offered to produce it as an enlarged issue of the journal, to appear in January 1954. In exchange they were to be relieved 'permanently of all extraneous duties' which, in the way of these things, had been piling up on them in lieu of anywhere else to assign them.

The volume duly appeared, published in hard covers and made available to army officers upon request.[9] Concise, clearly written and drawing on the best available secondary literature, it provided an excellent introduction and overview of a complex campaign with which most Australians would have had little familiarity. But although the Directorate honoured the agreement and the time-consuming extraneous tasks disappeared, in their place came an expectation built upon the success of the first volume that Keogh would now produce materials in support of the promotion examination system on a regular basis. As he later recalled:

> Since this could fairly be regarded as a direct contribution to
> the aim of developing an Australian military literature and
> the program was spread over ten years, we accepted it as a fair
> exchange for the distractions that always seemed to beset us at
> the worst possible moment.[10]

It must also have ensured some increase in financial resources (a recurrent problem in the journal's early years) while further emphasising the utility and relevance of the tasks they were embarked on.

Keogh produced a further five volumes in the same vein. All dealt with Australian campaigns from the two world wars and with one exception were published by the Directorate of Military Training. In published order they were:

> *The River in the Desert* (1955), which dealt with the
> Mesopotamian campaign in the Great War and in which
> Keogh himself had participated;
> *Suez to Aleppo* (1955), which covered the Suez and Palestine
> campaigns of 1916–18;

Middle East, 1939–43 (1959);
Malaya, 1941–42 (1962); and
South West Pacific, 1941–45 (1965).

Only the last-named had a commercial publisher.[11] The production standards were increasingly good, with lots of maps and some photographs and other illustrations; in *Middle East, 1939–43* the numerous tactical maps were reproduced in four colours and were admirably clear and easy to follow as they supported the analysis in the main text. The print-runs must have been fairly generous, since copies often turn up in secondhand bookshops to this day. While the historical literature dealing with all three conflicts has expanded voluminously since Keogh's day, and with the qualification that he drew on neither archival research nor materials produced by the opposing side, these volumes continue to represent good basic introductions to their subjects and a starting point for immersion in the field.

Keogh was a firm advocate of the importance of history to the education and development of army officers. As well as writing several pieces in the journal offering advice on military history and successful methods of studying it, he also offered advice on the more general function of reading and education in an officer's professional progress.[12] His was an appeal to utility, but his message was underpinned by a deep knowledge of history and his own voracious reading. He urged his audience to 'select and study – not merely read – the works which have a direct bearing on the subjects you have in mind' and to develop 'an alert, critical mind'. His endorsement of the importance of an educated mind to the profession of arms is worth restating and is as valid now as it was when he wrote it.

> The habit of regular, selective reading is the best method of enriching our minds with the experiences of the tens of thousands of soldiers, from generals to privates, whose thoughts and actions have been recorded in print. A rich and varied literature about World War II is already being

created ... [and] there are numerous biographies and personal narratives which help to colour and enliven the official volumes. Many of them are very human documents containing useful lessons on morale, administration, and man-management. In particular the service journals are full of articles analysing the experiences of the recent war from the point of view of statesmanship, strategy, tactics, equipment, and administration, together with suggestions for the application of the lessons adduced to present and future requirements.[13]

As the doyen of the field of War Studies, Professor Sir Michael Howard, would advise more than a decade later, Keogh was urging army officers to read widely and deeply and in context in order to gain the greatest benefit from their labours.

By the mid-1950s the *Australian Army Journal* was well established and publishing a wide range of articles, most of which were written by members of the army itself. The articles were clearly written, designed to appeal to a broad professional readership and, a feature of another age, refreshingly free of jargon and acronyms. Keogh himself nominally retired in April 1964, although he appears to have continued to contribute as editor until the following year when his article 'The Study of Military History' was published.[14] The article was republished in the journal in October 1973 and again in the reincarnated journal in 2007.[15] As the editorial that accompanied this latest iteration noted, 'how we use military history to shape both perceptions of the military and Australian history are important issues that need further exploration'. And as the editorial further noted, 'As Keogh was pointing out in 1965, Australians have long been celebrating Anzac Day without bothering to analyse what actually happened at Gallipoli. Not much has changed.'[16]

Keogh's belief in the importance of sound history sometimes manifested itself outside the journal and the other publications he produced within the army. As early as 1949 he published a detailed and closely argued refutation to an article on the conduct of Allied (which really meant Anglo-American) strategy in the recent war. '[A] critical analysis of our war effort is useful and desirable', he wrote, 'provided that it is directed towards obtaining a better appreciation of the nature of war and the principles governing its conduct'.[17] In a long and active retirement he continued to take a keen and well-informed interest in military history, international affairs and the army, and acted as military adviser to the long-running television series, *The Sullivans*, through which a new generation began to discover some of the events and issues of the war years as these had affected Australia and Australians. He died on 9 November 1981, aged 82.

As the lengthy obituary in the *Defence Force Journal* noted, Keogh made 'an important but now almost forgotten contribution' to military training and education in the Australian Army.[18] His own varied military experience in two world wars was an important source of his effectiveness in this area, as was his relationship with the senior officers of the post-war army. Timing was also fortuitous. Attempts to restart the *Commonwealth Military Journal* in the interwar period failed, partly through lack of resources and partly through the extreme smallness of the regular component of the force. The creation of an Australian Regular Army and the reformation of a large and invigorated CMF in the late 1940s meant that there was a professional constituency to which a journal of the profession of arms might cater, and while resources remained scarce for the first few years the almost continuous deployments in various parts of the region until the early 1970s ensured a steady flow of subject matter. The journal he founded was folded into a new, joint publication in 1976 and ceased, for a time, to have an independent identity. It was revived in 2003, and as an editorial in that year noted, 'although it is always impossible to verify warfighting ideas in peacetime, the real value of these ideas lies in the intellectual debate that they generate'.[19] This was fitting acknowledgment of Keogh's seminal role in promoting considered argument of professional affairs within the army, a legacy further recognised by the creation in 2014 of the E.G. Keogh Chair, a short-term visiting position held by a distinguished academic from outside Australia who can make a direct contribution to consideration of current and likely future issues of concern to the army. Keogh himself perhaps summed up his approach most succinctly when he wrote, 'Challenge everything; accept nothing without thinking about it . . . Our history is full of great military myths, most of which we thoughtlessly accept at their face value.'[20]

Further reading

E.G. Keogh, *Shenandoah, 1861–62*, Directorate of Military Training, Melbourne, 1954

———, *The River in the Desert*, Directorate of Military Training, Melbourne, 1955

———, *Suez to Aleppo*, Directorate of Military Training, Melbourne, 1955

———, *Middle East, 1939–43*, Directorate of Military Training, Melbourne, 1959

———, *Malaya, 1941–42*, Directorate of Military Training, 1962

———, *South West Pacific, 1941–45*, Grayflower Productions, Melbourne, 1965

9
THE CATALYST
Lieutenant-General Sir Thomas Daly

JEFFREY GREY

IT MIGHT SEEM COUNTER-INTUITIVE to suggest that a man who occupied the most senior position in the army for a period of five years and during a major war is nonetheless a shadowy figure. Daly was one of the most influential and consequential figures ever to hold the post of Chief of the General Staff (CGS) and one of the most talented soldiers the army has produced, but he generally abjured the limelight even when he was CGS; a strong and highly principled character, he was naturally averse to anything approaching a 'cult of personality'. The army he joined in the early 1930s looked appreciably like that formed after Federation; the structures and changes he set in play as CGS transformed the institution and served it well until the beginning of the 21st century.

Daly's career can be seen in two parts. Born on 19 March 1913, he was commissioned from Royal Military College (RMC), Duntroon, as a member of the Class of 1934, held the usual range of junior posts in militia units, and served in the Second World War in North Africa and the Pacific. He started the war as a captain and ended it as a

Lieutenant-General Sir Thomas Daly was one of Australia's most influential soldiers. His career culminated with his appointment as Chief of Australia's General Staff in 1966.
Australian War Memorial, AWM PJE/71/0183/VN

lieutenant-colonel, not an unusual time-and-rank progression given the enormous expansion of the army during the war. Nor was he the only regular officer to command an infantry battalion during the war – some 21 members of the Staff Corps commanded in this manner – but he was the only one to do so at the war's end, and his preparation and command of the 2/10th Battalion at Balikpapan further enhanced his reputation.[1]

For at least some of those Staff Corps officers who entered the army in the 1930s, the war provided an extensive and varied mix of experiences in different environments, tasks and levels, though only a relative handful exercised command at unit level. Daly was one of the most fortunate of this latter group.

This probably would not have mattered much if the Permanent Military Forces had reverted post-war to the role of administration and training in support of the militia as had occurred rapidly after 1918. Instead, the creation of the Australian Regular Army, albeit small and inadequately resourced in its early years, gave talented and ambitious young officers like Daly (he was 32 at the end of the Second World War) opportunities and options that their predecessors could not have dreamt of. He is a useful reminder of the part that timing and luck can play in a military career.

The second part of his career, and the part relevant to this discussion and the themes of this book, coincided with the establishment and development of the regular army and, like the army it was something of a work-in-progress, at least initially. For a decade after the war's end he filled a range of increasingly important positions in training and education roles, including two stints in Britain as both instructor and then student at the Staff College and the Imperial Defence College respectively. All of these were important posts but without any public profile. The same could not be said of his stint in command of the 28th Commonwealth Brigade in Korea at the height of the 'static war' there in 1952–53. Only two Australian brigadiers worked at this level in Korea – the other was John Wilton who, though Daly's senior by a handful of years in fact followed him in the appointment – but a general lack of understanding of the Korean War and the nature of the operations conducted meant, again, that neither officer attracted much public (as opposed to professional) attention.

Influence within an organisation can come in two forms: through personality and reputation and through the position occupied. When the two are combined the resultant impact is wide-ranging and frequently long-lasting, and so it proved with Daly. He possessed a strong moral compass informed by his quiet but intense devotion to his Catholic faith, allied to a strong sense of duty and obligation to those he led and a rigorous self-discipline. He had a powerful intellect and was well and widely read. Starting in late 1957 with his appointment as General Officer Commanding Northern Command in the rank of temporary major-general, Daly held a succession of senior 2- and 3-star appointments within the army for the next 15 years – a pattern that today would be unthinkable. Equally unlike today, the CGS really ran the army, while the senior officers who presided over the territorial commands and headed the staff divisions possessed real authority, were able to shape the organisation through the decisions they made, especially as members of the Military Board of Administration, and actually possessed significant resources in order to make things happen.

Several themes or issues ran through Daly's entire career and on which he focused whether commanding a battalion or running the entire army. One of these was a pervasive concern for 'his' people and for their well-being. As a battalion commander in 1945 he had felt the responsibility of command keenly, recognising as he must that 'some of them are going to die, and it may be your fault that they do. Not that you have much choice in the matter because you don't know what the enemy is going to do most of the time. But you do feel that.'[2] His sense of ultimate responsibility for the lives of Australian soldiers fighting in Vietnam when he was CGS was equally pronounced, if anything magnified by the fact that he felt his ultimate obligation was to his soldiers and the wider family of the army. Nor was his concern limited to the obvious sense of culpability for men's lives in combat zones. It is fashionable today to speak of a 'social contract' between the armed forces and their parent society, but for most of Daly's career there was no such thing.[3] Before the Second World War there was no superannuation scheme for service personnel, while into the 1970s pay was poor, conditions generally lagged behind the civil economy, and the provisions for families and dependants were generally pretty basic.

As a career soldier with a young and growing family, Daly had dealt with the housing shortages in both Australia and on posting to Britain after the war and had a keen appreciation of the ways in which severely inadequate accommodation could affect the willingness of soldiers to re-enlist because of the impact on families. Even when he became CGS, Daly always felt that he had to possess 'a log of claims to improve the soldier's lot' in attempting to persuade both politicians and civilian officials to spend money on improved facilities.[4] Mounting a public campaign or one sourced through the newspapers would have been completely out of character for Daly, and his quiet, determined and persistent advocacy within the system over a period of years contributed greatly to the establishment of the Kerr–Woodward and Jess inquiries into service pay and conditions, and superannuation respectively, in the period 1970–73.[5] Adopted more-or-less in their entirety by the Whitlam government, these reviews did more to advance the well-being of members of the armed forces than anything else for a generation, not least because they accepted the proposition that service in the armed forces should be treated broadly in the same way as any other category of employment, albeit one with some unique features specific to itself.

Daly's belief that people should be treated fairly and properly was demonstrated again in his first command as a senior officer: Northern Command from late 1957 to early 1961. This essentially covered Queensland with one important addition which made it a unique command within the army system, namely responsibility for the Australian territories of Papua and New Guinea and with this the command and administration of the Pacific Islands Regiment

(PIR), units manned by native soldiers recruited in those territories. In effect these were Australia's colonies; Australia was to that extent a colonial power and the PIR, consisting of native rank-and-file and white Australian officers, was a colonial military with broad similarities to the King's African Rifles or the *askaris* of the pre-1914 German colonies. This is now a largely unknown chapter in Australia's and the army's histories, but for 20 years from the early 1950s successive cohorts of young and recently commissioned Australians went north to officer units of the Australian Army which possessed only superficial similarities to the rest of the organisation.[6]

The PIR was in a troubled state when Daly assumed responsibility for it. Papuan and New Guinean soldiers had fought well in specially raised units during the Pacific War, but there were those both among the white settler population and the Department of Territories who doubted both the effectiveness and the wisdom of training and arming indigenous soldiers. Relations between the army and Territories – essentially the two key Australian instrumentalities with significant responsibilities in Papua New Guinea (PNG) – were usually fraught. There had been 'disturbances' among the men in the past, frequently arising from issues over differential pay rates and the strict discipline applied within the PIR, and in December 1957 Daly was faced with an outbreak of rioting, which posed a serious threat to the acceptance of the army within settler society. The causes were several and included tribal rivalries, tensions between civilians and soldiers and between soldiers and police, and underlying grievances over pay and conditions. The soldiers also felt aggrieved that their complaints had not been acted upon, while underlying a number of the other problems was the shortage of officers, both in numbers and experience, and the fact, as it emerged, that officers were being posted to the PIR who were not temperamentally suited to their roles.

The violence in late 1957 could well have led to the disbandment of the PIR, with serious medium-term consequences. Within a couple of days Daly flew to Port Moresby and his quiet but forceful interactions with all parties defused a situation that could easily have been further inflamed, not least through the commentary run in the *South Pacific Post*. He was forthright in his condemnation of the violence and disorder but equally clear as to where the ultimate responsibility lay: 'the breakdown in discipline was due principally to the officers not knowing their men sufficiently well and in consequence being unable to command their complete confidence and unquestioning obedience in an emergency'.[7] His first task, to rectify deficiencies within the unit, he effected quickly and thoroughly; the second and less tractable requirement, an improvement in relationships between the soldiers and the civilian populations, would take time and he devoted considerable energy during regular visits to the territory to help rebuild confidence and make good deficiencies as they emerged.

His primary concern, of course, was to ensure that the PIR was an effective and efficient constituent part of the army, able to meet its obligations for the defence of PNG since this was a direct responsibility of the Australian government. But his innate sense of fairness and decency predisposed him to address the men's grievances where he could and to ensure that a better selection process was applied to ensure that officers suited to their roles were sent for service with the PIR. One small but very telling sign of the changes he instituted was his insistence that officers be able to speak *tok pisin* fluently so that they could talk to their soldiers. (Despite the impression sometimes given, fluency in *tok pisin* is not easily attained.) He later assumed the role of Honorary Colonel of the regiment, standing down at Independence.

At the whole-of-institution level it was as Chief of the General Staff that he had most impact on the army and its future direction. Many of the issues with which he dealt were old, or at least familiar, and some recurred regularly to confront successive Chiefs. During the whole of Daly's tenure, the war in Vietnam was the 'main game' and consumed an enormous amount of his attention, but the army was more than the war. Running the army was a relentless task, running it while fighting a war that regularly threatened to overtax its resources even more so. Part of the problem was that the army grew in size in the face of additional demands upon it while army headquarters did not. Here perhaps lay the seed of the wholesale structural reorganisation of the army, including army headquarters, which Daly would initiate as the commitment to Vietnam wound down, and which would be implemented by his successors.

The remainder of this chapter examines three issues during Daly's period as CGS, all of which I would argue had enormous repercussions within the army long after his tenure in office had ended and all of which speak to his long-term influence on the institution he loved. In no particular order these were the expansion and consolidation of army aviation capabilities, the reorganisation noted above, and the domestic politics of Australia's commitment to Vietnam.

Daly did not create army aviation, but more than any other single senior officer he ensured that it survived the hostility of the Royal Australian Air Force (RAAF) and became a strong and vigorous capability. The opposition in the senior ranks of the air force to any but the most minimal and limited aviation capability in the army was implacable and entirely selfish, driven by the realisation that if the army acquired significant capacity in tactical air support it would, in time, take over responsibility for it – with the budgetary and related benefits that this would entail and the loss of resources and prestige that would inevitably follow for the RAAF. The latter had been forced to make the minimal possible concessions in terms of fixed-wing light aircraft but thereafter had dragged the chain or obstructed or ignored requests and suggestions from the army for several years. The Minister for Air (the RAAF's own minister), Peter Howson, concluded in his diary, 'army aviation ... has been neglected for many years in Australia. I am not sure who is to be blamed, but I suspect the RAAF more than the army.'[8] It was inter-service politics at its most naked, most destructive and most pointless.

Wilton had done the groundwork at army headquarters in the late 1950s for a review of the future direction of army aviation, but it was Daly who saw it through in the course of 1966, resulting in a decision from the Minister for Defence, Allen Fairhall, that responsibility for service aviation should be divided between the two services (the Royal Australian Navy (RAN), which maintained its own carrier-based capability through the Fleet Air Arm, seems to have studiously avoided involvement in the fight, perhaps in the interests of not drawing unwanted attention). The next step was the creation of an Army Aviation Corps and the setting up of the 1st Aviation Regiment in 1966–67 with two squadrons and two workshops and with other training and reconnaissance units under the command of the army Aviation Centre. The next step was to find a centralised home for these new assets, and Daly pushed successfully for the former civilian airfield at Oakey, outside Toowoomba, which the Department of Civil Aviation wanted to dispose of, to be allocated to the army. In due course this became the Army Aviation Centre. It was a skilful bit of opportunism on the part of the CGS, as was the agreement that the army should henceforth operate larger and more capable twin-engine aircraft as well as the single-engine airframes to which they had been restricted at the RAAF's insistence. In the latter instance, Daly played on the government's desire to bolster the domestic aircraft industry in the face of limited civilian markets for locally manufactured platforms.

The other major difficulty that senior attitudes in the RAAF presented for the army was their rather limited and unimaginative grasp of the helicopter and its potential on the tactical battlefield. The air force had acquired some Iroquois UH-1 'Hueys' in the early 1960s and, although these had been bought specifically for the army cooperation role, the RAAF refused the army's requests to deploy them operationally to Borneo in 1964 and declined to make them available for training the first units deployed to Vietnam; as a result the latter had never worked on real helicopters before they found themselves on helicopter insertions with the US Army. When Wilton had pointedly requested that Australian helicopters be deployed in support of the early ground commitment he was rebuffed, the Chief of the Air Staff arguing that any useful operational experience that might be 'gained in present conditions is doubtful and the complications of control would be difficult'.⁹ Such reasoning was simply perverse.

When the RAAF deployed No. 9 Squadron and its helicopters in support of the 1st Australian Task Force, the unit, in the opinion of the leading historian of the RAAF, 'was not prepared for war'.¹⁰ This was obviously unacceptable and, despite some additional early complications as the senior leadership of the air force gradually worked out that peacetime regulations and practices could not be applied sensibly in a war zone on active operations, it was gradually broken down. Daly did a great deal of behind-the-scenes work to this end, especially through the Chiefs of Staff Committee, which became doubly useful once the RAN began posting Fleet Air Arm personnel to fly with a US Army assault helicopter company. He also went out of his way to include air force perspectives through the annual CGS Exercise when it considered operational problems thrown up in Vietnam. The arguments were mostly had in Canberra, but for a time their consequences played out on the ground and in the air of Phuoc Tuy province.

The protracted squabble with the RAAF over helicopters in Vietnam pre-dated the commitment but nonetheless impacted upon it. It was a perfect demonstration of the antiquated machinery of command and control that existed within Defence, especially in joint matters involving cooperation between the services and which was an issue which Wilton, the Chairman of the Chiefs of Staff Committee, sought at length to rectify through a root-and-branch reform of the Defence machinery. This would be realised subsequently when Sir Arthur Tange became the Secretary of the Department of Defence in the course of the 1970s and, like Wilton before him, Tange would argue that Vietnam had demonstrated the weaknesses of Australian policy- and decision-making. The army's long war in Vietnam likewise exposed weaknesses in the army's structures and ways of doing business, while parallel developments in allied armies elsewhere further underlined the increasingly antiquated machinery at the disposal of the CGS. The army had been reformed and reorganised before, most recently in the late 1950s and early 1960s with the adoption and then abandonment of the short-lived experiment with the Pentropic formation, but the major impact had been on the field force and on the CMF (in particular) and with relatively few changes imposed on the higher headquarters machinery.

The Australian commitment to Vietnam would not end until 1972, but it was obvious after the election of President Nixon in the United States that US and allied forces would leave, and sooner rather than later, and in 1969 Daly authorised a review of the future organisation of the army. This was not as radical a move as it might seem – with the end of a long overseas commitment in sight, and in the knowledge by that stage that Britain was determined to remove its forces from 'East of Suez' (something that eventuated in 1971), it was clear that the contexts in which the army had operated for several decades were shifting. Daly also recognised that the end of the war would bring an end to the National Service scheme and with it a reduction in the size and strength of the army. The upside of this was that the government had committed to an authorised strength for the army at the end of the reduction, which allowed for rational forward planning. Subsequently, after the election of the Whitlam government in late 1972, a similarly wide-ranging review of the CMF would be conducted under Professor Tom Millar and this, too, would recommend far-reaching changes to old established structures. Although Daly had sought ways to reverse the decline in the CMF that had commenced in the 1950s, he has no claim to that particular reform, although the initial review team made explicit reference to the need for a similar and parallel approach to be taken with the CMF.

The review was announced in March 1970 and chaired by Major-General F.G. Hassett; it would produce *The Command and Organisational Structure of the Army in Australia* which, as its title made clear, combined restructuring of both the force in the field with the headquarters that commanded it and the supporting formations that maintained and supplied it. Although its terms were issued under the signature of the Minister for the Army, Andrew Peacock, its language and intent were unmistakably Daly's: the review 'must not be circumscribed by traditional organisational or procedural beliefs. I believe the review should not disregard the practicability of quite fundamental changes, even though these have been found inexpedient in the past.'[11]

In simple terms, the army had been organised on a geographic basis pretty much since Federation, with the various territorial commands more-or-less corresponding to the states of the Commonwealth. This meant that only army headquarters actually had oversight of the various components of the army in their totality and thus spent much of its time and resources dealing with relatively low level administrative matters rather than formulating and implementing policy. Daly thought the system was 'a relic of the pre-Federation era', and it certainly reflected an older reality when the CMF had been (or was believed to be) the mainstay of the land defence of the nation. That had not been true for some decades.

The most important departure from existing practice, and a move that brought the army into line with the RAN and RAAF, was the creation of a functional command system. The creation of Field Force, Training and Logistics Commands, concentrated and aligned functions and responsibilities within the army and permitted the replacement of the older territorial commands with much smaller military district headquarters in each state charged with a limited range of fairly low level responsibilities. It also permitted a major restructuring of army headquarters, which elevated the office of the CGS to an executive level of responsibility, and the hiving off of some responsibilities from army headquarters to the appropriate functional command. The emphasis increasingly was on policy, while the CGS was able to attend to the command of the army and to act as a principal adviser to the Minister for Defence.[12]

Implementation began in 1971 after approval for a three-stage process by the Military Board, and by that time Daly was on the verge of retirement. It fell to his successor, Lieutenant-General Mervyn Brogan, to see the reforms Daly had initiated bedded down (see Chapter 10). Like any such process, credit should be assigned to a number of individuals for the parts they played in the evolution and implementation of the reform process, but Daly as CGS was the initiator and sponsor of the process as it evolved, and without his strong early support it might well have stalled and failed. It was probably the single most important and wide-ranging reorganisation in the army since its foundation as a national institution in the decade after Federation.

The third area in which Daly proved highly influential on and within the army related to his conduct of his office with regard to the war in Vietnam. In what became an increasingly difficult and fraught position for the army – prosecuting an increasingly unpopular war in line with the policy and directives of established civilian authority while also dealing with the fallout from the casualties it sustained – Daly managed matters both internally and downwards and externally and upwards. With one significant exception this rarely attracted much public attention, which was very much the way he preferred things.

Like many senior officers, particularly of his generation, he disliked the media, and he was fortunate to work in a much more limited and less complex press environment than pertains today. At the same time he fully appreciated the desirability of managing the media environment in which the army had to operate, to the extent that this might prove possible. Wilton had noted that 'the spotlight of public interest' made it necessary for the whole army to be 'PR conscious and aware that all its actions had both PR and political implications', and this became even more true during Daly's period as CGS.[13] In particular, the operation of the National Service scheme and the despatch of conscripts on operational service in Vietnam led to heightened sensitivities within the government where any commentary about or from the army was concerned. Sensitivities were exacerbated by the fallout from the remarks made by Bruce White, Secretary of the Department of the Army, in November 1966 during which he made a number of fairly moderate criticisms of the American conduct of the war which, though widely shared, were indiscreet in the lead-up to a federal election.

As CGS, Daly thought his principal role was 'to try to keep the government off the soldier's back' through minimising political interference and commentary on their role.[14] He was deeply unimpressed with the ABC's handling of the 'bastardisation scandal' at RMC in 1969, noting in a letter to his minister, Phillip Lynch, more generally that 'to the news media the only news worth publishing is bad news, and the views of a relatively small number of articulate ill-wishers are given far more prominence than is fair or equitable'.[15] The 'civic action crisis' of March 1971 arose when an army decision to phase out activities, such as building schools and repairing roads, in preparation for a likely withdrawal from Vietnam, was leaked to the media. The ensuing public controversy led to the resignation of the Minister for Defence, Malcolm Fraser, and the fall of the Prime Minister, John Gorton. The issue stayed in the public arena far longer than it deserved because of poor judgment at the political level and as part of a wider campaign both within the government and among certain journalists to destabilise Gorton's leadership. Daly felt very strongly that officers of the armed forces had no business engaging in public controversy and that, in any case, 'over the years the army had become conditioned to not talking to anybody', something which he recognised was not necessarily in the army's best interests.[16] After the affair with Bruce White, senior officers were required to clear public statements in advance with the minister, and thereafter Daly generally declined speaking engagements while he remained in office.

The government made its own job harder through its failure to manage and shape an information campaign within Australia concerning the roles and purpose of the Australian forces in Vietnam. As Denis Warner, a long-serving correspondent based for many years in Asia (and for whose writing Daly had a high regard) observed, 'the Australian Government needed an informed public' where the war was concerned.[17] That it did not get one was a problem very largely of its own making. Daly knew that attacks on the army were usually a convenient device with which to attack the government, but this did not make it easier to stomach. Relations between the army and the press were 'not good', and his conscious decision to avoid press conferences and public comment undoubtedly contributed to that, as he himself again recognised clearly. The result was that 'a group of influential people were denied a firsthand view of matters of great public interest'. On the other hand, and as the civic action crisis in 1971 served to confirm, by consciously staying out of the fray to the greatest extent possible Daly undoubtedly helped the army avoid much of the opprobrium which would otherwise have been directed at it as a result of the 'complete, utter nonsense' that was sometimes reported in the press and that came to characterise the military–media relationship in the United States. This was especially the case after the Tet Offensive in the first part of 1968, the reporting of which Daly described as 'the lunatic hallucinations of the daily press which have achieved transcendental levels in the past week'.[18]

Daly was a conservative by instinct and very much a man of his time. As he was to show in his retirement, and especially during his time as Chairman of the Council of the Australian War Memorial, this did not in any sense close his mind to the possibility of doing things in new ways or departing from established practices where these could be shown to need overhauling or replacing. His strong personal identification with the army meant that he would fight tenaciously in defence of its interests, but equally that he was amenable to new approaches that would help to strengthen it as an institution, make it more effective and help safeguard its members and their families. That he chose to do so within the structures of his time made him doubly effective, but his refusal to seek the limelight on his own behalf has served to obscure the very substantial contributions that he made.

Further reading

J. Grey, *A Soldier's Soldier: A Biography of Lieutenant-General Sir Thomas Daly*, Cambridge University Press, Melbourne, 2013

G. Pratten, *Australian Battalion Commanders in the Second World War*, Cambridge University Press, Melbourne, 2009

10
POST-WAR PLANNER
Lieutenant-General Sir Mervyn Brogan

TRISTAN MOSS

ON 29 FEBRUARY 1972 Lieutenant-General Sir Mervyn Brogan, Chief of the General Staff (CGS), watched as the last Australian combat troops boarded HMAS *Sydney* in Vung Tau, South Vietnam. In inspecting the loading of troops and equipment, and speaking to the men as they settled aboard the ship, Brogan was witness to the final phase of one of Australia's longest wars, and to the end of a 20-year period of almost continuous Australian deployments in Asia, from Korea to Vietnam. Like other senior Australian officers of his generation, much of Brogan's career had been dedicated to preparing for and fighting of these wars; now he was responsible for the army as it finished its long involvement in South-East Asia. Yet, while the period in which Brogan served is best remembered for its conflicts – and often controversy – his career was an illustration of the vast and vital, if quotidian, task of managing an army. This was no more the case than during Brogan's time as CGS, from 1971 to 1973, during which the Australian Army underwent a series of fundamental changes in composition and structure in addition to the withdrawal

Lieutenant-General Sir Mervyn Francis Brogan (right), Chief of the General Staff 1971–73, in a key period when Australian troops withdrew from Vietnam and the army fundamentally modernised its command structure.
Australian War Memorial, AWM FOD/72/0035/VN

from Vietnam: national servicemen were released en masse, the army's system of regional command was replaced, Papua New Guinean units formed a separate defence force, and the Citizen Military Forces (CMF) was overhauled.

Brogan was one of a succession of strong Chiefs of the General Staff who guided the institution through its longest period of continuous deployment and combat. Like his two predecessors, Lieutenant-Generals Sir John Wilton and Sir Thomas Daly, Brogan was commissioned during the 1930s, had his first taste of combat during the Second World War, and gradually rose through the ranks as a result of his competency as a leader and manager of soldiers and the structures they inhabited in the army. He was, according to his successor, Lieutenant-General Frank Hassett, a 'commonsense' officer, who gave 'clear and unmistakable orders', but was not overbearing in the exercise of command, preferring to allow individuals to work as they saw fit. Known as an officer who had a strong rapport with those around him, and for his wit and sense of humour, Brogan saw the value in cultivating networks, both within the army and in wider circles.[1] Equally, he had little hesitation in taking action when necessary, and demanded plain speaking from himself and those who worked with him.

Brogan was guided by his interest in the army as a profession, and recognised that good management, organisation and planning was as essential as leadership. Appreciative of the opportunity the army afforded him to study and practise engineering, Brogan was deeply engaged in the institution and its future. He understood that the army was not something that existed only to be directed, but that it also had to be carefully managed and cared for. Citing Churchill, he believed that the army 'is a living thing. If it is harried it gets feverish; if it is sufficiently disturbed, it will wither and almost die'.[2] While his predecessors commanded the army during an era of conflict, and are remembered for it, Brogan's achievement was in guiding it through an intense period of reorganisation, which represented the most significant period of upheaval since the army's inception prior to the First World War. The withdrawal from Vietnam, and the period of belt-tightening that followed, could easily have been the beginning of a nadir for the army; instead, the early 1970s was a time of challenging, but ultimately positive, redevelopment. Brogan's achievements as CGS are largely unremarked upon because of the skill with which he navigated the difficulties of the period, managing the army as 'a living thing', composed of both people and ideas.

Born on 10 January 1915, Mervyn Francis Brogan was one of a small cohort of Australian officers who had their foundational experiences in the small pre–Second World War Australian Army, and retired as it became the modernised force that we know today. Growing up in the Sydney beachside suburb of Manly, Brogan was a conscientious student. During his final year of high school in 1932, he received a scholarship to attend the Sydney Technical College free of charge, one of just three students in the state to do so.[3] However, the 17-year-old Brogan aimed higher and, with the permission of his father, applied and was accepted into Royal Military College (RMC), Duntroon. He joined what was a small peacetime army, orientated towards providing a base from which to manage part-time units of the CMF, and aid in their expansion in the event of war. Consequently, there was only a handful of cadets in Brogan's year. Indeed, the financial constraints on the army at the time were such that the college had been relocated to Sydney for much of the 1930s, sharing space in Victoria Barracks, Paddington. Cadet Brogan excelled at sport, particularly rugby, which won him friends and respect, as well as demonstrating his leadership and other masculine virtues the army believed could be detected on the sporting field before they were applied in battle. It was during this period that Brogan earned the sobriquet 'Basher', a reference to his prowess in the boxing ring as much as temperament and stature.[4] Indeed, Brogan thrived at RMC and was awarded the 'sword of honour' for graduating top of his class.

Shortly after leaving RMC as a new member of the Royal Australian Engineers, Brogan joined the construction project for new fortifications on Rottnest Island, part of the defences of Fremantle.[5] After this practical experience of the army engineer's craft, he began his degree at the University of Sydney in 1936, graduating two years later. During the 1930s the opportunity to attend university was still a rare one for men like Brogan, and he valued the experience, throwing himself into university life, not least the rugby team in which he maintained an interest throughout his life. When war broke out in 1939, Brogan was not immediately given an opportunity to serve overseas, and was instead posted to Duntroon to train the significantly larger intake of cadets for wartime service.

Brogan found his chance for active service with the entry of Japan into the war, serving with Second Australian Army headquarters staff as General Staff Officer 2 and aiding the organisation of supplies to the Kokoda Trail. He was mentioned in despatches, an early recognition of his efficiency and aptitude as an officer in this vital but unglamorous task. Brogan was promoted to Assistant Quartermaster-General New Guinea Force, again displaying his capacity to organise complex but essential parts of the military machine in managing the air resupply to Australian and American forces in the campaign to retake Salamaua in 1943. Brogan's subsequent OBE for these efforts stated that the entire air supply scheme during the campaign was thanks to his 'skill and ability'.[6] That the young officer – with a permanent rank of captain – was fulfilling the role of a lieutenant-colonel was an additional sign of the qualities that would propel him to higher rank, and of the administrative tasks that would be the hallmark of his career.

The final years of the war saw Brogan posted back to Australia to the Directorate of Military Training – another organisational task – and then back to headquarters Australian First Army. In 1945 Brogan was chosen to travel as an observer with the British Army in Germany, as part of a broader Australian military effort to expand the corporate knowledge of future leaders by exposing them to operations different from those then being fought in the Pacific. However, while presumably a different and enlightening experience after New Guinea, Brogan was laid low by malaria shortly after his arrival, much to the surprise of the British doctors who, in the snow-covered ruins of the Third Reich, did not consider this tropical diseases when determining the cause of Brogan's admission to hospital. In his account of his hospital visit, Brogan woke to find that the hospital staff had simply assumed that their antipodean visitor was suffering the effects of excessive alcohol consumption![7]

Following the war, Brogan returned to his earlier teaching role as Commanding Officer School of Military Engineering. Being based in Sydney, Brogan played a minor role in the Chifley government's controversial response to striking coal-miners when he was tasked with mobilising Royal Australian Engineers personnel in Eastern Command to assist in mining coal. The pressure placed on the young colonel was evident in his recollection of the words of Lieutenant-General Berryman, Brogan's superior: 'If you don't get it [coal], Brogan, someone's head is going to roll and it isn't going to be mine.'[8]

Brushes with federal politics aside, Brogan spent the 1950s in the hectic cycle of a field officer moving his way up the ranks. In this period he saw a wide variety of postings, both as trainer and, importantly for a middle-ranking officer, as trainee. As such, Brogan returned to Britain to study at the Joint Services Staff College from 1950 to 1952. He began to make his mark on the army as a whole with his reappointment as Director Military Training in 1954, a time when the Australian Army was attempting to relearn and re-establish its previous expertise in the jungle tactics it had developed during the Second World War, but had let deteriorate in the following decade as the army focused on the war in Korea and the plan to support Britain in the Middle East, should a global conflict break out again. Brogan was instrumental in reopening the jungle-training establishment at Canungra, drawing on the British experience in Malaya through a visit there in September 1954.[9]

As the head of training and doctrine formation in the Australian Army, Brogan was engaged with his art, but not necessarily overawed by the shifts in technology and tactics occurring during the 1950s. In 1955 he penned an article on 'Tactics and Atomics' – subsequently republished in the prestigious American journal *Military Review* – in which he emphasised what he considered to be the foundational ideas of warfare, and argued that 'the old principles, varied in application in degree only, will still prove sound'.[10] Moreover, seconded as a brigadier in the Far East Land Forces Headquarters from 1956 to 1958, Brogan also recognised that in the types of coalition warfare Australia engaged in at the time, diplomacy and integration with allies played a role alongside tactics. He again drew on his experiences to contribute to the development of the army of which he was a part, writing an article on British Commonwealth integration in which he expressed his support for a close relationship between Commonwealth forces, but argued that the relationship, as a result of the drift between Great Britain and Australia, needed to be constantly maintained within the army.[11] Brogan's own experience working with the British was reinforced by attendance at the Imperial Defence College in 1959, a step that was both his last period of study and a clear indicator of an officer destined for senior rank.[12]

Brogan's rise to the position of CGS was decided a decade before he assumed the role, in 1961, when discussions between the Secretary of the Department of Defence and his minister determined the succession of the position from the then CGS, Lieutenant-General Reginald Pollard: Wilton, Daly, Brogan, Hassett.[13] Brogan was appointed to his first senior command in 1962, as General Officer Commanding (GOC) Northern Command, during a period in which the Australian Army underwent a dramatic expansion. Prior to the changes of the 1970s, which Brogan would later oversee, the role of a GOC of a regional command was a challenging one, as each headquarters was responsible for administering all the training and logistics functions of the army units in its jurisdiction, as well as exercising command over them. Practices could therefore differ between these commands, as each represented a world unto itself in many respects.

Northern Command was a particularly complex entity as it encompassed the Australian territories of Papua and New Guinea, making it responsible for the Pacific Islands Regiment (PIR), based in Port Moresby. This unique unit had its origins in the Second World War, when Papuan and New Guinean men were recruited to fight the Japanese, a task they fulfilled with distinction. Their unit was disbanded in 1946, partly from fear of 'arming the natives', only to be raised again in 1951 as Australia's northern defences looked increasingly shaky with the advent of the Cold War. (See Chapter 9 for a description of the troubled period 1957–61 under Lieutenant-General Sir Thomas Daly's command.) In 1962, Australia's strategic situation worsened, and the PIR again grew in importance. After years of Australian diplomatic resistance, Indonesia was granted the formerly Dutch possession of West Papua, which meant that for the first time, Australia shared a land border with a potentially hostile country. Alongside a much wider army expansion announced by Prime Minister Robert Menzies in 1962, therefore, the PIR was also expanded. Planning for the largest military build-up in Papua New Guinea (PNG) since the Second World War fell to Brogan and his staff, who recommended the expansion of the PIR from one to three battalions and a host of ancillary units, under the aegis of a new PNG Command, separate from Northern Command.

Brogan did not see the PIR as simply another unit of the Australian Army, and framed his plan for its expansion in terms of 'the transition of a country from a dependent to an independent status', which could only be 'non violent and administratively harmonious' if the structures of state, such as the military, were already established.[14] In doing so, Brogan looked beyond his immediate task of raising new units for Australia's defence to see the PIR not simply as part of the army, but also as the beginning of a future independent PNG defence force. That he supported this idea during a time when the PIR was expanding in response to Australian defence needs, rather than those of a then only theoretical independent PNG, is all the more remarkable. Overseeing the expansion of the army in PNG, Brogan also supported fundamental changes in the previously segregated relationship between Australian and Papua New Guinean soldiers, such as the integration of Messes in 1962 following the removal of restrictions on alcohol consumption for Papua New Guineans by the colonial government.[15]

In February 1965 Brogan was appointed the first Director of Joint Service Plans, a role that necessitated a close working relationship with the Department of Defence in Canberra for the first time. Brogan's appointment by Wilton, then the CGS, was part of a wider effort to encourage a closer working relationship between the three services; Brogan's selection for the task of establishing a 'war room' – as a precursor to a joint tri-service staff – was testament to his organisational and interpersonal skills at a time when the concept of 'jointery' was still a future aspiration.[16] As Director, Brogan was also involved in the maintenance of Australia's political and military alliances, accompanying the Chairman, Chiefs of Staff Committee, Air Chief Marshal Sir Frederick Scherger, and the foreign minister, Sir Paul Hasluck, to the South East Asia Treaty Organization (SEATO) military advisers' conference in April 1965.

Drawing on these experiences, Brogan developed an understanding of the broader strategic and social context in which the army operated, and knew that it could not delude itself into thinking that it only had to focus on the business of war. Following his trip to SEATO, he emphasised to members of Parliament that Australia was a 'small country in the military sense', and that its 'preservation lies in contracting political and military alliances with like-minded powerful allies'.[17] Similarly, as Quartermaster-General, a role he assumed in 1966, Brogan came to realise that the army had 'in many other instances planned our facilities in isolation from the current and foreseeable needs and desires of the rest of the community'.[18] This belief continued into his last command before his appointment as CGS, as GOC Eastern Command, the largest and most significant of the regional commands. Referring to the media's treatment of the Australian Army in the Vietnam War, which was frequently the subject of controversy, Brogan told other senior officers that the army was 'under constant critical assessment by an unsympathetic, if not hostile, press'. Nonetheless, while public opinion was 'not listed in our manuals', Brogan argued, 'in the event it is a Principle of Peace and we must learn to live with it'.[19]

From 1970, the Australian Army began to shift from a force orientated towards war in South-East Asia alongside its allies, to one with few direct threats and an uncertain role. As Robert O'Neill notes, the period from 1971 to 1975 was 'the most consequential five years for Australian defence policy since the Second World War'.[20] Brogan's appointment as CGS from 19 May 1971 to 19 November 1973 meant that he held responsibility for the raft of changes occurring during this watershed period. Brogan had a clear vision for the army's future, seeing the period as one 'of peace with no imminent threat, a challenging time to consolidate and learn from what we have been doing in the field, a much needed time to put our house in order and to clarify where we are heading'.[21] He believed that to do this, the army must be modern, well organised and well educated.[22] Indeed, Brogan himself was at the forefront of the professionalisation of the officer cohort, being the first CGS with a university degree.

As CGS, Brogan administered and commanded the army as the Chairman of its executive body, the Military Board, which he both led and contributed to through the management of his own areas of responsibility in training, operations and force development. His role was therefore one that both focused on the day-to-day running of the army and on planning for its future. In addition, the CGS was the main source of advice for the government, usually through the Minister for the Army, and the Defence Minister, as well as the Chiefs of Staff Committee, which dealt with issues affecting the three services, and the Defence Committee, which focused on broader strategic issues.[23] Brogan's time as CGS, like those before him, was therefore composed of a broad range of activities, from visiting troops to conferring with government ministers.

Faced with the task of managing the army during a period of uncertainty and transition, and having already served on the Military Board as Quartermaster-General, the third most senior member, Brogan wasted little time imposing his own style of no-nonsense management on the body. For instance, shortly after becoming CGS, Brogan directed that the Military Board Minutes, which were the principal means by which policy was decided and communicated, were 'to be promulgated in a more abridged form than in present use'.[24] He was also plain spoken in his comments on the myriad reports and submissions that landed on his desk, sometimes annotating reports with 'rot', 'rubbish' and 'here we go again'.[25]

The Military Board's role in deciding the army's future required a close working relationship with both government ministers and civilian members of the Departments of the Army and Defence. This relationship depended to a large extent on the personal relationship between the men concerned. Colonel Ian Mackay commented on the sobering move from his position as CO of 7th Battalion, Royal Australian Regiment (7RAR), to assistant to Brogan in 1973: 'the bureaucrats were in control, and I could see that in the peace time army, even a lieutenant general didn't have too much authority'.[26] Clashes between the military and their civilian counterparts in government are a feature of defence life, then as now, but the situation was serious enough in 1973 for Brogan to write to the senior members of army headquarters, acknowledging their concerns of 'unwarranted interference in professional matters, unreal deadlines, withholding of information for which the Services have a need to know, uninformed supervision, delays, wrong levels of action'. However, characteristic of the capable manager and administrator that he was, Brogan refused to give voice to these concerns beyond his immediate circle until his subordinates provided him with 'specific areas of legitimate complaint' that he could cite.[27]

The end of the Australian involvement in the Vietnam War in 1972 was the most recognisable shift in the Australian Army's posture during Brogan's tenure as CGS. The process had begun in 1970 when the 1st Australian Task Force's third battalion, 8RAR, was not replaced, in response to the new US policy of Vietnamisation and withdrawal from the conflict. The task force gradually contracted in size until August 1971, when Prime Minister William McMahon announced the withdrawal of combat troops. The last infantry battalion, 4RAR/NZ, left Vietnam in December 1971, with the remaining support troops withdrawing by February the following year, save for a small team of advisers. While the Australian presence in Phuoc Tuy province had helped create a broad level of peace and stability, with fewer attacks by Viet Cong and North Vietnamese troops, most commentators within the army and among the public were pessimistic about the ability of the South Vietnamese to ensure the security of the province, and indeed the entire country, without the support of foreign troops.[28]

The gradual withdrawal of Australian troops had provided the army with time to assess its post-war future, which it began during Daly's tenure as CGS. In 1969 the army completed the *Review of the Size and Shape of the Army Post Vietnam*, which called for an army of 28,000 men, of which around 11,000 would be allocated to a field force in infantry battalions and other combat arms. Under this plan, combat troops composed a smaller percentage of the total force, reflecting a broader trend among modern Western militaries, in which the tail far outnumbered the teeth.[29] The 1969 review helped coalesce army thinking on its future size, but the expansion and contraction of the army was not new, having occurred during the two world wars, and throughout the growth of the early 1960s. Unlike these periods, the army also used the looming withdrawal from Vietnam as an opportunity to reorganise its basic structure, and set up the Army Review Committee (ARC) in early 1970, under Major-General Frank Hassett and the Chief Defence Scientist, Dr John Farrands. The ARC was charged with examining the structures of command within the army, principally the regional commands and army headquarters. This review had been a long time coming, as the problems associated with the decentralised command system, which dated back to Federation, had been acknowledged from the 1950s.

As Brogan had experienced in Northern and Eastern Commands, each regional command was essentially its own army, responsible for training, logistics and everyday functions. Yet, the Australian Army was a national force. Equally important, any invasion of Australia was unlikely to affect a single state, or require the resources and units of only a single region. The army had refrained from addressing these issues prior to the 1970s because of its overseas commitments; it feared that any wholesale reorganisation would adversely affect combat operations. With Australian troops withdrawing from Vietnam in the 1970s, and no likelihood of operations elsewhere, the army was free to reorganise.

In its January 1971 report, *The Command and Organisational Structure of the Army in Australia*, the ARC advocated a new command structure that centralised and rationalised command within the army. In particular, the ARC recommended that the regional commands be replaced by three 'functional commands'. The first was Field Force Command, which, broadly, oversaw all combat units in Australia, such as the infantry battalions, engineers, armour and artillery. Logistics Command would have responsibility for all transport, supply, maintenance and support units, and would command all Support Area and Communication Zone units. Finally, Training Command directed all army schools, training battalions and centres, and was charged with formulating training doctrine, although RMC Duntroon remained under the oversight of the CGS.[30] This arrangement would, the ARC hoped, address the issue of differing policies and practices, particularly in training, between the different regional commands, while streamlining the duplication of effort that had existed previously. It would also bring the army in line with the other two services, which already operated functional commands.

Complementing the reorganisation of the regional commands was the ARC's recommendation that army headquarters be more efficiently structured so as to better focus on policy-making for the army, rather than simply its day-to-day operation. Up to this point, army headquarters had directly commanded around 140 units; these were largely passed to the functional commands under the ARC's proposals. At the same time, the headquarters was reorganised into four branches – Operations, Personnel, Logistics and Material – in which policy planning for each individual area of the army would take place; the latter two branches were eventually combined. With the removal of direct planning responsibility, the CGS and his staff could be elevated to a more executive role, overseeing the army as a whole and formulating policy, rather than being mired in detail.[31]

The army's reorganisation was not without its critics; one cynical officer quoted to Brogan a Roman officer under Nero, who said of his own army's constant reorganisation 'we tend to meet any new situation by reorganising, and a wonderful method it can be for creating the illusion of progress while producing confusion, inefficiency and demoralization'.[32] However, such views were in the minority, and few could claim that the system of command in Australia did not need an overhaul. It fell to Brogan to implement these recommendations from late 1971, assisted by Hassett in the newly revived role of Vice CGS. Existing regional commands were used as the basis for the new functional commands, and by mid-1973, both the functional command system and the army headquarters reorganisation had been largely completed, rationalising an organisational structure that was better suited to pre-First World War defence than the varied activities of a large, permanent and professional peacetime army.

The reorganisation was in hand by the election of the Whitlam government in December 1972. While inextricably associated with the end of the war in Vietnam, the Labor government did little to change the number of Australians deployed in the war zone, as the overwhelming majority of troops had already been returned to Australia. Shortly after coming into office, Prime Minister Gough Whitlam did, however, unequivocally end the decade-long Australian involvement when he withdrew from Vietnam the remaining advisers. More important to the army was the swift end of the National Service scheme in December 1972. All recruits already in the selection and training pipeline were released, and all national servicemen were permitted to leave the army as soon as they wished, although some elected to serve out their terms.

Brogan did not oppose the end of conscription, particularly as many in the army maintained an ambivalent attitude towards a scheme that on the one hand provided much-needed, and often well-educated and motivated, young men for the army, but at the same time attracted the ire of many members of the public (although certainly not all), and was a drain on army manpower. Brogan's principal concern over the end of conscription was that any changes to the National Service scheme occur gradually for, he rightly believed, 'stop and go is fatal to rational Army development'.[33] Nonetheless, National Service in 1972 was a social issue first and a defence one second and the scheme was wound up swiftly.

With the army's strength so drastically and immediately reduced, Brogan was faced with a difficult situation unforeseen in the plans for the post-Vietnam army. Almost overnight, 12,000 national servicemen were lost to the army, which Brogan believed had 'an immediate and vital impact on the Army's capacity to fulfill its function and perform its various roles'.[34] Not only did the exodus leave many units dangerously under strength, other army initiatives also had to be cancelled, such as the innovative use of national servicemen with teaching degrees in PNG to educate Papua New Guinean soldiers. Characteristically of Brogan, he believed this significant challenge could be mitigated with good management: 'this event, drastic as its effect may be in the short term, if properly handled need not, in the long run, impair the Army's capability to meet its foreseeable tasks'.[35] Brogan planned to preserve the army's nine infantry battalions by hollowing them out. Three units would be maintained at their full strength of around 600 men, two around half strength, and four battalions would be reduced to training units of 200 men each. Under this plan, Brogan hoped the army would retain the divisional structure of nine battalions, if not its total manpower, by keeping the battalions in 'suspended animation'. He believed strongly that the army should retain a division framework, otherwise, he stated, 'we have no capability to field an independent, balanced force'.[36] However, Brogan's wish was an attempt to 'save the silverware after Vietnam', and the hope for the maintenance of a complete division was untenable after the mass removal of national servicemen.[37] Moreover, the proposed policy of expanding infantry battalions undercut the role of the CMF as the basis for expansion in times of war.

The army bit the bullet in May 1973, at the insistence of the Department of Defence, reducing the RAR from nine battalions to six.[38] Strongly supported by Brogan and other officers, the division structure was retained by the army, but was based around three task forces of two infantry battalions, rather than the usual three. Even a reduced strength division was desirable, planners felt, as it allowed the army to maintain particular skills and techniques, such as the command of large formations, and was the smallest formation in which all arms of the army would operate together. Equally, many in the army felt that a division represented a clear statement of Australia's military power. As David Connery has argued, the maintenance of a division, no matter how small, was probably an important part of the army's self-image as a credible force.[39] This structure, based around the six infantry battalions of 1st Division, remained the basis for the Australian Army into the 1990s.

At the same time as the army was reorganising itself in Australia, it was also instrumental in creating an entirely new defence force in PNG. Having planned for the creation of PNG Command in 1963, Brogan oversaw the next and final revision of the Australian Army's units there, with the raising of the Joint Force PNG in January 1972, which preceded the creation of the Papua New Guinea Defence Force (PNGDF) the following year. It was only at this point that Papua New Guinean soldiers ceased to be the largest minority in the Australian Army, and instead began to serve their own country as it moved towards independence.

Brogan welcomed the shift to a joint defence force in PNG, feeling that the Department of Defence had at last 'grasped the nettle' and taken a strong interest in PNG, which had largely been an army concern prior to this point. Moreover, Brogan believed that having a greater involvement from the other two services and their departments offered an opportunity for the army to advance its own interests.[40]

Within the Australian defence establishment, the Department of Defence's leadership in the planning of the PNGDF reflected its growing power over the service departments, which would eventually be formalised in the amalgamation of the Army, Navy and Air Departments in the Tange reforms of the late 1970s, for which Brogan was consulted.[41]

Much of the planning for the PNGDF was done hastily, as the timetable for independence was sped up under the Whitlam government. Indeed, the plan approved by Brogan in 1963 formed a significant part of the basis for the independent PNGDF, and was essentially a localised PNG Command, combined with air and naval elements. There was simply no time to construct a radically different force. Efforts focused on bringing existing units up to strength, and replacing Australian soldiers with their Papua New Guinean counterparts. In 1975 the Australian commander in PNG, Brigadier Jim Norrie, handed command to Papua New Guinean Brigadier Ted Diro, the first local commander of the PNGDF, although Australia contributed around 500 personnel to the total force of 3500 at independence.

Brogan's time as CGS also saw the decline of the CMF as Australia's 'second army'. Although authorised at around 60,000 men, the CMF was by 1970 only half that number, with the result that most of its units were woefully under strength.[42] The force had been eroded by diminishing public interest and declining links with the community, unwillingness to reorganise the force and an unclear sense among politicians about what the force was for, most notably in the government's refusal to send a CMF battalion to Vietnam. The release of national servicemen from their obligations further hit the CMF, as those men who had joined the citizens forces as an alternative to National Service left in droves.

Addressing the CMF's troubles was a painful process for the army. Brogan had a sentimental attachment to the CMF; like many of his peers, he had served in the force at one stage of his career, in his case in the Sydney University Regiment. While believing that the 'present malaise must be cured [and] the decline arrested', Brogan recognised that 'the drift may be sociological', as the enthusiasm with which men joined the CMF prior to the 1950s was no longer universal.[43] Nonetheless, Brogan, alongside many other officers, had accepted the Regular Army's new status as the primary defender of Australia. His support for the divisional structure on the grounds of 'credible' defence, for instance, demonstrated his belief that this force, rather than the much larger civilian forces, would be Australia's main line of defence.

During the final year of Brogan's tenure, the Whitlam government charged political scientist Professor Tom Millar with assessing the future of the CMF. Millar's final report, delivered in 1974, found that Australia should abandon the two-army system. Instead, the CMF was to be constituted as the reserve force supporting the Regular Army (incorporating the pre-existing but smaller Regular Army Reserve and Regular Army Emergency Reserve) in what was termed a 'total force'.[44] The army acted quickly on Millar's recommendations, and completed much of the changes during Hassett's term as CGS from 1973 to 1975. While the CMF had declined over the course of the 1960s in numbers and importance, the significance of this shift is not to be underestimated. The implementation of the Millar Report marked the end of the idea that Australia was to be defended by citizen soldiers called out in a time of need, and was an acknowledgment of not only the new speed with which a threat might arise, but also the variety of deployments Australia might be called on to undertake short of outright war, such as the 'wars of choice' in South-East Asia. Brogan was characteristically forthright on the issue of the CMF's role in Australia's defence, believing that 'the days of instant armies are gone' and that Australia's defence now rested largely on the professional army. Given the change in strategic circumstances and the decline in numbers of the CMF, Brogan believed that to rely on it as the foundation for Australia's defence was as 'impractical as it was outmoded'.[45]

Alongside organisational changes to the regular force and CMF, the army also addressed long-standing issues of service conditions and morale. A committee under Sir John Kerr was established by the McMahon government to investigate salaries and allowances within the army and, in a series of reports released between 1971 and 1973, aimed at reorganising the complex and opaque pay system while simultaneously recognising the army as an 'industry'.[46] This appreciation was long overdue, as Australian servicemen and their families had laboured under poor service conditions for decades. As the army transitioned almost overnight into a fully volunteer force that needed to recruit and retain skilled men, the need for it to address the problems identified by the Kerr Committee only became more important. Fortunately, Brogan had a strong supporter in the Minister for Defence, Lance Barnard, whose own service experience and willingness to advocate on the army's behalf against opposition within the Labor Party earned him Brogan's respect and gratitude.[47]

At the same time, many in the army were concerned about a decline in morale among soldiers after Vietnam as the army adjusted to financial constraints and offered fewer opportunities for exciting work. Although Brogan denied it publicly, he and other officers believed that arresting any drop in morale was an important step that complemented other structural adjustments to peacetime service conditions.[48] In discussing the use of the army in the coming decade, Brogan and his colleagues on the Military Board emphasised 'the need for a sense of purpose in addition to training for war', as well as encouraging more interesting training activities and sport to raise morale in the ranks.[49]

Brogan retired from his position in 1973 and was succeeded by Hassett. He continued to have a strong academic interest in the army and in particular in the continuation of the changes he had begun as CGS. He was an active contributor to the debate over the defence of Australia, for instance, and only one year after leaving the army one of his articles was used in debate in Parliament.[50] Based in Sydney, Brogan was also Colonel Commandant of the Royal Australian Engineers and of the University of New South Wales Regiment, and served on the board of the Australian War Memorial. He died in 1994.

The mark an individual officer of senior rank, such as Brogan, might make on the Australian Army was dependent on the political, strategic and financial context facing the army of which they were a part. Lieutenant-General Sir John Wilton, CGS, and Chairman Chiefs of Staff Committee during the mid-1960s, for instance, assumed the position at a time of expansion and overseas deployment, and so had a profound influence on the organisation's development; this same expansion saw Brogan influence the construction of PNG Command and, as a result, the PNGDF.[51] Yet, in contrast to Wilton, Brogan's tenure as CGS came during a period of changing strategic circumstances, with restricted funding, a new government, and a concentrated period of review within the army. His role, therefore, was one of manager in which a deft hand, administrative mind and, as Hassett said of him, not a small degree of 'steel', was required to guide the army through its most significant shifts in its peacetime history.[52]

When Brogan began in the position, the Australian Army was still involved in active combat operations, and was the largest it had ever been, containing 12,000 national servicemen and 3000 Papua New Guineans. When he left in 1973, the army was a smaller force that had a new and streamlined system of command, had amalgamated six of its battalions and lost two in the PIR. Brogan was also the last head of the army to visit his troops in a war zone until Australian troops were deployed to Afghanistan in 2001. Brogan's constant engagement with the army, its doctrine, structure and future throughout his career demonstrated his suitability for this role. The changes were not as dramatic or controversial among the general public as the army's deployment to South-East Asia during the preceding decade, but were of similar long-term importance in shaping the army's future. Indeed, the reorganisation managed by Brogan framed the basis for the army as it exists today.

Further reading

'Functional Commands', *Australian Army Journal*, no. 283, December 1973, pp. 2–18

M. Brogan, 'The Australian Army – Points and Problems', *The RUSI Journal*, vol. 118, no. 1, 1 March 1973, pp. 54–60

D. Connery, *Which Division? Risk Management and the Australian Army's Force Structure after the Vietnam War*, Australian Army Historical Unit Occasional Paper Series, Canberra, July 2014

A. Ekins and I. McNeill, *Fighting to the Finish: The Australian Army and the Vietnam War, 1968–1975*, vol. 9, *The Official History of Australia's Involvement in Southeast Asian Conflicts 1948–1975*, Allen & Unwin, Crows Nest, 2012

J. Grey, *A Soldier's Soldier: A Biography of Lieutenant-General Sir Thomas Daly*, Cambridge University Press, Melbourne, 2012

D.M. Horner, *Strategic Command: General Sir John Wilton and Australia's Asian Wars*, Oxford University Press, Melbourne, 2005

D. McCarthy, *The Once and Future Army: A History of the Citizen Military Forces, 1947–1974*, Oxford University Press, Melbourne, 2003

A. Palazzo, *The Australian Army: A History of Its Organisation 1901–2001*, Oxford University Press, Melbourne, 2001

A. Tange, *Defence Policy-Making: A Close-Up View, 1950–1980*, Peter Edwards (ed.), Canberra Papers on Strategy and Defence, no. 169, ANU E Press, Canberra, 2008

NOTES

Introduction
John Connor

1. M. MacMillan, *History's People: Personalities and the Past*, House of Anansi Press, Toronto, 2015, p. 270.
2. MacMillan, *History's People*, pp. 2–3, 79–80, 344.
3. G. Walsh, *Australia: History & Historians*, School of History, Australian Defence Force Academy, Canberra, 1999, p. 19; J. Black and D.M. MacRaild, *Studying History*, 2nd ed., Macmillan, Basingstoke, 2000, p. 100; S.B. Oates, *Biography as History: The Twelfth Edmondson Historical Lectures*, Markham Press Fund, Waco, Texas, 1991, p. 11.

1 The First Commander: Lieutenant-General Sir Edward 'Curley' Hutton
Craig Stockings and Tom Richardson

1. R. Adams, 'The Military View of the Empire 1870–1899: As Seen through the Journal of the Royal United Services Institution', *Journal of the Royal United Services Institution*, vol. 143, no. 3, June 1998.
2. D. Morton, 'Authority and Policy in the Canadian Militia, 1874–1904', PhD thesis, University of London, 1968, p. 360; J. Buchan, *Lord Minto, A Memoir*, T. Nelson and Sons, Ltd., London, 1924, <http://gutenberg.net.au/ebooks05/0500261h.html>, accessed 12 July 2012 (chapter 6).
3. 'Notes for Lecture on "Personal Recollections of the Zulu War"', 1880, Hutton Papers (hereafter HP), Reel F-1, UNSW Canberra Library.
4. D. Morton, *Ministers and Generals: Politics and the Canadian Militia, 1868–1904*, University of Toronto Press, Toronto, 1970, p. 134.
5. R. Aubrey, 'Major-General E.T.H. Hutton: A Study of his Relations with the Canadian Government', BA Thesis, Carleton University, Ottawa, 1957, pp. 7–8.
6. Hutton to Alderson, 3 June 1902, HP, A-6.
7. W. Perry, 'Lieutenant-General Sir Edward Hutton: The Creator of the Post-Federation Army', *Australian Army Journal*, No. 291, August 1973, p. 19.
8. 'Commonwealth Defence Bill', 1901, NAA CP103/12 Bundle 3/A8.
9. *Ibid.*

10 'A Study in British Commonwealth Co-operation. Australian Defence Policy to 1938', NAA A5954, 784/2; *Sydney Morning Herald*, 24 July 1901, NAA A6, 1901/201.
11 'A Study in British Commonwealth Co-operation. Australian Defence Policy to 1938', NAA A5954, 784/2.
12 Hutton to Minto, 8 March 1902, HP, A-1.
13 Hutton to Ommanney, 24 February 1902, HP, A-2.
14 R.J.R. Lehane, 'Lieutenant-General Edward Hutton and "Greater Britain"': Late-Victorian Imperialism, Imperial Defence and the Self-governing Colonies', PhD thesis, University of Sydney, 2005, p. 239. Emphasis in original.
15 N. Leckie, *Country Victoria's Own: 150 Years of 8/7 Royal Victoria Regiment and its Predecessors, 1858–2008*, Australian Military History Publications, Sydney, 2008, p. 22.
16 *Official Yearbook*, no. 1, 1908, p. 1082; no. 12, 1919, pp. 1080–1; no. 13, 1920, pp. 999–1012.
17 'Report of the Federal Military Committee', AWM 3, [1].
18 'Memoirs', HP, F-2.
19 'Second Annual Report by Major-General Sir Edward Hutton, K.C.M.G., C.B., Commanding the Military Forces of the Commonwealth' (hereafter *Second Annual Report*), 1 May 1904, NAA A1195, 45.30/27793; 'Military Forces of the Commonwealth – Annual Report' (hereafter *First Annual Report*), E.T.H. Hutton, 1 May 1903, NAA A1195, 45.30/27793; Correspondence (various) Hutton / Forrest / Collins, February–May 1902, NAA B168, 1902/867 Part 1.
20 'Minute Upon the Defence of Australia' (hereafter *Minute, 1902*), E.T.H. Hutton, 7 April 1902, NAA A1195, 45.30/27793.
21 *Ibid.*
22 *Ibid.*
23 *Ibid.*
24 *Ibid.*
25 'Scheme of Organisation of the Military Forces of the Commonwealth into a Field Force and into Garrison Troops', AWM 3, 677.
26 Barton to Hutton, 6 April 1902, HP, A-4.
27 *Sydney Morning Herald*, 24 April 1902, p. 6.
28 *West Australian*, 28 April 1902, p. 4.
29 Collins to Hutton, July 1902, NAA B168, 1902/2688.
30 *Ibid.*
31 Hutton to Prince Arthur, 29 April 1902, HP, A-2.
32 Hutton to Bigge, 29 April 1902, HP, A-2.
33 Bigge to Hutton, 17 July 1902, HP, A-2.
34 'Memoirs', HP, F-2.
35 *Second Annual Report*.
36 'The Military Forces of the Commonwealth Tables', AWM 3, [22].
37 Hutton to Ommanney, 19 August 1903, HP, A-2.
38 Hutton to Bigge, 21 October 1902, HP, A-2.
39 *Ibid.* Hutton subsequently sent a copy of the letter to Northcote to Bigge.
40 Lehane, 'Greater Britain', pp. 227–8.

NOTES

41 Tennyson to Forrest, 1 July 1903, Forrest Papers, NLA, MFM G 660.
42 *Second Annual Report*; 'Draft of Commonwealth Military Regulations', NAA A2657, vol. 1.
43 Hutton to Ommanney, 19 April 1904, HP, A-2.
44 Hutton to Balfour, 27 June 1904, HP, A-2.
45 *Ibid*. Hutton sent a copy of this letter to Lord Balfour.
46 Collins to Hutton, 28 November 1902, NAA B168, 1902/2688.
47 Appendix A to *Organisation of the Military Forces of the Commonwealth, Commonwealth Parliamentary Papers* (*CPP*), vol. 2, 1903, p. 60.
48 C. Stockings, *The Making and Breaking of the Post Federation Australian Army, 1901–09*, pp. 81–2.
49 *Sydney Morning Herald*, 27 June 1904, p. 9.
50 *Monaro and Southern District Advertiser*, 12 March 1903, and *Cooma Express*, 26 May 1903, NAA B168, 02/1823 & 02/2688.
51 *Adelaide Advertiser*, 15 June 1902 (clipping), HP, A-3.
52 Hutton to Forrest, 16 November 1903, NAA B168, 1902/2688.
53 See, for example, Price to Bridges, NAA B168, 02/2688.
54 W. Kelly, *Commonwealth Parliamentary Debates*, 2nd Parliament, 3rd Session, p. 609.
55 Hutton to Ward, 7 June 1904, HP, C-4.
56 J. Mordike, 'Control by Committee: The First Military Board', paper presented to the Australian War Memorial Conference, Canberra, 1987.
57 Hutton to Collins, 12 March 1902, AWM3, 02/359; Wilcox, 'Relinquishing the Past', p. 57.
58 'Select Committee: Case of Senator Lt. Col. Neild. Minutes of Evidence', NAA A1194, 45.30/27794.
59 'Estimates of the Defence Department for the Financial Year, 1903–04', NAA A1194, 05.13/2472.
60 W. Vamplew (ed.), *Australians: Historical Statistics*, Fairfax, Syme & Weldon Associates, Sydney, 1987, pp. 133, 412.
61 Hutton to Forrest, 4 May 1903, HP, A-4.
62 Hutton to Tennyson, 4 May 1903, HP, A-3.
63 *First Annual Report*.
64 Hutton to Chapman, 16 March 1904, NAA B168, 1902/867.
65 *Second Annual Report*.
66 Hutton to Minto, 16 May 1904, HP, A-1; *Second Annual Report*.
67 *Second Annual Report*.
68 *Second Annual Report*.
69 *First Annual Report*.
70 'Narrative of Instructional Operations by a Cavalry Division,' 4 May 1904, NAA B168, 1903/618.
71 *First Annual Report*; 'Comparative Statement for Militia and Volunteers', NAA MP84/1, 1937/1/68.
72 Hutton to Chapman, 1 March 1904, NAA A2657, vol. 1.
73 Chapman to Hutton, 4 March 1904, NAA A2657, vol. 1.
74 R. McMullin, *So Monstrous a Travesty*, Scribe Publications, Melbourne, 2004, pp. 103–4.

75 Hutton to Minto, 16 May 1904, HP, A-1.
76 Mordike, 'Control by Committee: The First Military Board, 1905', pp. 10–11.
77 J. Wood, *Chiefs of the Australian Army*, Australian Military History Publications, Loftus, 2006, p. 45.
78 'Memorandum by a Committee in Regard to the Command and Administration of the Military and Naval Forces', NAA B168, 1904/184 Part 3. Emphasis in the original.
79 *Ibid.*
80 *Ibid.*
81 'An Act to amend the Defence Act 1903', NAA B168, 1904/184 Part 3.
82 Hutton to Collins, 20 August 1904, HP, A-6.
83 Hutton to Collins, 20 August 1904, HP, A-6.
84 McCay to Deal, 7 September 1904, HP, A-6.
85 *Major-General Sir Edward T. H. Hutton, K.C.M.G., C.B*, Biographical Press Agency, London, 1905, pp. 14–15.
86 *Ibid.*
87 'Memoirs', HP, F-2.
88 'Memoirs', HP, F-2.
89 E.T.H. Hutton, 'The Bond of Military Unity', *The Empire and the Century*, John Murray, London, 1905, pp. 239–40.
90 Wood, *Chiefs of the Australian Army*, p. 46 (quoting from the *Argus*, 10 November 1904).
91 C.E.W. Bean, *The Story of ANZAC*, vol. 1, Angus & Robertson, Sydney, 1921, p. 178.

2 Duntroon to the Dardanelles: Major-General Sir William Bridges
Chris Clark

1 C.E.W. Bean, *Two Men I Knew: William Bridges and Brudenell White, Founders of the A.I.F.*, Angus & Robertson, Sydney, 1957, pp. 17, 75.
2 Bean, *Two Men I Knew*, p. 76.
3 P. Pedersen, 'Burning Bridges', *Wartime: Official Magazine of the Australian War Memorial*, no. 50, 2010, pp. 20–5.
4 J. Grey, *The War with the Ottoman Empire*, vol. 2 of *The Centenary History of Australia and the Great War*, Oxford University Press, South Melbourne, 2015, p. 65.
5 Pedersen, 'Burning Bridges'.
6 P.S. Sadler, *The Paladin: A Life of Major-General Sir John Gellibrand*, Oxford University Press, South Melbourne, 2000, pp. 59, 70.
7 N. Meaney, *A History of Australian Defence and Foreign Policy, 1901–23, vol. 1: The Search for Security in the Pacific, 1901–14*, Sydney University Press, Sydney, 1976, pp. 62–3.

8   Bridges to Chauvel, 20 August 1914, Chauvel Papers (consulted when this material was in the possession of Lady Chauvel; possibly now in records donated to Australian War Memorial in 1994 as PR00535).
9   C.D. (Coulthard-)Clark, *A Heritage of Spirit: A Biography of Major-General Sir William Throsby Bridges, KCB, CMG*, Melbourne University Press, Carlton, 1979, pp. 118, 121.
10 J. Connor, *Anzac and Empire: George Foster Pearce and the Foundations of Australian Defence*, Cambridge University Press, Melbourne, 2011, pp. 47–8.
11 Clark, *A Heritage of Spirit*, pp. 136–8.
12 D. Moore, *Duntroon: A History of the Royal Military College of Australia, 1911–2001*, Royal Military College of Australia, Canberra, 2001, see Appendix 11, pp. 518–25.
13 Clark, *A Heritage of Spirit*, p. 105; Chris (Coulthard-)Clark, *Duntroon: The Royal Military College of Australia, 1911–1986*, Allen & Unwin Australia, North Sydney, 1986, pp. 224–7.
14 Hutton draft memoirs, British Library, MS 50113, pp. 15–17.
15 *Argus* (Melbourne), 6 March 1896, p. 5.
16 Clark, *A Heritage of Spirit*, pp. 25–6.
17 Undated 'Historical Notes' in Bean Papers, Australian War Memorial (AWM) Series 38 (5), 3DRL 8042, item 34.
18 *Sydney Morning Herald*, 27 April 1896, p. 4; *Australian Town & Country Journal* (Sydney), 2 May 1896, p. 10.
19 Clark, *A Heritage of Spirit*, p. 27; C.D. (Coulthard-)Clark, *The Citizen General Staff: The Australian Intelligence Corps 1907–1914*, Military Historical Society of Australia, Canberra, 1976, p. 10.
20 Clark, *A Heritage of Spirit*, p. 38; C. Wilcox, *Australia's Boer War: The War in South Africa 1899–1902*, Oxford University Press, South Melbourne, 2002, p. 75.
21 Clark, *A Heritage of Spirit*, pp. 42–44; C.D. Clark, 'The "Invasion" of New Caledonia', *Australian Army Journal*, no. 279, August 1972, pp. 9–19; Chris (Coulthard-)Clark, 'Australia's Monroe Doctrine: An Attempt to Keep the Islands English', *Pacific Islands Monthly*, vol. 57, no. 12, December 1986, pp. 40–2; Chris (Coulthard-)Clark, 'Australia's First Spy', in J. Laffin and P. Badman, *Special and Secret*, Time-Life Books Australia, North Sydney, 1990, pp. 12–13.
22 J. Mordike, *An Army for a Nation: A History of Australian Military Developments 1880–1914*, Allen & Unwin, North Sydney, 1992, p. 158.
23 C.D. (Coulthard-)Clark, *The Citizen General Staff: The Australian Intelligence Corps 1907–1914*, Military Historical Society of Australia, Canberra, 1976, p. 8; Clark, *A Heritage of Spirit*, p. 47.
24 Clark, *A Heritage of Spirit*, pp. 47–8.
25 *Ibid.*, pp. 50–1.
26 *Ibid.*, pp. 52–3.
27 *Ibid.*, pp. 53–4, 56–7.
28 Clark, *The Citizen General Staff*, pp. 12–16.
29 G. Serle, *John Monash*, Melbourne University Press, Carlton, 1982, p. 170.
30 P.A. Pedersen, *Monash as Military Commander*, Melbourne University Press, Carlton, 1985, p. 23.

31 *Punch* (Melbourne), 24 September 1914, p. 536.
32 C.D. (Coulthard-)Clark, *Australia's Military Map-Makers: The Royal Australian Survey Corps 1915–96*, Oxford University Press, South Melbourne, 2000, pp. 8–11.
33 Clark, *A Heritage of Spirit*, pp. 78–80.
34 *Ibid.*, pp. 80–3.
35 *Ibid.*, pp. 84–5.
36 *Ibid.*, pp. 91–4.
37 *Ibid.*, pp. 101–2.
38 A.J. Hill, *Chauvel of the Light Horse: A Biography of General Sir Harry Chauvel, GCMG, KCB*, Melbourne University Press, Melbourne, 1978, p. 42.
39 C.D. Clark, 'General Bridges: The Reluctant Commandant', *RMC Historical Journal*, vol. 2, 1973, pp. 34–5.
40 *Punch* (Melbourne), 11 May 1911, p. 688.
41 Clark, 'General Bridges: The Reluctant Commandant', pp. 33–4.
42 *Argus* (Melbourne), 17 March 1914, p. 10.
43 Clark, *A Heritage of Spirit*, p. 113.
44 Hamilton to Sir John French, 10 March 1914, Hamilton Papers, Liddell Hart Centre for Military Archives, King's College, London, Item 7/8/5.
45 Clark, *A Heritage of Spirit*, pp. 113–14.
46 *Ibid.*, p. 185.
47 General Brudenell White, quoted in Bean, *Two Men I Knew*, p. 75; see also Chris (Coulthard-)Clark, 'Major-General Sir William Bridges: Australia's First Field Commander', in D.M. Horner (ed.), *The Commanders: Australian Military Leadership in the Twentieth Century*, Allen & Unwin, Sydney, 1984, pp. 13–25.

3 The Enigma: General Sir Cyril Brudenell Bingham White
Peter Stanley

1 'Tiny Victorian town hosts military ceremony to honour "forgotten" war hero', ABC News, <www.abc.net.au/news/2015-09-27/victorian-town-honours-war-hero-general-white/680872>, accessed 5 January 2016.
2 C.E.W. Bean, *Two Men I Knew: William Bridges and Brudenell White Founders of the A.I.F.*, Angus & Robertson, Sydney, 1957; R. Derham, *The Silence Ruse: Escape from Gallipoli*, Oryx Publishing, Melbourne, 2000; M. Derham, *Brudenell White: An AIF Legend*, Oryx Publishing, Melbourne, 2015.
3 J. Bentley, 'Champion of Anzac: General Sir Brudenell White, the First Australian Imperial Force and the emergence of the Australian military culture 1914–18', PhD, University of Wollongong, 2003.
4 G. Verney, 'General Sir Brudenell White: The Staff Officer as Commander', in D. Horner (ed.), *The Commanders: Australian Military Leadership in the Twentieth Century*, Allen & Unwin, Sydney, 1984, pp. 26–43; J. Grey, 'Sir Cyril

Brudenell White (1876–1940), *Australia Dictionary of Biography*, Vol. 12, <adb.anu.edu.au/biography/white-sir-cyril-brudenell-1032>, accessed 5 January 2016. Verney's essay came out of research he conducted for his thesis 'The Army High Command and Australian Defence Policy, 1901–1918', PhD thesis, University of Sydney, 1982, the research papers for which he donated to the Australian War Memorial (AWM) as Series PR85/083.
5   Bean, *Two Men I Knew*, pp. 80–1.
6   *Ibid.*, pp. 12–13.
7   Bentley, 'Champion of Anzac', p. 95, quoting the *Herald* (Melbourne), 16 March 1940.
8   Bean, *Two Men I Knew*, p. xii.
9   J. Mordike, *An Army for a Nation: A History of Australian Military Developments 1880–1914*, Allen & Unwin, Sydney, 1992, p. 197, quoting White to Hutton, 3 September 1908, in the Hutton Papers in the British Library.
10 G. Serle, *John Monash: A Biography*, Melbourne University Press, Melbourne, 2002, p. 190.
11 Even as his admirers extol White as a gentleman they reveal behaviour that would seem to contradict his reputation for probity. Bentley reveals that he was engaged simultaneously to Amy Ricardo and to Ethel Davidson (whom he married after extricating himself from the entanglement). So much, Bentley concedes, for the maxims of 1895 ('never telling a lie' and 'being straightforward').
12 Mordike, *An Army for a Nation*, pp. 239–42.
13 C.D. (Coulthard-)Clark, *A Heritage of Spirit: A Biography of Major-General Sir William Throsby Bridges*, Melbourne University Press, Melbourne, 1979, pp. 146–7.
14 D. Winter, *25 April 1915: The Inevitable Tragedy*, University of Queensland Press, St Lucia, 1994, p. 226; sourced to 'AWM38/606/5' – actually Australian War Memorial (AWM) 38, 3DRL 606/5/1, Diary, Charles Bean, April–May 1915.
15 Bentley, 'Champion of Anzac', p. 203, quoting Bean, *Two Men I Knew*, p. 96 and J.L. Treloar, *An Anzac Diary*, Alan Treloar, Armidale, 1993, p. 142.
16 Birdwood to Munro Ferguson, 17 May 1915, Birdwood Papers, AWM, 3DRL3376, 31; quoted in Bentley, 'Champion of Anzac', p. 217. Note that Bentley incorrectly but consistently renders Munro Ferguson as 'Munro-Ferguson'.
17 P. Sadler, *The Paladin: A Life of Major General Sir John Gellibrand*, Allen & Unwin, Sydney, 2000, pp. 73–5.
18 M. Derham, *Brudenell White: An AIF Legend*, Oryx Publishing, Melbourne, 2015, p. 43.
19 'Note on the Withdrawal from Anzac', Folio 1, Box 7, AWM4/3, 3 DRL/1400.
20 'Dardanelles Operations Evacuation of Anzac and Suvla', The National Archives (UK), Series WO158, Item 580.
21 A. Hill, *Chauvel of the Light Horse*, Melbourne University Press, Melbourne, 1979, p. 62.
22 Bean, *Two Men I Knew*, p. 124.

23 P. Pedersen, *Monash as Military Commander*, Melbourne University Press, Melbourne, 1985, p. 133.
24 Bentley, 'Champion of Anzac', p. 274, quoting letter Brudenell White to Ethel White, 24 April 1916. (The letter was cited to 'in possession of Lady Rosemary Derham' but is now presumably in the collection of the National Library of Australia (NLA)).
25 Bean, *Two Men I Knew*, p. 130.
26 As White's account makes clear, the celebrated drip guns were 'fired after the men had finally left the trenches' – that is, after the evacuation had actually succeeded ('Note on the Withdrawal from Anzac', Appendix II, Box 7, AWM 4/3, 3 DRL/1400).
27 'General Sir Brudenell White by Field Marshal Sir William Birdwood of Anzac', AWM 2DRL 1212.
28 The episode is described in Bean's official history (Vol. III, p. 633), his *Two Men I Knew* (p. 137) and in many subsequent secondary sources, including Bentley, 'Champion of Anzac', pp. 310–11. Haig's phrase comes from his diary, 2 September 1916; Gary Sheffield and John Bourne (eds), *Douglas Haig: War Diaries and Letters*, Weidenfeld & Nicolson, London, 2005, p. 225.
29 Bentley, 'Champion of Anzac', p. 311.
30 C.D. (Coulthard-)Clark, *No Australian Need Apply: The Troubled Career of Lieutenant-General Gordon Legge*, Allen & Unwin, Sydney, 1988, p. 157.
31 Bean, *Two Men I Knew*, p. 149.
32 M. Hampton, *Attack on the Somme: 1st Anzac Corps and the Battle of Pozières Ridge, 1916*, Helion, Solihull, 2016, pp. 171–3.
33 P. Pedersen, *Monash as Military Commander*, p. 298; quoted in M. Derham, *Brudenell White*, p. 49.
34 White to Gellibrand, 8 June 1917, Brudenell White, NLA, MS 5172/2.4/27.
35 Sadler, *The Paladin*, p. 139.
36 'German Withdrawal, 1st Anzac Corps', AWM 26, 152/8, 153/1, 153/2.
37 Bean, *The Story of Anzac*, Vol. I, p. 74.
38 R. McMullin, *Pompey Elliott*, Scribe, Melbourne, 2008, p. 437.
39 Ibid., pp. 427–9.
40 Bean, *Two Men I Knew*, p. xi.
41 J.D. Millar, 'A Study in the Limitations of Command: General Sir William Birdwood and the AIF, 1914–1918', PhD thesis, UNSW, Canberra, 1993, p. 113.
42 White to Bean, 17 June 1932, Brudenell White, NLA, MS5172/2.4/27, Box 33.
43 White to Bazley, 14 June 1935, Brudenell White, NLA, MS5172/2.4/27, Box 33.
44 White to Bean to White, 17 June 1932, Brudenell White, NLA MS5172/2.4/27, Box 33.
45 For example, the papers of Brigadier-General Ramsay McNicoll suggest that the corps commander's chief of staff did not impinge upon even a brigade commander's life. In his biography of Sir William Glasgow, who commanded the 13th Brigade, Peter Edgar does not mention White, and in his study of the 13th Brigade White appears once, when he visited Glasgow's headquarters: P. Edgar, *Sir William Glasgow: Soldier, Senator and Diplomat*, Big Sky

Publishing, Newport, 2011; P. Edgar, *To Villers-Bretonneux with Brigadier-General William Glasgow, DSO*, privately published, 1998.
46 R. Derham, *The Silence Ruse*, p. 231.
47 *Ibid.*, p. 53.
48 Brudenell White diary, 3 May 1917, AWM 1/25, 3DRL/1400, Box 3.
49 C.E.W. Bean, 'Celebrities of the A.I.F. (8): Cyril Brudenell White', *Reveille*, 31 March 1931, p. 15.
50 Bentley, 'Champion of Anzac', p. viii.
51 *Ibid.*, p. 115.
52 Verney, 'General Sir Brudenell White', in Horner, *The Commanders*, pp. 42–3.

4 Not Up to the Job?
Major-General Gordon Legge
Chris Clark

1 P. Edgar, *Sir William Glasgow: Soldier, Senator and Diplomat*, Big Sky Publishing, Newport, NSW, 2011, p. 222.
2 C.D. (Coulthard-)Clark, *No Australian Need Apply: The Troubled Career of Lieutenant-General Gordon Legge*, Allen & Unwin, Sydney, 1988, pp. 15–17.
3 Clark, *No Australian Need Apply*, pp. 5, 7–8.
4 *Ibid.*, pp. 6–7.
5 USI NSW *Journal and Proceedings*, 1897, pp. 19–35, 46–7; *Sydney Morning Herald*, 22 October 1897, p. 3.
6 USI NSW *Journal and Proceedings*, 1899, pp. 1–22; *Sydney Morning Herald*, 29 August 1899, p. 6.
7 Claim made not in 1899 but in the *Bulletin* (Sydney), 27 May 1915, p. 7.
8 Clark, *No Australian Need Apply*, pp. 24–5.
9 B.H. Travers, *William Holmes: Secretary and Soldier*, Echo Books, Canberra, 2016, pp. 125–8, 526.
10 C. Wilcox, *Australia's Boer War: The War in South Africa 1899–1902*, Oxford University Press, South Melbourne, 2002, p. 160.
11 Wilcox, *Australia's Boer War*, pp. 214, 381.
12 *Reveille*, 1 June 1938, p. 8.
13 Clark, *No Australian Need Apply*, pp. 40–1.
14 NSW *State Reports*, 1904, pp. 297–316.
15 USI NSW *Journal and Proceedings*, 1905, pp. 87–99.
16 Ewing to Bridges, 19 June 1907, National Australian Archives (NAA), Series MP84/1, Item 1856/4/4.
17 Clark, *No Australian Need Apply*, p. 46.
18 *Commonwealth Parliamentary Debates*, vol. 17, pp. 7527–36.
19 Bridges to Hutton, 17 December 1907, *Hutton Papers*, Vol. 7, MS 50/089, pp. 58–9.
20 *Punch* (Melbourne), 26 January 1911, p. 112.

21 C.E.W. Bean, *Two Men I Knew: William Bridges and Brudenell White, Founders of the A.I.F.*, Angus & Robertson, Sydney, 1957, pp. xii–xiii.
22 Clark, *No Australian Need Apply*, pp. 49, 52.
23 *Ibid.*, pp. 52–53.
24 C. (Coulthard-)Clark, *Breaking Free: Transforming Australia's Defence Industry*, Australian Scholarly Publishing, Melbourne, 1999, pp. 10–13.
25 Wallack to Bridges, 29 September 1909, letter formerly in possession of Mr C.W. Bridges-Maxwell of Bellevue Hill, NSW (now deceased).
26 Clark, *No Australian Need Apply*, pp. 56–7.
27 *Commonwealth Parliamentary Papers*, 1910, vol. II, pp. 83–104.
28 Minute, Legge to Secretary, Department of Defence, 12 November 1910, NAA, B197, 1804/1/7.
29 Clark, *No Australian Need Apply*, pp. 62, 66–8, 216–21.
30 *Ibid.*, pp. 78–9.
31 Clark, *No Australian Need Apply*, pp. 76–7.
32 *Age* (Melbourne), *Argus* (Melbourne), *Sydney Morning Herald*, 10 August 1914.
33 *Argus*, 10 August 1914, p. 8.
34 *Sydney Morning Herald*, 10 September 1914, p. 8.
35 G. Verney, 'The Army High Command and Australian Defence Policy, 1901–1918', PhD thesis, University of Sydney, 1985, p. 177.
36 Clark, *No Australian Need Apply*, pp. 92–7, 175–6.
37 *Ibid.*, pp. 98–102.
38 M. Hampton, *Attack on the Somme: 1st Anzac Corps and the Battle of Pozières Ridge, 1916*, Helion Publishing, Solihull, 2016, chapters 2 and 6.
39 R. Blake (ed.), *The Private Papers of Douglas Haig 1914–1919*, Eyre & Spottiswoode, London, 1952, p. 155.
40 Telegram: Legge to Birdwood, 27 January 1917, AWM 3DRL/3376, Birdwood papers, 9/3d.
41 Clark, *No Australian Need Apply*, pp. 167–9.
42 Clark, *No Australian Need Apply*, pp. 178–85; C.D. (Coulthard-)Clark, *The Third Brother: the Royal Australian Air Force 1921–39*, Allen & Unwin, 1991, North Sydney, chapter 1.
43 Clark, *No Australian Need Apply*, pp. 189–91.
44 *Ibid.*, 196–200.
45 *Ibid.*, pp. 201–12.
46 *Military Order*, No. 62 of 1924.
47 Chris (Coulthard-)Clark, *Duntroon: The Royal Military College of Australia, 1911–1986*, Allen & Unwin, North Sydney, 1986, p. 113.

5 The Soldier as Technocrat: Brigadier John William Alexander O'Brien
Jeffrey Grey

1. D.P. Mellor, *The Role of Science and Industry*, G. Long (ed.), *Australia in the War of 1939–1945, Series 4: Civil*, Vol. 5, Australian War Memorial, Canberra, 1958, pp. 24–5.
2. A.J. Sweeting, 'O'Brien, John William Alexander', *Australian Dictionary of Biography*, Vol. 15, Melbourne University Press, Melbourne, 2000. G. Rimmer, *In Time for War: Pages from the Life of the Boy Brigadier*, Mulavon, West Ryde, 1991, offers a biography heavily based on O'Brien's extensive personal diaries and correspondence.
3. His extensive service dossier is at NAA, B883, VX15127.
4. Rimmer, *In Time for War*, pp. 65–6.
5. *Ibid.*, p. 67.
6. *Ibid.*, p. 103.
7. Mellor, *The Role of Science and Industry*, p. 239.
8. Rimmer, *In Time for War*, p. 69.
9. Mellor, *The Role of Science and Industry*, pp. 550–72, devotes an entire chapter to the issue.
10. Rimmer, *In Time for War*, pp. 95–6.
11. *Ibid.*, p. 104.
12. *Ibid.*, p. 107.
13. Mellor, *The Role of Science and Industry*, p. 453.
14. Rimmer, *In Time for War*, p. 109.
15. *Ibid.*, pp. 114–15.
16. Takemae Eiji, *Inside GHQ: The Allied Occupation of Japan*, Continuum, New York, 2002, p. 179.
17. There are numerous references to O'Brien's role in B.C. Dees, *The Allied Occupation and Japan's Economic Miracle: Building the Foundations of Japan's Science and Technology, 1945–1952*, Routledge, New York, 2013. See Rimmer, *In Time for War*, pp. 159–75.
18. Rimmer, *In Time for War*, p. 117.
19. *Ibid.*, pp. 117–18.

6 The Quiet Achiever: Lieutenant-General Sir John Northcott
Robert Stevenson

1. *Graduation List of Officers of the Australian Military Forces*, Vol. 1, The Active List, Wilke & Co. Pty Ltd Printers, Melbourne, 7 March 1946, p. 1.
2. J. Hetherington, *Blamey, a Controversial Soldier: A biography of Field Marshall Sir Thomas Blamey, GBE, KCB, CMG, DSO, ED*, Australian War Memorial

(AWM) and the Australian Government Publishing Service, Canberra, 1973; D.M. Horner, *Blamey: The Commander-in-Chief*, Allen & Unwin, Sydney, 1988; B. Lodge, *Lavarack: Rival General*, Allen & Unwin, St Leonards, 1998; I.D. Chapman, *Iven G. Mackay Citizen and Soldier*, Melway Publishing, Melbourne, 1975; D.M. Horner, 'Lieutenant-General Sir Vernon Sturdee: The Chief of the General Staff as Commander', D.M. Horner (ed.), *The Commanders: Australian Military Leadership in the Twentieth Century*, George Allen & Unwin, Sydney, 1984, pp. 143–58.

3   Unlike some of the subjects in this volume, Northcott has no substantial biography and secondary material on his life is limited to an entry in the *Australian Dictionary of Biography* (*ADB*) and an article published in the *Australian Army Journal* (*AAJ*). Fortunately he did leave a collection of personal papers in the State Library of New South Wales (SLNSW), while his army personnel file is available at the National Archives of Australia (NAA). H.J. Coates, 'Northcott, Sir John (1890–1966)', *ADB*, Vol. 15, Melbourne University Press, Melbourne, 2000, pp. 493–4; L.E. Beavis, 'General Northcott: A Wartime Chief of Staff', *AAJ*, No. 215 (April 1967), pp. 3–11; SLNSW: Sir John Northcott Papers ML MSS1431; NAA: Series B2458, Item 32.

4   NAA: B2458, 32; Beavis, 'General Northcott', p. 3.

5   Secondary and tertiary educations were considered luxuries at this time with just 6.5 per cent of males aged between 15 and 19 remaining in full-time education. C. Campbell and H. Proctor, *A History of Australian Schooling*, Allen & Unwin, Crows Nest, 2014, p. 108.

6   Coates, 'Northcott, Sir John (1890–1966)', p. 493.

7   L.M. Newton, *The Story of the Twelfth*, John Burridge Military Antiques, Swanbourne, 2000, p. 42.

8   Northcott was joined in Britain by his fiancée, Winifred Paton, who travelled from Australia to join him. The pair married on 14 September 1915 at the parish church in Oxted, Surrey, NAA: B2458, 32.

9   Beavis, 'General Northcott', p. 5; NAA: B2458, 32.

10 Honorary major (A&I Staff) dated 1 January 1919, brevet major (A&I Staff) 1 January 1920, brevet major (Staff Corps) 1 October 1920, and substantive major (Staff Corps) 1 October 1923. NAA: B2458, 32.

11 A.R. Godwin-Austen, *The Staff and the Staff College*, Constable and Company, London, 1927, p. 286.

12 Major-General E. Ironside, 'Confidential Report Staff College', 1 December 1926, Australian War Memnorial (AWM), Series 182, Item A1.

13 Australian CGS letters January 1934–February 1940, NAA: A6828.

14 Major-General Charles 'Digger' Brand, CB CMG DSO (1873–1961), Australian-born regular army officer, served in the Anglo–Boer War, as Commanding Officer 8th Battalion, AIF (1915–16), Commander 4th Infantry Brigade, AIF (1916–18) and as a post-war politician.

15 'Report of the Committee appointed to investigate the Mechanisation of the AMF', nd [June 1928]; Military Board agenda, 51/1928, 20 June 1928, both NAA: A2653, 1928, vol. 1.

16 On AMF's interwar mechanisation efforts see James Morrison, *Mechanising an Army: Mechanisation Policy and Conversion of Light Horse 1923–1940*, Land Warfare Studies Centre (LWSC), Study Paper No. 307, LWSC, Duntroon, June 2006; R.N.L. Hopkins, *Australian Armour: A History of the Royal Australian Armoured Corps 1927–1972*, Royal Armoured Corps Tank Museum, Puckapunyal, 1993, pp. 13–32.
17 Promotion to brevet lieutenant-colonel (Staff Corps) dated 1 July 1935, to substantive lieutenant-colonel (Staff Corps) 1 January 1936, NAA: B2458, 32.
18 IDC was open to officers of the three British uniformed services and the Civil Service, and also to small numbers of dominion officers. Usually the Australian quota of two officers per year was not filled. The other Australian Army IDC attendees were John Lavarack, Henry Wynter, Vernon Sturdee, Sydney Rowell and William Bridgeford. Lodge, *Lavarack*, p. 5; D.M. Horner, *High Command: Australia and Allied Strategy 1939–1945*, AWM and George Allen & Unwin, Canberra and Sydney, 1982, p. 12.
19 Major-General Leslie Beavis, CB CBE DSO psc (1895–1975), Australian-born regular army officer, served as Director of Ordnance Services, AIF (1940–42), Master-General of the Ordnance, AMF (1942–46) and as Australian High Commissioner to Pakistan (1952–54).
20 Beavis, 'General Northcott', p. 6.
21 Northcott, IDC paper 'Imperial Defence', SLNSW: ML MSS 1431/28.
22 Beavis, 'General Northcott', p. 6.
23 D.M. Horner, *Defence Supremo: Sir Frederick Shedden and the Making of Australian Defence Policy*, Allen & Unwin, St Leonards, 2000.
24 Sir Robert Archdale Parkhill, KCMG (1878–1947), Australian-born politician, served as Minister for Home Affairs (1932), Minister for the Interior (1932), Post-Master General (1932–34) and Minister for Defence (1934–37). Parkhill has been described as not 'a brilliant minister' but 'certainly the best among those who held the defence portfolio in the interwar years', J. McCarthy, *Australia and Imperial Defence 1918–39: A Study in Air and Sea Power*, University of Queensland Press, St Lucia, 1976, p. 83.
25 The Lavarack–Parkhill incident is covered in Horner, *Defence Supremo*, p. 48; Lodge, *Lavarack*, p. 53.
26 Promotion to brevet colonel (Staff Corps) dated 1 July 1937, substantive colonel (Staff Corps) 13 October 1939, NAA: B2458, 32.
27 J. Grey, *The Australian Army*, Oxford University Press, South Melbourne, 2001, p. 97; Hopkins, *Australian Armour*, pp. 26–7.
28 Local promotion to major-general (Staff Corps) dated 13 October 1939, substantive promotion 1 July 1940, NAA: B2458, 32.
29 Beavis, 'General Northcott', p. 6.
30 C.E.W. Bean, *Two Men I Knew*, Angus & Robertson, Sydney, 1957, p. 203.
31 D.M. Horner, *Inside the War Cabinet: Directing Australia's War Effort 1939–45*, Allen & Unwin, St Leonards, 1996, pp. 9–10.
32 C. Edwards, *Bruce of Melbourne, Man of Two Worlds*, Heinemann, London, 1965, p. 284.
33 Casey, Cable C4 to Menzies, 5 November 1939, NAA: A2671, 34/1939.
34 Northcott, Cable C7 to Squires, 6 November, NAA: A2671, 34/1939.

35 Beavis, 'General Northcott', p. 8.
36 The Defence Committee normally comprised the Chiefs of Staff of the three uniformed services and a representative of the Secretary of the Department of Defence, Frederick Shedden. When the Chiefs met without the Secretary's representative the meeting was known as the Chief of Staff Committee. Horner, *Inside the War Cabinet*, p. 10.
37 The War Cabinet was responsible for directing Australia's war effort. The formation of the War Cabinet was announced on 15 September 1939 and it comprised the Prime Minister along with the ministers for Supply, Defence, Commerce, Information and the Attorney-General. Shedden was dual 'hatted' as Secretary of the Department of Defence and Secretary of the War Cabinet. The Chiefs of Staff were only invited to attend the War Cabinet in an advisory capacity on matters concerning the military conduct of the war. Horner, *Inside the War Cabinet*, pp. 2–3.
38 Record of Decisions of Full Cabinet, 20 November 1939, NAA: A5954/46, 803/1.
39 Squires, Signal to Northcott, 21 November 1939, NAA: A5954/69, 582/2; 'Report by the Military Board on the Raising of a Special Force for Continuous service Either in Australia or Overseas', 13 September 1939, NAA: A2653/1, 1939, vol. 3.
40 The Singapore strategy was a naval defence policy of the British Empire that evolved in a series of war plans between 1919 and 1941. It aimed to deter Japanese aggression by stationing a Royal Navy fleet in the Far East, based at Singapore. Peter Dennis, 'Australia and the Singapore Strategy', in B.P. Farrell and S. Hunter (eds), *The Great Betrayal?: The Fall of Singapore Revisited*, Marshall Cavendish Editions, Singapore, 2010, pp. 20–31.
41 Statement by the Right Honourable the Prime Minister, House of Representatives, 29 November 1939, NAA: CRS A816/1, 52/302/135,
42 V. Schofield, *Wavell: Soldier and Statesman*, John Murray, London, 2006.
43 Northcott quoted in Bean, *Two Men I Knew*, p. 224 fn. 3.
44 Bean, *Two Men I Knew*, p. 218.
45 *Ibid.*, pp. 220–1.
46 Vasey letter to wife, 15 August 1940, quoted in D.M. Horner, *General Vasey's War*, Melbourne University Press, Carlton, 1992, p. 67.
47 The raising of the AIF's 7th Division was announced on 28 February 1940, the 8th Division on 22 May 1940, the 9th Division in early June 1940 and the 1st Armoured Division on 1 January 1941. A. Palazzo, *The Australian Army: A History of its Organisation 1901–2001*, Oxford University Press, South Melbourne, 2001, pp. 144–5.
48 F.R. Sinclair, Memorandum SS.1823 'Major-General J. Northcott – Deputy Chief of the General Staff to Secretary Department of the Army', 4 October 1940, AWM182, 1A.
49 Shedden, Memorandum to Secretary Department of the Army, 4 October 1940, NAA: MP729/6, 2/401/15.)
50 Report of Singapore Defence Conference – Review by Chief of Staff, 16 November 1940, NAA: A2671/1, item 254/1940.

51 War Cabinet Minute 632, 26 November 1940, NAA: A5954/46, 804/2. The Advisory War Council was an initiative of Menzies who, in the absence of a bipartisan government, formed the Council to include the War Cabinet and members of the political Opposition. Horner, *Inside the War Cabinet*, p. 6.
52 Churchill, Cable 510 to Menzies, 23 December 1940, NAA: A2671, 254/1940.
53 War Cabinet Minute 689, 8 January 1941, NAA: A5954 805/1, folio 516.
54 *Ibid.*
55 Hopkins, *Australian Armour*, p. 61.
56 P. Beale, *Fallen Sentinel: Australian Tanks in World War II*, Big Sky Publishing, Newport, 2011, p. 98.
57 War Cabinet Agendum 150/1940, NAA: A2671, no identifying number.
58 Hopkins, *Australian Armour*, p. 63.
59 Northcott, Minute to Fitzgerald (Secretary, Department of the Army), 20 March 1941, NAA: MP729/6, 50/401/144.
60 Command of the 9th Division went to Leslie Morshead. B. Maughan, *Tobruk and El Alamein*, G. Long (ed.), *Australia in the War of 1939–1945, Series 1: Army*, Vol. 3, AWM, Canberra, 1966, p. 8.
61 S.F. Rowell, *Full Circle*, Melbourne University Press, Carlton, 1974, p. 98. Lieutenant-General Sir Sydney Fairburn Rowell, KBE CB (1894–1975), Australian-born regular army officer. He and Northcott shared similar experiences during the First World War, with Rowell being invalided from Gallipoli in November 1915. In the interwar period Rowell followed Northcott to Britain in 1925 to attend staff college, again in 1935 as an exchange officer, and succeeding him as DCGS in 1941. D.M. Horner, 'Lieutenant-General Sir Sydney Rowell: Dismissal of a Corps Commander', in Horner (ed.), *The Commanders*, pp. 225–43.
62 'The Formation of an Armoured Division', 13 November 1940, NAA: MP729/6, 37/401/228.
63 Hopkins, *Australian Armour*, pp. 81, 88–89.
64 *Ibid.*, p. 50.
65 Substantive promotion to major-general (AIF) dated 1 September 1941, NAA: B2458, 32.
66 NAA: B2458, 32; Frank Legg, *The Gordon Bennett Story*, Angus & Robertson, Sydney, 1965, p. 196.
67 Northcott letter N3/1/9 to HQ Home Forces, 27 January 1942, AWM54, 44/1/4.
68 Lieutenant-General Sir Horace Clement Hugh Robertson, KBE DSO psc (1894–1960), Australian-born regular officer, commanded 19th Brigade (1940–41), returned to Australia where he was involved in the so-called 'revolt of the generals' against Blamey, served as GOC 1st Armoured Division (1942–43), GOC 5th Division (1945), GOC 6th Division (1945), and succeeded Northcott as C-in-C BCOF (1946–50) and later served as C-in-C British Commonwealth Forces, Korea (1950–51). Jeffrey Grey, *Australian Brass: The Career of Lieutenant General Sir Horace Robertson*, Cambridge University Press, New York, 1992, pp. 95–6, 100. On the 1st Armoured Division see Z. Lambert, 'The Birth, Life and Death of the 1st Australian Armoured Division', *AAJ*, vol. IX, No. 1 (Autumn 2012), pp. 89–103.

69 Hopkins, *Australian Armour*, p. 94.
70 P. Handel, *The Vital Factor: A History of the 2/6th Australian Armoured Regiment 1941–1946*, Australian Military History Publications, Loftus, 2004, pp. 25, 38, 45, 48.
71 *Ibid.*, pp. 125–52; Beale, *Fallen Sentinel*, p. 164; D. McCarthy, *South-West Pacific Area First Year*, G. Long (ed.), *Australia in the War of 1939–1945*, Series 1: Army, Vol. 5, AWM, Canberra, 1959, pp. 363, 452.
72 Temporary promotion to lieutenant-general (AIF) dated 6 April 1942, substantive promotion to lieutenant-general (Staff Corps), 1 December 1945, and substantive promotion to lieutenant-general (AIF) 6 December 1946, NAA: B2458, 32.
73 Hopkins, *Australian Armour*, p. 95; Palazzo, *The Australian Army*, pp. 170–1.
74 Horner, *General Vasey's War*, p. 178; Stuart Sayers, *Ned Herring: A Life of Sir Edmund Herring KCMG, KBE, DSO, MC, ED, KStJ, MA DCL*, Hyland House in association with the AWM, Melbourne/Canberra, 1980, p. 210.
75 NAA: B2458, 32.
76 Blamey quoted in 'High Tributes to General Northcott', *Argus* (Melbourne), 1 April 1946, p. 2.
77 Beavis, 'General Northcott', p. 10.
78 *Ibid.*, pp. 8–9.
79 Blamey letter to Curtin, 24 September 1942, Blamey papers 23.81.
80 Blamey letter to Curtin, 8 October 1942, SLNSW: ML MSS1431/14; Hetherington, *Blamey, Controversial Soldier*, p. 299.
81 Northcott demi official letter CGS 54 to Sturdee, 21 November 1942, p. 3, AWM113, MH 1/87.
82 Northcott letter CGS 115 to senior Australian army commanders, 6 April 1944, SLNSW: ML MSS1431, 14 (CY Real 3072).
83 'High Tributes to General Northcott', *Argus* (Melbourne), 1 April 1946, p. 2.
84 Interview with Berryman, Sydney, May 1952, AWM172, 70. Lieutenant-General Sir Frank Berryman, KCVO CB DSO psc (1894–1981), Australian-born regular army officer, served as Commander Royal Artillery 7th Division (1941), Brigadier General Staff I Corps (1941–42), Major-General General Staff First Army (1942), DCGS (1942), Chief of Staff New Guinea Force (1942–43), GOC II and I Corps (1943–44), and Chief-of-Staff Advanced Land Headquarters (1944–45).
85 P. Dean, *The Architect of Victory: The Military Career of Lieutenant-General Sir Frank Horton Berryman*, Cambridge University Press, Port Melbourne, 2011, p. 171.
86 Blamey letter to Northcott, 7 December 1942, SLNSW: ML MSS1431/14.
87 Dunstan to Rowell, 29 September 1942, Rowell papers, 9, AWM: 3DRL6763.
88 Beavis, 'General Northcott', p. 10.
89 Northcott demi official letter CGS 54 to Sturdee, 21 November 1942, p. 3. AWM113, MH 1/87.
90 Northcott letter to Blamey, 7 November 1942, SLNSW: ML MSS1431/14.
91 Blamey letter to Northcott, 14 November 1942, SLNSW: ML MSS1431/14.
92 Blamey minute to Northcott, 14 November 1942, SLNSW: ML MSS1431/14.

NOTES

93 Northcott letter CGS 53 to Blamey, 19 November 1942, SLNSW: ML MSS1431/14.
94 Hopkins, *Australian Armour*, pp. 50–51.
95 *Ibid.*, p. 51.
96 'Re-organization of Infantry Formations in the AMF', 13 February 1943, AWM54, 721/2/11.
97 *Ibid.*, pp. 2, 4. On the development of the jungle fighting army see A. Threlfall, *Jungle Warriors: From Tobruk to Kokoda and Beyond, How the Australian Army Became the World's Most Deadly Jungle Fighting Force*, Allen & Unwin, Crows Nest, 2014.
98 Northcott letter A12/1943 to Sturdee, 21 December 1943, p. 3, AWM113, MH 1/87. Northcott visited the South-West Pacific theatre eight times between October 1942 and October 1945. NAA: B2458, 32.
99 Beavis, 'General Northcott', p. 9.
100 This issue is discussed in P. Hasluck, *The Government and the People, 1942–1945*, G. Long (ed.), *Australia in the War of 1939–1945, Series 4: Civil*, Vol. 2, AWM, Canberra, 1970, pp. 371–442; Horner, *Inside the War Cabinet*, pp. 150–63; Palazzo, *The Australian Army*, pp. 172–8.
101 'Review of the War Effort of the Services in Light of the Present Situation With Particular Reference to the Provision Being Made for the Defence of the Mainland', March 1944, NAA: A5954/1, 309/2.
102 J. Robertson, *Australia at War, 1939–45*, William Heinemann, Melbourne, 1981, pp. 159–60.
103 Northcott, letter A5/1944 to Lieutenant-General E.K. Smart, 25 May 1944, p. 2, AWM113, MH 1/88, part 2.
104 'The Australian Direct War Effort', 14 June 1945, AWM: 3DRL6643, 2/23.12.
105 This incident is related in Beavis, 'General Northcott', p. 10.
106 G. Long, *The Final Campaigns*, in G. Long (ed.), *Australia in the War of 1939–1945, Series 1: Army*, Vol. 7, AWM, Canberra, 1963, p. 73.
107 *Ibid.*, p. 581.
108 Northcott, letter to Rowell, 30 October 1945, SLNSW: ML MSS1431. Dr Herbert Vere Evatt (1894–1965), Australian-born Labor politician and High Court judge, served as Attorney-General and Minister for External Affairs (1941–49).
109 War Cabinet Minute 4400, 19 September 1945, NAA: A2671, 426/1945.
110 Horner, *Defence Supremo*, p. 233.
111 'Northcott as Leader in Japan', *Courier-Mail* (Brisbane), 31 October 1945, p. 2.
112 R.J. Bell, *Unequal Allies: Australian-American Relations and the Pacific War*, Melbourne University Press, Carlton, 1977, p. 195; Grey, *Australian Brass*, pp. 129–31.
113 'Plan for a British Commonwealth Force to Participate in the Occupation of Japan', Joint Chiefs of Staff in Australia, Melbourne, 15 May 1946, AWM114, 422/7/8 (hereafter 'Plan for BCOF').
114 A. Bryant, *Triumph in the West 1943–1946*, Collins, London, 1959, pp. 512, 514; Auchinleck letter to Mountbatten, 14 October 1945, Auchinleck papers, item 1104, John Rylands Library, University of Manchester, quoted in Grey, *The Australian Army*, p. 164.

115 B2458, 32; P. Bates, *Japan and the British Commonwealth Occupation Force 1946–1952*, Brassey's, London, 1993, pp. 13–16; J. Wood, *The Forgotten Force: The Australian Contribution to the Occupation of Japan, 1945–1952*, Allen & Unwin, Sydney, 1998, p. 52.
116 'Directive to the Commander-in-Chief, British Commonwealth Occupation Forces in Japan', AWM114, 376/2/4.
117 'Plan for BCOF', AWM114, 422/7/8.
118 'BCOF Working Smoothly Says C-in-C. Co-Operation Speaks Well for Future', *Argus* (Melbourne), 6 May 1946, p. 20.
119 Ibid.
120 Rowell, *Full Circle*, pp. 161–2.
121 Private Ronald Govey, transcript of oral history recording, Kure, Japan, 13 February 1947, AWM: S00016.
122 Grey, *Australian Brass*, p. 133.
123 'Plan for BCOF', p. iii, AWM114, 422/7/8.
124 'New State Governor Gen. Northcott Appointed', *Sydney Morning Herald*, 1 April 1946, p. 1; NAA: B2458, 32.
125 Coates, 'Northcott, Sir John (1890–1966)', p. 494. In addition to being a state Governor, Northcott was appointed as Administrator filling in for Sir William McKell for five months as Governor-General in 1951 and again for nearly three months in 1956 for Sir William Slim. C.D. (Coulthard-)Clark, *Soldiers in Politics: The Impact of the Military on Australian Political Life and Institutions*, Allen & Unwin, St Leonards, 1996, p. 60.
126 'State Funeral for Sir John Northcott', *Canberra Times*, 6 August 1966, p. 4.
127 NAA: B2458, 32.
128 Rowell, *Full Circle*, pp. 98, 162.
129 Beavis, 'General Northcott', p. 10.
130 'Unveiling By Gen. Northcott', *Canberra Times*, 23 November 1963, p. 3; Beale, *Fallen Sentinel*, p. 143; Hopkins, *Australian Armour*, p. 225.
131 P. Handel, *Fifty Years of the Royal Australian Armoured Corps*, Royal Australian Armoured Corps Memorial and Army Tank Museum, Puckapunyal, nd, p. 74; Handel, *The Vital Factor*, dedication.
132 The tank was removed and placed in the collection of the Australian War Memorial.

7 Fall and Rise:
Lieutenant-General Sir Sydney Rowell
Karl James

1 Cablegram, part B of 2117, Blamey to Prime Minister John Curtin and General Douglas MacArthur, 28 September 1942, Australian War Memorial (AWM), AWM67 11/2.
2 Rowell letter to CGS, 14 October 1942; Blamey letter to Curtin, 1 October 1942, AWM: AWM67 11/2.

NOTES

3. Blamey letter to Curtin, 27 December 1942, National Archives of Australia, (NAA), Canberra: A5954 266/1.
4. Cited in David Horner, 'Lieutenant-General Sir Sydney Rowell: Dismissal of a Corps Commander', in David Horner (ed.), *The Commanders: Australian Military Leadership in the Twentieth Century*, Allen & Unwin, Sydney, 1984, p. 228.
5. 'Who Will Be Australia's Atomic Age Army Chief', *News*, 29 August 1949.
6. See Horner, 'Lieutenant-General Sir Sydney Rowell', pp. 225–43; Dudley McCarthy, *South-West Pacific Area First Year: Kokoda to Wau*, AWM, Canberra, 1959, pp. 236–40; and John Hetherington, *Blamey, Controversial Solider: A Biography of Field Marshall Sir Thomas Blamey, GBE, KCB, CMG, DSO, ED*, AWM and the Australian Government Publishing Service, 1974, pp. 239–58.
7. Rowell also acknowledged Lieutenant-General Sir John Lavarack as a supporting influence. 'Remember the Blamey–Rowell "Trouble" during the War?', *Herald* (Melbourne), 23 November 1954.
8. S.F. Rowell, *Full Circle*, Melbourne University Press, Melbourne, 1974, p. 1.
9. Rowell, *Full Circle*, p. 39.
10. First report by Lieutenant-General E.K. Squires, Inspector-General of the Australian Military Forces, AWM: AWM54, 243/6/58.
11. Gavin Long diary, interview with Menzies, 20 June 1946, AWM: AWM67, 1/11.
12. Rowell letter to Long, 20 January 1947, AWM: AWM67, 3/338, part 2.
13. Rowell letter to Long, 20 December 1951, AWM: AWM67, 3/338, part 2.
14. Rowell letter to Long, 20 January 1947, AWM: AWM67, 3/338, part 2; Rowell interview with David Horner, 26 June 1974, AWM: S00346.
15. Cited in Horner, 'Lieutenant-General Sir Sydney Rowell', p. 226.
16. Cited in David Horner, *Blamey: The Commander-in-Chief*, Allen & Unwin, St Leonards, 1998, p. 199.
17. Rowell interview with Horner, 26 June 1974, AWM: S00346.
18. Sydney Rowell, 'General Sturdee and the Australian Army', *Australian Army Journal*, no. 207, 1966, p. 6.
19. Comments on history by Lieutenant-General V.A.H. Sturdee and Lieutenant-General S.F. Rowell, AWM: AWM67, 5/31.
20. Sturdee letter to A.J. Sweeting, 11 December 1956, AWM: AWM67, 3/384.
21. Command of Australian forces in Ambon; Rowell letter to Lieutenant-Colonel L.N. Roach, 14 January 1942, AWM: AWM54, 573/6/10.
22. David Horner, 'Lieutenant-General Sir Vernon Sturdee: The Chief of the General Staff as Commander', in Horner, *The Commanders*, pp. 156–8.
23. Rowell, *Full Circle*, p. 107.
24. Comments on draft chapters of the official history, Major-General B. Morris, p. 8, AWM: AWM67, 3/274.
25. Report on operations of the New Guinea Force, 11 August to 28 September 1942, p. 3, AWM: AWM123, 270.
26. Clowes letter to Rowell, 30 August 1942, AWM: 3DRL6763 (A), 3.
27. Vasey letter to Rowell, 28 August 1942, AWM: 3DRL6763 (A), 7.
28. Rowell letter to Vasey, 30 August 1942, AWM: 3DRL6763 (A), 7.
29. Rowell letter to Vasey, 8 September 1942, AWM: AWM54, 225/2/5.

30 'Defending Port Moresby', *Sydney Morning Herald*, 11 September 1942; 'Sold Buttons while Waiting for Moresby News', *The Australian Women's Weekly*, 26 September 1942.
31 'Tough Men, Tough Task', *Argus*, 16 September 1942.
32 Blamey letter to Rowell, 20 September 1942, AWM: 3DRL6763 (A), 7.
33 Rowell letter to William Dunstan VC, 24 September 1942, AWM: 3DRL6763, 9.
34 Rowell questionnaire on the Greek campaign, 20 January 1947, p. 10, AWM: AWM67, 3/338, part 2.
35 The irony of Blamey's remark was not lost on Lavarack given their own untrusting relationship. Lavarack diary, 28 October 1942, Lieutenant-General Sir John Lavarack papers, courtesy of James W. Lavarack and Peter J. Dean.
36 Horner, 'Lieutenant-General Sir Sydney Rowell', p. 242.
37 Interview, Rowell with Horner, 26 June 1974, AWM: S00346.
38 Rowell letter to Clowes, 28 September 1942, AWM: 3DRL6763 (A), 2.
39 Discussions with Commander-in-Chief, South-West Pacific Area, 20–26 October 1942, NAA: A5954, 266/1.
40 War Cabinet minute, 'Change in command in New Guinea Forces', 5 October 1942; Rowell letter to Shedden, 1 January 1943; and, Extract from Prime Minister's statement at secret session of Parliament, 8 October 1942, NAA: A5954, 266/1.
41 Cable Z134, Blamey to Shedden, 9 November 1942, NAA: A5954, 266/1.
42 War Cabinet minute 11 January 1944; Blamey letter to Curtin, 27 December 1942, NAA: A5954 266/1.
43 Case of Lieutenant-General Rowell, 26 January 1943, NAA: A5954 266/1.
44 Rowell letter to Shedden, 22 April 1943, NAA: A5954, 46/24.
45 Rowell letter to Long, 28 August 1943, AWM: AWM67, 3/338, part 2.
46 Blamey letter to Shedden, 10 August 1943, NAA: A5954, 46/24.
47 Rowell letter to Shedden, 26 August 1944, NAA: A5954, 46/24.
48 Rowell, *Full Circle*, p. 139.
49 Rowell, *Full Circle*, p. 159.
50 Sturdee letter to Forde, 29 November 1945, NAA, Melbourne: MP729/8, 2/431/32.
51 Sturdee minute to Forde, 9 January 1946, NAA, Melbourne: MP729/8, 2/431/44.
52 Sturdee minute to Forde, 9 January 1946, NAA, Melbourne: MP729/8, 2/431/44.
53 Sturdee letter to Forde, 29 November 1945, NAA, Melbourne: MP729/8, 2/431/32.
54 Post-war defence policy minute paper, 7 January 1944, NAA: A816, 14/301/275.
55 G. Sligo, 'The development of the Australian Regular Army, 1944–1952' in P. Dennis and J. Grey (eds), *The Second Fifty Years: The Australian Army 1947–1997*, Australian Defence Force Academy, Canberra, 1997, pp. 28–9.
56 The Post-War Army – Policy paper no. 1, 6 March 1946, NAA: A816/1, 52/301/245.

57 Rowell letter to Shedden, 26 July 1946, NAA: A5954, 69/11.
58 A. Palazzo, *The Australian Army: A History of its Organisation 1901–2001*, Oxford University Press, Melbourne, 2002, p. 204.
59 Summary of army post-war plan, 19 May 1947, AWM: AWM124, 5/94.
60 Rowell, *Full Circle*, p. 172.
61 Shedden letter to Rowell, 12 October 1949, NAA: A5954, 69/11.
62 Rowell, *Full Circle*, p. 196; Directorate of Army Public Relations, Retiring CGS reviews the army, 20 December 1954, p. 5, NAA: A816, 58/301/361.
63 Minutes of Council of Defence meeting, 20 April 1948, NAA: A9787, 111.
64 'Blunt Warning by General Rowell', *Advertiser*, 8 November 1948.
65 Australian Military Mission to Malaya, Report on Malaya July–August 1950, p. 1, AWM: AWM51, 171.
66 R. O'Neill, *Australia in the Korean War 1950–53: vol. 1: Strategy and Diplomacy*, AWM and the Australian Government Publishing Service, Canberra, 1981, p. 106.
67 S. Rowell, '1915 and Today', *Stand-to*, vol. 3, no. 4, April–May 1952, p. 2; Sydney Rowell, 'Lessons from Korea', *Australian Army Journal*, no. 52, September 1953, pp. 5–7.
68 Rowell, *Full Circle*, p. 183.
69 Cited in J. Grey, *The Australian Army*, Oxford University Press, South Melbourne, 2001, pp. 187–9.
70 Farewell message from General Sir Sydney Rowell, 15 December 1954, NAA: A816, 58/301/361
71 Cited in I. McNeill, *To Long Tan: The Australian Army and Vietnam War 1950–1966*, Allen & Unwin in association with the AWM, Canberra, 1993, p. 7.

8 A Military Intellectual: Colonel E.G. Keogh
Jeffrey Grey

1 N. Jans with D. Schmidtchen, *The Real C-Cubed: Culture, Careers and Climate and How They Affect Military Capability*, Strategic and Defence Studies Centre, Canberra, 2002, pp. 74–5.
2 The condition was his father's stipulation that he not be sent for overseas service until he turned 19. According to his dossier, this stipulation was ignored and he disembarked in Basra in late August 1916.
3 There is virtually nothing written about Keogh. Details of his life are drawn from his service dossier (NAA, B883, VX11986) and an obituary: W. Perry, 'Good-Bye Colonel Keogh: First Editor of the *Australian Army Journal*', [Australian] *Defence Force Journal*, 37, November–December 1982, pp. 11–16. This latter is wrong in some minor particulars; for instance, it states that he enlisted for service in the Great War in Adelaide, whereas his attestation

papers are clearly marked Melbourne. There is a photograph of the young Driver Keogh in the Australian War memorial (AWM), negative DA15828.
4   There is a short and clear discussion of the evolution of the *FSR* volumes between 1909 and the 1930s in I.M. Brown, *British Logistics on the Western Front, 1914–1919*, Praeger, New York, 1998, pp. 224–7.
5   Introduction, ATM 1, August 1941. The introduction appears from internal evidence to have been written in about February 1942, probably following the fall of Singapore.
6   A.B. Lodge, *The Fall of General Gordon Bennett*, Allen & Unwin, Sydney, 1986, p. 216.
7   E.G. Keogh, 'Birth of the Army Journal', *Australian Army Journal*, no. 329, October 1976, p. 5.
8   'Promotion Examinations', *Australian Army Journal*, no. 1, June–July 1948, p. 15.
9   E.G. Keogh, *Shenandoah, 1861–62*, Directorate of Military Training, Melbourne, 1954.
10 Keogh, 'Birth of the Army Journal', p. 8.
11 E.G. Keogh, *South West Pacific, 1941–45*, Grayflower Productions, Melbourne, 1965.
12 For example, E.G. Keogh, 'How to Study Military History', *Australian Army Journal*, no. 5, February–March 1949.
13 [Keogh], 'Promotion Examinations', p. 16.
14 E.G. Keogh, 'The Study of Military History', *Australian Army Journal*, no. 188, January 1965.
15 Keogh, 'The Study of Military History', *Australian Army Journal*, vol. 4, no. 2, Winter 2007.
16 'Retrospect', *ibid.*, p. 145.
17 E.G. Keogh, 'Allied Strategy in World War II – A Rejoinder', *The Australian Quarterly*, vol. 21, no. 1, March 1949, p. 12.
18 Perry, 'Goodbye Colonel Keogh', p. 11.
19 'Intellectual Mastery and Professional Military Journals', *Australian Army Journal*, vol. 1, no. 2, December 2003, p. 10.
20 E.G. Keogh, 'The Study of Military History', Jeffrey Grey ed., *Chief of Army's Reading List*, rev. ed., Land Warfare Studies Centre, Canberra, 2012, pp. 9, 10.

9 The Catalyst: Lieutenant-General Sir Thomas Daly
Jeffrey Grey

1   G. Pratten, *Australian Battalion Commanders in the Second World War*, Cambridge University Press, Melbourne, 2009, p. 293. Details of Daly's early career are discussed in J. Grey, *A Soldier's Soldier: A Biography of Lieutenant-General Sir Thomas Daly*, Cambridge University Press, Melbourne, 2013, pp. 1–57.

NOTES

2 Lieutenant-General Sir Thomas Daly, interview with B. Breen, 14 September 1992.
3 This idea has a number of names. In Britain it is described as a Military Covenant, while its specifically Australian variant is the Military Accord.
C. Carter, 'Dealing with Defence: The Problems with a Military Covenant', *The Conversation*, 20 January 2015, <http://theconversation.com/dealing-with-defence-the-problems-with-a-military-covenant-34022>, accessed 12 February 2016.
4 Breen, notes of interview with Daly, 19 January 1994. This was the only one of the interviews Breen conducted that could not be located and that hence has no transcript.
5 'From 1947 to 1985, Service pay and allowances were under the control of standing Departmental committees, with ad hoc external advisory committees established from time to time. The most important of these, the Kerr/Woodward Committee of Inquiry, which was appointed in 1970, produced seven reports on formal conditions of service during the period 1970 to 1973. These introduced much-needed principles to govern subsequent deliberations, as well as reforming the structure of Service pay. For example, the traditional complex daily rate of pay was replaced with a civilian-style salary structure, including a Service Allowance to compensate for the disabilities of Service life, with a major component being payment in lieu of overtime. The system of numerous trade skill margins was replaced by six broad-banded pay levels ranging from unskilled to technicians. This broad-banded wage structure was, in fact, far in advance of the prevailing civilian wages systems, with their untidy multiplicity of awards and relativities, and formed the basis for the broad-banded system in place today.' D. Anderson, *The Challenge of Military Service: Defence Personnel Conditions in a Changing Social Context*, Parliament of Australia, Background Paper 6, 1997–98.
6 By far the best, and the only serious modern treatment of the PIR, is T. Moss, 'Guarding the Periphery: The Australian Army in Papua New Guinea, 1951–1975', PhD thesis, Australian National University, 2015.
7 Daly, report, 20 December 1957, NAA MP927/1, A5/1/132.
8 P. Howson, *The Life of Politics: The Howson Diaries*, Viking, Melbourne, 1984, pp. 199–200.
9 Murdoch minute to Wilton, 13 September 1965, NAA, A1945, 248/4/128.
10 A. Stephens, *Going Solo: The Royal Australian Air Force, 1946–1971*, AGPS, Canberra, 1995, p. 292.
11 CGS's remarks, army headquarters briefing, 27 October 1969, p. 73. Copy in the Army History Unit (AHU), Canberra.
12 A. Palazzo, *The Australian Army: A History of its Organisation 1901–2002*, Oxford University Press, Melbourne, 2001, pp. 283–92, goes into the detail of these changes and the resultant structures that emerged.
13 Military Board minute 1/1966, 21 January 1966, Military Board Proceedings, AHU.
14 Daly, interview with Breen, 22 April 1994.
15 Daly letter to Lynch, 31 October 1969, NAA A6853, 2.
16 Daly, interview with I. McNeill, 4 June 1975.

17 D. Warner and T. Payne, *War and Words: The Australian Press and the Vietnam War*, Oxford University Press, Melbourne, 2007, p. 298.
18 Daly, cable 4311 to COMAFV, 14 February 1968, NAA A6853, 1.

10 Post-war Planner: Lieutenant-General Sir Mervyn Brogan
Tristan Moss

1 F. Hassett, 'Officer with a Gift for Friendship', *Australian*, 23 March 1994.
2 M. Brogan, 'The Australian Army – Points and Problems', *The RUSI Journal*, vol. 118, no. 1, 1 March 1973, p. 57.
3 'Scholarships', *Sydney Morning Herald*, 4 March 1932.
4 Leader of the WA opposition to Brogan, 27 April 1973, NAA A6836, 9.
5 'To Work on Fort', *Daily News (Perth)*, 12 October 1936.
6 'Awards for Gallantry: Lengthy List of Australians', *Age*, 27 April 1944.
7 Conversation with Edward Brogan, 5 November 2015. My thanks to Edward Brogan for allowing me access to his father's private papers, and for taking the time to discuss his father with me.
8 M. Brogan, cited in P. Deery, 'Chifley, the Army and the 1949 Coal Strike', *Labour History*, no. 68, 1 May 1995, p. 84.
9 M.C.J. Welburn, *The Development of Australian Army Doctrine, 1945–1964*, Canberra Papers on Strategy and Defence, no. 108, Strategic and Defence Studies Centre, Canberra, 1994, p. 38; 'Officer to Study Jungle Warfare', *Newcastle Sun*, 16 September 1954.
10 M. Brogan, 'Tactics and Atomics', *Military Review*, March 1957.
11 M. Brogan, 'British Commonwealth Integration: An Australian Viewpoint', *Australian Army Journal*, no. 88, September 1956, pp. 5–16.
12 J. Grey, *A Soldier's Soldier: A Biography of Lieutenant-General Sir Thomas Daly*, Cambridge University Press, Melbourne, 2012, p. 86.
13 D.M. Horner, *Strategic Command: General Sir John Wilton and Australia's Asian Wars*, Oxford University Press, Melbourne, 2005, p. 195.
14 Northern Command, 'Organisation of the Army – Papua New Guinea – Subsequent Phase', 13 August 1963, AWM90 WPI.
15 Military Board Minute No. 181/1962, 'Visit by QMG to Papua/New Guinea Sep 62', October 1962, Australian Army History Unit (AHU).
16 Horner, *Strategic Command*, p. 262.
17 Joint Planning Committee, Department of Defence, notes used by Major-General Brogan, chairman JPC, in addressing members of the Government Members Defence Committee, 26 August 1965, Brogan private papers (hereafter BPP).
18 M. Brogan, 'Opening Address – GOC's Exercise, 24/25 October 70', October 1970, BPP.
19 M. Brogan, 'Address by Major General M.F. Brogan, CBE, on Closing of the Chief of the General Staff's Exercise', August 1968, BPP.

20 R. O'Neill, 'Defence Policy', W.J. Hudson (ed.), *Australia in World Affairs, 1971–75*, Allen & Unwin, Sydney, 1980, p. 11.
21 M. Brogan, 'CGS Exercise 1972, Opening Remarks by the CGS', 1972, BPP.
22 M. Brogan, 'Address to Joint Services Staff College', 26 June 1973, BPP.
23 Horner, *Strategic Command*, pp. 194–202.
24 Military Board Minute 281a, 'Military Board Minutes – Format and Procedure', 29 July 1971, AHU.
25 See for instance annotations on 'FYRP – Army Manpower Levels – Interim and Long Term', 14 December 1972, NAA A6840, 3.
26 Interview with Ian Mackay, No. 1501, Australians at War Film Archive, <www.australiansatwarfilmarchive.gov.au/aawfa/interviews/327.aspx?keywords=1501>, accessed 1 January 2016.
27 Brogan to VCGS and many, 'Activities of the Three Services', 13 July 1973, NAA A6835, 4.
28 A. Ekins and I. McNeill, *Fighting to the Finish: The Australian Army and the Vietnam War, 1968–1975*, vol. 9, *The Official History of Australia's Involvement in Southeast Asian Conflicts 1948–1975*, Allen & Unwin, Crows Nest, 2012, pp. 640–1.
29 A. Palazzo, *The Australian Army: A History of Its Organisation 1901–2001*, Oxford University Press, Melbourne, 2001, p. 282.
30 'Army Reorganization', *Australian Army Journal*, no. 283, December 1972, *passim*.
31 Palazzo, *The Australian Army*, pp. 283–92.
32 Brogan, 'CGS Exercise 1972, Opening Remarks by the CGS', 1972, BPP.
33 Brogan, 'The Australian Army – Points and Problems', p. 57.
34 'Cessation of National Service: Statement by CGS – DFDC Meeting', 18 December 1972, NAA A6480, 3.
35 *Ibid*.
36 Brogan, 'The Australian Army – Points and Problems', p. 58.
37 D. Connery, *Which Division? Risk Management and the Australian Army's Force Structure after the Vietnam War*, AHU Occasional Paper Series, July 2014, pp. 16–17.
38 J. Grey, *The Australian Army*, Oxford University Press, Melbourne, 2001, p. 225.
39 Connery, *Which Division?*, p. 18.
40 See Brogan to Assistant Secretary of the Department of the Army, 4 July 1972, NAA A6846, 5.
41 A. Tange, *Defence Policy-Making: A Close-Up View, 1950–1980*, Peter Edwards (ed.), Canberra Papers on Strategy and Defence, no. 169, ANU E Press, Canberra, 2008, p. 62.
42 Palazzo, *The Australian Army*, p. 294.
43 'The Citizen Soldier', foreword by Lieutenant-General Sir Mervyn Brogan, KBE, CB, Chief of the General Staff, June 1972, NAA A6836, 8.
44 D. McCarthy, *The Once and Future Army: A History of the Citizen Military Forces, 1947–1974*, Oxford University Press, Melbourne, 2003, p. 176.
45 M. Brogan, 'The Place of the CMF', *Canberra Times*, 28 March 1974.
46 Horner, *Strategic Command*, p. 363.

47 Brogan to Barnard, 19 November 1973, BPP.
48 'Retiring General Denies Drop in Morale', *Canberra Times*, 4 October 1973.
49 Military Board Minute No. 307/1973, 'The Employment of the Army in the Seventies', 21 June 1973, AHU.
50 See for instance M. Brogan 'Men, Money and Material in Defence of Mainland Australia', *Pacific Defence Reporter*, August 1974, pp. 6–9.
51 Horner, *Strategic Command*, p. 194.
52 F. Hassett, 'Officer with a Gift for Friendship', *Australian*, 23 March 1994.

INDEX

Individuals with page numbers in **bold** indicate chapters dedicated to those individuals.

1RAR (1st Battalion, Royal Australian Regiment) 174
1st AIF (Australian Imperial Force)
  doubling 67–68
  governance 68–69
  raising 37, 38–39, 62–63, 64
1st Australian Armoured Division 132, 161
1st Australian Division 37, 38, 56, 65–66, 81, 98–99, 225
1st Australian Task Force 203
1st Aviation Regiment 202
1st Mounted Infantry Brigade 10, 22
1st New South Wales Mounted Rifles 86–87
2/6th Armoured Regiment 134
2/10th Battalion 196
2nd AIF (Australian Imperial Force) 107–8, 125, 126, 127, 128, 133, 158, 185
2nd Australian Division 71, 81, 99
2RAR (2nd Battalion, Royal Australian Regiment) 174
3RAR (3rd Battalion, Royal Australian Regiment) 174
6th Australian Division 126–27, 158, 159, 161–62
7th Australian Division 107–8, 158, 161–62
8th Australian Division 129–30, 186
  23rd Brigade 161
9th Australian Division 69, 131, 158, 167

ABC 207
Afghanistan 229
Ambon 161
American Civil War 188–89
Anderson, Colonel W.M. 132, 133
Antill, John 34
ANZAC 65, 98

Anzac Day 1, 191
army aviation 201–2
Army Aviation Centre 202
Army Aviation Corps 202
Army Education Service 188
army headquarters (AHQ) 205, 222–23
Army Training Memorandums (ATMs) 185–87
Arthur, Duke of Connaught 19
Aspinall, Cyril 67
atom bomb 143–44, 145–46
Auchinleck, Field Marshal Sir Claude 71, 168
Australia
  American alliance 105
  Australianists vs imperialists 62–63, 82, 85
  Japan: post-war occupation 143–44
  Japanese threat 95–96, 97–98, 124–25, 126, 135
  Japanese threat: lack of preparedness 161
  Papua and New Guinea colonial territories 198–200
  post-war strategic interests and threats 171–72
  WWII as foundational 105–6
Australian Armoured Corps 130
Australian Army Journal 187–88, 192
Australian Army Reserve 97
Australian Army restructuring *see also* Citizen Military Forces; Commonwealth Military Forces
  AMF reformed as Australian Regular Army 155, 171–72, 177–78, 183, 192, 196
  divisional structure 224–25
  reorganisations 203–4
  review and implementation 204–6, 221–23

257

Australian Army Review Committee 221–23
Australian contingents for South African wars 19, 21, 22, 86–87
Australian Corps 70–71, 73, 75
Australian Defence Committee 126–27, 173, 219
Australian Defence Force 85–86
Australian Defence Force Academy 40
Australian Engineers Corps 20
Australian Intelligence Corps 50–52, 63
Australian Labor Party 30–31
Australian Military Committee 16
Australian Military Mission to Washington 169
Australian National Defence League 90
Australian Naval and Military Expeditionary Force 96–97
Australian Shipbuilding Board 112–13
Australian Staff College 182, 188
Australian Staff Corps 121, 156–57, 167, 196
Australian Tank Corps 122
Australian War Memorial 67, 208
Australian Women's Army Service 176
aviation branch 95

Balikpapan 196
Balkan War 64
Barnard, Lance 228
Barton, Edmund 13, 14–15, 18, 20, 23
Bean, Charles 34, 37, 44
  hagiography of White 59–63, 65, 68, 69, 72, 74–75, 78
  influence on Legge's reputation 82
  White's influence on 75
Beavis, Major-General Leslie 123, 124, 135, 171
Bennett, Lieutenant-General Henry Gordon 129, 137, 186
Bentley, John 60, 71, 76–77
Berryman, Sir Frank 137, 169–70, 173
Bigge, Sir Arthur 20, 21
Birdwood, General Sir William 39, 65, 66, 68, 70–71, 72–73, 74, 75, 99
Black, Jeremy 2
Blamey, General Sir Thomas 69, 119–20, 134, 143, 158
  as C-in-C AMF 135, 162
  Greek campaign 159–60

  Northcott and 135–39
  in Papua and New Guinea 164–65
  retirement 169
  Rowell and 155, 158–60, 166–67, 168, 170
  Rowell sacking 136, 153–54, 165–66
Boer Wars *see* South African wars
Borneo 202
Bostock, Air Vice-Marshal William 136
Brand, Brigadier Charles 122–23
Bridgeford, Brigadier William 159, 171, 175
Bridges, Major-General Sir William Throsby 3, 34, **37–56**
  AIC formation 50–52
  AIF raising 38–39, 64
  as Assistant Quartermaster-General 45–46
  background and early years 40–42
  as Chief of Intelligence 47–48
  as Chief of the General Staff 52–53, 91
  family 43–44, 54–55
  Hutton and 39, 43, 46, 56
  on Imperial General Staff 53
  as Inspector-General 39, 55–56
  Legge and 88, 89, 90–91, 94
  military career 40, 41–43, 44–45, 66, 98
  personality 34
  RMC Duntroon establishment 53–55
  White and 62, 65, 66
British Army 21–22, 29, 46, 182
British Army Council 185
British Committee of Imperial Defence 49, 124
British Commonwealth Occupation Force 143–44, 169, 172, 173
British Empire
  Australian forces command 15, 18–19
  East of Suez 204
  Greek campaign 159–60
  imperial defence coordination 10–11
  Japan: post-war occupation 143–44
  Japan: war against 129
  London blitz 169
  Malaya 175
  Russia 83
  Singapore defence 126
British Expeditionary Force 126
British Experimental Mechanised Force 122
British Foreign Office 123–24

INDEX

British Imperial Defence College 123–24, 157, 216
British Imperial General Staff 52, 53, 94–96, 122
British Staff College 29, 121–22
British Territorial Force 123
British War Office 21, 38, 39, 44, 46, 51, 123, 168–69
Brodrick, William St John 14
Brogan, Lieutenant-General Sir Mervyn 6–7, 205, **211–29**
 air supply scheme 214
 army restructuring implementation 223–25
 as Chief of the General Staff 211–13, 216, 219–29
 as Director of Military Training 214, 215–16
 education 213–14
 as GOC Eastern Command 218
 as GOC Northern Command 216–18
 military career 215–16
 retirement 228–29
 'Tactics and Atomics' 215–16
Brooke, Field Marshal Sir Alan 122, 168
Bruce, Stanley 126

cadet system 17, 49
Canada 17, 41
Canberra 54
Canungra 215
Caroline Islands 96, 97
Casey, Richard 125–26, 168
CGS Exercise 203
Chamberlain, Joseph 15
Chamberlain, Neville 126
Chapman, Austin 24, 30
Chauvel, Colonel H.G. 34, 39, 54, 98, 100
Chiefs of Staff Committee 173–74, 203, 219 *see also* Joint Chiefs of Staff
Chifley, Ben 143, 169, 170, 172, 173, 174, 215
China
 Japan and 98
 South-East Asian influence 175
 Soviet influence on 171
Churchill, Winston 126, 130, 212
Citizen Military Forces 13, 123, 156–57, 161, 167, 171–72, 173, 188, 192, 226–27 *see also* Commonwealth Military

Forces; *under state militias*
 review 203–4, 205
civic action crisis 207, 208
Clark, Chris 71
Clowes, Major-General Cyril 107–8, 163–64, 166, 171
coal-miners strike 173, 215
Cold War 175, 177
Collins, Captain Robert Henry Muirhead 13, 31, 32–33
Colonial Conferences, London 20, 38, 52
Colonial Defence Committee 13, 24
The Command and Organisational Structure of the Army in Australia 204–6, 222–23
command responsibility 115
command structures 221–23
Commonwealth Military Forces *see also* Citizen Military Forces
 as both garrison troops and field force 17–19, 25
 budget 27–28
 command 47–48
 officer corps 29
 six colonial militias formed into 15–16
Commonwealth Military Journal 187, 192
Commonwealth Naval Forces 48
Commonwealth of Australia 45, 87–88
Commonwealth Transport Committee 122
communism 175
compulsory service vs volunteers 18, 37, 38, 48–49
Connery, David 225
conscription 223–24
conscription referenda 100
Cook, Joseph 39, 53
corps commander role 158
Council of Defence 32, 47–48, 98
Curtin, John 135–36, 137, 153, 154, 162, 166, 167

Daly, Lieutenant-General Sir Thomas 6, 174, **195–208**, 212
 as 28th Commonwealth Brigade commander 196–97
 character 197
 as Chief of the General Staff 195, 197, 198, 200–208, 216
 as GOC Northern Command 197, 198–200

259

military career 195–98
Pacific Islands Regiment 198–200
the press and 206–8
Darwin Mobile Force 158
Dawson, Senator Andrew 30–31
Deakin, Alfred 30, 48–50, 52, 53, 89–90, 91, 92–93
Defence Act 1903 32, 88
Defence Act 1904 3, 22–23, 32–33
Defence Bill 13–15, 16, 18, 45, 92–93
defence budget 140–41, 172
Department of Army 109, 226
Department of Civil Aviation 202
Department of Defence 12–13, 16, 89, 95, 218, 225–26
Department of Territories 199
Department of Treasury 125
Derham, Mark 66
Derham, Rosemary 76
Directorate of Military Training 184, 186–88
Directorate of Water Transport 113
Diro, Brigadier Ted 226
doctrine
   Army Training Memorandums (ATMs) 185–87
   Field Service Regulations (British Army) 184–85
Dominions Conference, London 125–26
Drake, Senator James 30
Drayton Grange 62
Dunstan, William 137
Dutch East Indies 161

Edgeworth David, Sir 182
education for officers 181–82 *see also* Royal Military College Duntroon
Edward, Prince of Wales 19–20
Egypt 39, 68, 99, 127–28, 167
Elizabeth II 150
Elliott, Pompey 71, 74
equipment *see* ordnance (equipment)
Evatt, Dr H.V. 143
Ewing, Thomas 50, 52, 89, 90, 91

Fairhall, Allen 202
Farrands, John 221
federation 45, 87–88
Field Force Command 205, 222
Field Service Regulations (British Army) 184–85

Finn Report 16
First Army 134
First World War *see* Great War
Fisher, Andrew 52–53, 54, 91
Forde, Frank 137
Forrest, John 13, 14, 16, 20, 22, 23, 25–28, 30
Foster, William 66
France
   Vichy 160
   in Vietnam 175
Fraser, Senator James 142
Fraser, Malcolm 207
French, Colonel G.A. 44
French, Major-General John 26, 45
Fuller, Colonel J.F.C. 122

Gallipoli 38, 156
   evacuation 66–67, 99
   invasion 64–65, 120, 121
   lack of critical analysis 191
Gellibrand, Major John 66, 73
General Officer Commanding (GOC) role 10, 32, 33, 47
General Staff 51, 52
Germany
   colonial territories in Pacific 96
   German New Guinea 96
   Pacific Squadron 39, 96–97
   Panzerarmee Afrika 69
   V1 and V2 rockets 169
   on Western Front 126
Godley, Major-General Alexander 64
Gordon, Brigadier Joseph 64
Gorton, John 207
Great War 2, 56, 64, 96, 156 *see also* Gallipoli; Western Front
Greek campaign 159–60
Grey, Jeff 60
guides corps 50

Haig, Douglas 71, 75, 99
Haldane, Viscount 62
Hamilton, General Sir Ian 55, 64–65
Hampton, Meleah 72
Handcock, Lieutenant Peter 15
Hasluck, Sir Paul 218
Hassett, Lieutenant-General F.G. 204, 212, 216, 221, 223, 226, 228, 229
Hawley, Colonel R.B. 29

INDEX

helicopters 202–3
Herring, Major-General Edmund 135, 137
Hetherington, John 154, 155
Hill, Alec 67
Hoad, Major-General John 46–47, 52, 53, 55–56, 92, 94
Home Forces Command 134
Hopkins, Lieutenant-Colonel Ronald 132–33, 139–40, 150
Horner, David 155, 162
housing 198
Howard, Professor Sir Michael 191
Howson, Peter 201
Hughes, William Morris 14, 76, 100
Hutton, Lieutenant-General Sir Edward ('Curley') 2–3, **9–34**
   Australian Army structure 14, 42–43
   birth and education 10
   Bridges and 39, 43, 46, 56
   conversion of infantry to mounted units 24
   conversion of volunteers to militia 23–24
   as GOC 10, 12, 32–33, 45
   Hoad and 46–47
   Legge and 84
   military career 10–11, 45
   'Minute Upon the Defence of Australia' 16–19
   national tour 20
   personality 11–12
   White and 61, 62, 63

I Anzac Corps 70–71, 73, 75, 99
I Australian Corps 158–60, 161–62
II Australian Corps 134–35
III Australian Corps 134
India 84
Indian Army 29
Indonesia 217
intellectuals 181
intellectual characteristics of AA 182
Ironside, Major-General Edmund 122
Italians in Libya 159

Japan 46, 89
   Australia, threat to 95–96, 97–98, 124–25, 126, 135
   entry into Second World War 161
   local elections 145
   Pacific Theatre 161, 186
   in Papua and New Guinea 153, 162–65
   post-war occupation 114–15, 143–47
   post-war reconstruction 145–46
   Soviet influence on 171
   US aerial bombing 146
   US atomic bombing of 143–44, 145–46
   US Navy blockade 146
   war against 129
Jess inquiry 198
Joint Chiefs of Staff 144, 145, 147
Joint Service Plans 218
jointery 218
Jones, Air Vice-Marshal George 136

Kanga Force 163, 165
Kelly, William 25
Kemsley, Sir Alfred 78
Keogh, Colonel Eustace Graham 5–6, **181–93**
   birth and military career 183–84
   campaign volumes 188–90
   in Directorate of Military Training 184, 186–88
   E.G. Keogh Chair 192–93
   importance of educated mind 190–91
   importance of history 190
   retirement 192
   roles 183
   'The Study of Military History' 191
Kerr, Sir John 228
Kerr–Woodward inquiry 198
Kirkpatrick, Major-General George 55, 94
Kitchener, Field Marshal Lord 93–94, 98
Korean War 174, 175, 196–97

language acquisition: *tok pisin* 200
Lavarack, Lieutenant-General John 119–20, 124, 134, 137, 160, 165
Lawrence, General Sir Arthur 10
Lealofi, Tupua Tamasese 44
Lease Lend program 141
Legge, Major-General Gordon 4, **81–101**
   as 1st Australian Division commander 98–99
   as 2nd Australian Division commander 99
   as AIF commander 98–99
   background and education 82–83

Bean and 82
Bridges and 88, 89, 90–91, 94
   as Chief of the General Staff 96, 100
   as Director of Defence Organisation 93–94
   Hoad and 92
   Hutton and 84
   on Imperial General Staff 94–96
   as Inspector-General 100
   Kitchener and 93
   on Military Board 91–92
   military career 83, 84–86, 88
   as Quartermaster-General 91–94
   as RMC Duntroon commandant 100–101
   South African wars 86–87
   universal service introduction 89–91
   White and 71–72, 100
Legge's Reports 84
Lend Lease program 141
Lewis, Essington 125
Light Horse 24
Lisle, Lieutenant-Colonel Beauvoir de 87
Lloyd, Major C.E.M. ('Gaffer') 107, 110
Logistics Command 205, 222
Long, Gavin 168
Lynch, Phillip 207
Lyne, Sir William 18–19

MacArthur, General Douglas 165, 166, 167
McCarthy, Dudley 155
McCay, Colonel James Whiteside 32–33, 50–51, 98
Mackay, Colonel Ian 220
Mackay, Iven 119–20, 134
McMahon, William 220–21, 228
MacMillan, Margaret 1–2
McMullin, Ross 74
MacRaild, Donald 2
Maginot Line 126
Mahdist rebels in Sudan 42, 83
Malaya 129–30, 175, 190
Manchuria 46
mapping 51
Maroubra Force 163, 164
Maxwell, Sir John 39
media *see* the press
medical service 20
Mediterranean 69

Mellor, D.P. 110, 113
Menzies, Robert 127, 157–58, 174, 175, 176, 217
Menzies, Sydney 109–10
Mesopotamian campaign 183, 189
Middle East 190
migration to Australia 105, 176
Milford, E.J. 107–8
Military Board
   armoured division 130
   army morale 228
   army restructuring 205
   CGS role 52, 173, 205, 219–20, 223
   clashes between military and civilian members 220
   establishment 22, 32, 33, 47–48
   expansion under Legge 90–92
   as functional headquarters 92
   general mentions 50, 63, 125, 185, 188
   mechanisation of AMF 122–23
   Military Secretary role 91
   Quartermaster-General role 91–92
   reconstitution by Sturdee 169, 170–71
   women 176
militia *see* Citizens Military Forces
Millar, Dermot 75
Millar, Professor Tom 204, 226
Millen, Senator Edward 54, 55–56, 96
Milne Force 163
Monaro District 24
Monash, Lieutenant-General Sir John 63, 98, 158
Montgomery, General Sir Bernard 122, 168
morale 228
Morant, Lieutenant Harry ('Breaker') 15
Morshead, Sir Leslie 71, 137
Munro Ferguson, Sir Ronald 66
Murison, Blanche ('Peggy') 156

national guard 49
National Service scheme 155, 175–76, 177–78, 204, 206, 223–24, 226 *see also* universal service
Nauru 96
Naval Board 32, 48
Neild, John Cash 26–27
New Caledonia 46
New Guinea 110, 134, 136, 138, 140–41, 162–65, 169

INDEX

New Guinea Force 138–39, 153–54, 162–65, 214
New Guinean soldiers *see* Pacific Islands Regiment; Papua New Guinea Defence Force
New South Wales 17, 134
New South Wales militia 15, 16, 24, 42, 44, 83, 84, 86–87
Newcastle 135
Nixon, Richard 204
Norrie, Brigadier Jim 226
Northcote, Lord 21
Northcott, Lieutenant-General Sir John 4–5, **119–50**
  as acting CGS 128–29
  background 121
  Blamey and 135–39
  British secondment 123–24
  as Chief of the General Staff 135, 139–40
  as C-in-C British Commonwealth Occupation Force 144–47
  as Deputy Chief of General Staff 125–28, 132, 133
  as Director Military Operations and Intelligence 124–25
  as Director Supply and Transport 122–23
  as GOC 1st Australian Armoured Division 132–34
  as governor of New South Wales 120, 147
  in Great War 120–21
  as II Australian Corps commander 134–35
  military career 119–22, 147–50
Northcott Drive, Canberra 149–50
Northern Command 197, 198–200, 216–18
nursing service 20

Oates, Stephen B. 2
O'Brien, Brigadier John William Alexander 4, **105–16**
  in 2nd AIF 107–8
  background 106–7
  as chairman Army Inventions Directorate 105
  as Deputy Master-General of Ordnance (Equipment) 109–14, 115–17

  as Director of Artillery 108–9
  in post-war Japan 114–15
  Toyoda trial 115
  in United States 115
Ommanney, Sir Montagu 21, 23
O'Neill, Robert 219
operational level of war 184–85
ordnance (equipment) 109–10
  2nd AIF shortages 127
  AC1 Cruiser tank 111–12, 130–31, 133–34
  AC3 Thunderbolt tank 149–50
  development and acquisition 113–14
  field gun-howitzer (Short 25) 108–9
  M3 light tank (Stuart) 131
  Owen submachine-gun 111, 138–39
  watercraft 112–13

Pacific Islands Regiment (PIR) 198–200, 216–18
Pacific Theatre 142–43, 185, 190, 199
Palazzo, Albert 172
Palestine 69, 128, 189
Papua New Guinea 224 *see also* New Guinea
Papua New Guinea Command 225
Papua New Guinea Defence Force 225–26
Papuan carriers 163
Papuan soldiers *see* Pacific Islands Regiment
Parkhill, Sir Robert 124
Paulet, Eleanor 10
pay and conditions 25, 188, 198, 199, 228
Peacock, Andrew 204
Pearce, Senator George 53, 54, 64, 74, 94, 97
Pentropic formation 203–4
the Philippines 162, 169
Playford, Sir Thomas 49, 50
Pollard, Lieutenant-General Reginald 216
Port Kembla 135
Post War Army Planning Committee 171–72
the press
  Australian Army and 206–8
  Hutton 18, 24, 30, 31
  South Pacific Post 199–200
  Vietnam 218–19
professional mastery 187
promotion examinations 188–90
public interest 207–8

263

Quartermaster-General role 218
Queensland 134, 197, 216–18
Queensland Defence Force 44, 62
Queensland militia 14

Rabaul, New Britain 161
recruitment 141–43, 172–73
Reid, George 33, 34
Reid–McLean government 31
responsibility of command 197–98
Review of the Size and Shape of the Army Post Vietnam 221–23
Rifle Brigade 60
rifle clubs 17, 89
Rimmer, Gordon 109, 112
Roach, Lieutenant-Colonel L.N. 161
Roberts, Tom 9
Robertson, Major-General Horace ('Red Robbie') 134, 146, 147, 149, 162, 169–70
Rosenthal, Charles 81
Rottnest Island 213
Rowell, James and Zella 155–56
Rowell, Lieutenant-General Sir Sydney 5, **153–78**
  as AIF Detail commander 167
  background and education 155–56, 157
  Blamey, relations with *see* Blamey
  in British War Office 168–69
  as Chief of the General Staff 155, 173–74
  as Cold War warrior 175
  concern for reputation 168
  as Deputy Chief of General Staff 132, 133, 160, 162, 173
  Full Circle 155
  Great War 156
  Greek campaign 159–60
  as I Australian Corps commander 134, 162
  Keogh and 186
  military career 154–55, 177–78
  National Service scheme 176
  as New Guinea Force commander 162–65
  Pacific Theatre 161
  policy paper on strategic interests and threats 171–72
  retirement 176–77
  South African wars 155–56
  Squires, relations with *see* Squires
  Sturdee, relations with *see* Sturdee
  as Vice Chief of General Staff 155, 169–71, 173
  views on Northcott and BCOF 146, 147
Royal Australian Air Force 100, 161, 201–3, 205
Royal Australian Armoured Corps 149–50
Royal Australian Artillery 20
Royal Australian Engineers 51, 173, 215
Royal Australian Navy 49, 107, 202, 203, 205
Royal Military College Duntroon 17, 29, 37, 39–40, 53–55, 94, 100–101, 156, 171
  Australian Army restructuring 222
  bastardisation scandal 207
  at Victoria Barracks 213
Royal Regiment of Australian Artillery 150
Royal Women's Australian Army Corps 176
Russia 46, 83, 89
  as Soviet Union 167, 171

Sadler, Peter 66
St George's English Rifles 26–27
Samoa 44
Scherger, Air Chief Marshal Sir Frederick 218
School of Gunnery 43
School of Infantry 85
Science Council of Japan 114
SEATO (South East Asia Treaty Organization) 218
Second Army 134
Second World War 69, 105–6, 119–20, 158, 214
shearers' strike (1891) 14
Shedden, Frederick 124, 166, 167, 173
Shenandoah campaign 188–89
shipbuilding 112–13
Sinclair, Frank 109
Singapore 126, 128–30, 133, 161–62, 186
Smuts, Jan 87
social contract 197–98
social role of militia 23–24, 28–29
Solomon Islands 169
South African wars 19, 21, 22, 44–45, 86–87, 155–56

INDEX

South Australia 134
South Australian 3rd Light Horse
  Regiment 156
South Australian militia 15, 25, 87
South East Asia Treaty Organization 218
Soviet Union 167, 171
  as Russia 46, 83, 89
Spender, Percy 130, 131
Squires, Lieutenant-General Ernest 126,
    127, 128, 129
  background and military career 157
  as Inspector-General 157–58
  Rowell and 155, 157
Street, Geoffrey 128–29
Sturdee, Lieutenant-General Vernon
    119–20, 124–25, 135, 187
  as acting C-in-C AMF 169–70
  as Chief of the General Staff 129, 131,
    144, 170, 173
  recall of Australian divisions 161–62
  Rowell and 155, 159–60, 169–70
Sudan 42, 83
Suez campaign 189
The Sullivans (TV show) 192
superannuation 198
Survey Corps 51
Swiss militia system 48–49, 86
Sydney 135
Syrian campaign 108, 160

Tange, Sir Arthur 203, 226
Tasmania 121, 134
Tasmanian militia 15, 18, 25, 26
Tennyson, Lord Hallam 27
territorial commands 205
territorial military districts 134
Throsby clan 41
Thursday Island 62
Timor 161
Toyoda, Admiral Soemu 115
training
  close order drill 85
  CMF 17, 28–30
  National Service scheme 176
  universal service 85–86, 89–91
Training Command 205, 222
Treloar, Major John 66, 75
Tropical Force 97–98

United Service Institutions 84–85, 89, 188
United States
  American war in Vietnam *see* Vietnam
  Australian alliance with 105
  Australian shipbuilders 112–13
  Japan: atomic bombing of 143–44,
    145–46
  Japan: post-war occupation 114–15,
    143–44
  Japan: war against 129
  Korean War 174
United States Air Force 146
United States Army 202, 203
United States Navy 146
universal service 85–86, 89–91 *see also*
    National Service
University of Sydney 48, 88

Vansittart, Sir Robert 123–24
Vasey, Major-General George 113, 114,
    129, 135–36, 144, 153, 162, 164,
    171–72
Verney, Guy 60, 78
Victoria, Queen 10
Victoria 134
  cadet system 17
  Melbourne Cavalry 24
  militia 107
Vietnam 175, 197, 200–204, 207, 208
  Australian adviser withdrawal 223
  Australian troop withdrawal 211,
    220–21
  CMF and 226
  the press 218–19
  public opposition to war 206

Walker, Major-General Harold ('Hooky')
    65
Wallack, Colonel E.T. 92
Walsh, Gerry 2
War Cabinet 134, 135
War Railway Council 94, 122
war room 218
War Studies 189–91
Warner, Denis 207
watercraft 112–13
Watson, Prime Minister 31
Watson, Colonel W.D. 134
Wavell, General Sir Archibald 127–28
West Papua 217

Western Australia 134
Western Australian militia 15, 18, 25, 26
Western Front
  Bullecourt 73–74, 76
  in general 69, 70–71, 72
  Polygon Wood 75
  Pozières 71, 72, 81, 99
  Somme 72
  Ypres 74
White, Bruce 206, 207
White, General Sir Cyril Brudenell Bingham 3–4, 34, **59–78**
  AIF role 59, 64, 67–69, 73–74, 76–77
  Australianists vs imperialists 62–63
  background and education 60–61
  Bean, influence on 75 *see also* Bean, Charles
  Birdwood and 70–71, 72–73, 74
  Bridges and 62, 65, 66
  in British War Office 62–63
  Buangor grave 59
  character 63, 76, 78
  as Chief of the General Staff 128, 129
  as Director of Military Operations 64
  Elliott and 74
  Gallipoli 64–67
  Haig and 71
  Hutton and 61, 62, 63
  Legge and 71–72, 100
White, Eustace 61
White, Maria and John 60–61
Whitlam government 198, 204, 223, 226
Wilmot, Chester 167
Wilson, Lieutenant-General Sir Henry 160
Wilton, Lieutenant-General Sir John 196–97, 201, 202, 203, 206, 212, 216, 218, 229
Wolseley Ring 10, 22
Wynter, Major-General Henry 131, 136

Yamashita, General 115

www.ingramcontent.com/pod-product-compliance
Ingram Content Group UK Ltd.
Pitfield, Milton Keynes, MK11 3LW, UK
UKHW041306180426
11947UKWH00009B/733